dirtbag

dirtbag

ESSAYS

AMBER A'LEE FROST

ST. MARTIN'S PRESS
NEW YORK

First published in the United States by St. Martin's Press,
an imprint of St. Martin's Publishing Group

DIRTBAG. Copyright © 2023 by Amber A'Lee Frost. All rights reserved.
Printed in the United States of America. For information, address
St. Martin's Publishing Group, 120 Broadway, New York, NY 10271.

www.stmartins.com

Designed by Omar Chapa

The Library of Congress Cataloging-in-Publication Data
is available upon request.

ISBN 978-1-250-26962-1 (hardcover)
ISBN 978-1-250-26963-8 (ebook)

Our books may be purchased in bulk for promotional, educational,
or business use. Please contact your local bookseller or the Macmillan
Corporate and Premium Sales Department at 1-800-221-7945, exten-
sion 5442, or by email at MacmillanSpecialMarkets@macmillan.com.

First Edition: 2023

10 9 8 7 6 5 4 3 2 1

For the first word I ever spoke, the first word
I ever wrote: Mom

contents

introduction

Men make their own history, but they do not make it as they please; they do not make it under self-selected circumstances, but under circumstances existing already, given and transmitted from the past. The tradition of all dead generations weighs like a nightmare on the brains of the living. And just as they seem to be occupied with revolutionizing themselves and things, creating something that did not exist before, precisely in such epochs of revolutionary crisis they anxiously conjure up the spirits of the past to their service, borrowing from them names, battle slogans, and costumes in order to present this new scene in world history in time-honored disguise and borrowed language.

—KARL MARX, *THE EIGHTEENTH BRUMAIRE OF LOUIS BONAPARTE*

If she says she can do it, she can do it.
She don't make false claims.

—DAVID BOWIE, "QUEEN BITCH"

Call me Amber.

I know, opening my self-important little book of essays with a nod to a masterpiece is brass-neck, pretentious, try-hard, self-indulgent, cringe, etc., but aren't we all sometimes? And anyway, all those pretty little horses bolted the moment I signed a book contract for a "memoir," so I'm having fun with it, and I encourage you to do the same whenever possible.

I want this book to be informative and useful, but I also want it to be entertaining, well written, and a pleasurable read—not an obligation. My story is easy enough to ignore; I'm not standing on your front lawn blasting the audiobook through a boom box. No one is making you read it (I hope), least of all me (and if someone voluntarily slogs through an entire book they don't like or don't care about, that's on them). So if you're reading this, I have to (at least) assume it's because you want to know what I saw and what I have to say about it.

My credentials were often acquired by happenstance: right place, right time. I started out in Indiana, working on Planned Parenthood and anti–Tea Party activism, and I started a chapter of a then-obscure organization, now fairly well-known as Democratic Socialists of America. From there I moved to New York. I was on the ground for Occupy Wall Street, and I worked for the Working Families Party before being hired as one of DSA's four employees at the time. I wrote about arts and culture and eventually left politics in Jacobin and other outlets, before jumping into the first Bernie campaign and taking a job cohosting the podcast Chapo Trap House with Will Menaker, Matt Christman, Felix Biederman, and Virgil Texas, just in time for the second Bernie campaign. Not a bad résumé when you're trying to justify (to others or yourself) writing a book about socialism in the here and now. Unfortunately, I frequently take on too many labor-intensive projects at once, which often leads to panic, guilt, and eventually a state of obsessive work-ethic-induced self-loathing so severe that I eventually just go catatonic and stare at a wall for a week. It's a similar irony to opening a food delivery app, seeing six hundred options, and becoming so overwhelmed that you lose your appetite. This was difficult to start writing, and even more difficult to finish.

So in preparation for this book of essays on my experiences with socialist politics before and after the two campaigns of Bernie Sanders, I decided to get a shrink. But not just any shrink. I sought and acquired a shrink who specializes in a technique called cognitive behavioral therapy, a hypermanagerial approach to mental health based on eliminating negative thought and behavior "patterns" and supplanting them with "healthier" ones; the idea is that the subject can create new habits to live a more functional and productive life regardless of any underlying suffering (which they are now better able to endure with stoic resilience, thanks to CBT). It's not that the approach actually *discourages* the subject from looking inward, but it allows her to function without looking too *deeply*. This was ideal for me lest the void gaze back, and it become a whole thing where I might have had to put "real" work on hold in order to "work on *myself*," which is what I came to CBT to avoid doing in the first place. I call it "psychoanalysis for Protestants," and it might not be as healthy as a deep dive, but it's way less of a hassle.

My therapist was a right-wing Orthodox Jew who openly abhorred Bernie Sanders; he was exactly what I needed. I never actually asked him whether he googled me and found my writing or my podcast, but at some point I had to assume. He never mentioned the election per se, but he had a tendency to suddenly and without provocation speak glowingly of people like Dennis Prager, the virulently anticommunist Jewish talk-radio host who went from never-Trump conservative to The Donald's biggest cheerleader. My shrink managed to regularly work Dennis Prager quotes into our sessions. I found this funny, and somewhat charming. Mostly it gave me some distance.

He was always telling me that I should go to church, get married, and have children, so that I'd have a sense of my value as a human being beyond politics and work, those being the two abstractions that motivated my every major decision (and which, for me, existed independently of one another only as a distinction without a difference). I also found this funny, and somewhat charming. Like most people, he was a little right and a little wrong. I like most people. And I liked him.

He once asked in earnest if I had ever considered the possibility that I was unconsciously overextending myself to the point of exhaustion because that's the only kind of rest I felt I deserved; it's an explanation that flattered my sense of duty, but the reality is just that I have the memory of a goldfish, and I compulsively repeat the same cycle of overwork to the point of collapse without even noticing until it's too late. (Unless, of course, I write things down.)

He also once asked if I had considered the possibility that *perhaps* I chase quixotic political ambitions because I know that no matter how hard and smart I work, they will most likely never come to fruition in my lifetime. This may seem counterintuitive, but he has correctly identified a certain type of person who runs rampant on "the left." For these Sisyphean radicals, politics offers an identity as a beloved archetype—the righteous underdog, the beautiful loser, the brilliant outsider, etc. They find a perverse sense of security in the job that they will never complete; if it was ever finished, who would they even *be* anymore? Again, my therapist didn't quite get me right. While it's true that I don't feel I exist if I'm not working, I've always preferred working on almost anything other than politics.

Generally speaking, I like writing about politics, and I like podcasting about politics. In the right company, I even enjoy talking about politics. But actually *doing* politics—campaigns, protests, activism, organizing . . . what a fucking drag. I've done all those things, and since I'm a lifer, I know I will again, but they will *always* be a chore for me. It's just not my idea of fun. But I don't do it for fun.

Neither do I do it for a sense of identity, belonging, or camaraderie (I had friends before I had politics, and I would keep an eye on anyone in your organization who didn't), and I certainly don't do it for the warm fuzzies (gross). I do it because I want socialism, and socialism for me is simply a chore that *needs to be done.* It's like Dorothy's old chestnut, "I hate writing, I love having written." Much of my exasperation with "doing politics" is that socialism is something I wish was *already* done, so I could get back to reading the short stories of Deborah Eisenberg, convincing my friends to rent a picturesque woodland cabin in bumblefuck California one more time, trying to diagnose my dogs' skin allergies, learning to play the Appalachian dulcimer, etc. Socialists become irrelevant to the masses when they forget that "the work" is intended as a means to an end; the goal isn't to "be a socialist" (whatever that means). The goal is to change the world so that we can *live under socialism* (or at least as much socialism as we can manage under the circumstances).

Socialism was only ever a means to an end for me; I first threw myself into politics out of frustration with an economy that sabotaged the talents, desires, and ambitions of so many people I knew and loved. What I want—what I have always wanted—is nothing more or less than a relatively democratic workers' state that runs smoothly and fairly, one where enough injustice has been resolved that for the average person, "politics" may be relegated to a minorly inconvenient aspect of civic responsibility, like taking out the trash. I want a socialism that runs mostly on autopilot, so people can spend most of their short time on this earth focusing on what they'd rather be doing if you gave them the time and the money and the freedom.

I explained this to my therapist, but I'm not sure if he believed me. Nonetheless, we shared an amity. He was always funny, friendly, and sympathetic without being condescending or going easy on me. He has been indispensable in writing this book (along with some occasional chemical help from my prescribing psychiatrist, a left-wing, secular Jew who listens to a podcast called *Cum Town* and goes to a CrossFit gym).

I sought out both of them because I was starting to panic. I felt deeply compelled to write my own account of the unlikely rise of a post–2008 wave of social democratic politics, and I was becoming overwhelmed by the sense of responsibility I felt to it; my involvement with Occupy Wall Street, Democratic Socialists of America, and the Bernie Sanders campaign finally felt whole enough to form a complete picture, if I could just get it right. Not only did I feel a duty to posterity but, on a personal level, I also desperately needed for people to understand what actually happened, at least as I saw it.

So I secured the only therapist in my insurance network who practiced within thirty miles of my apartment and specialized in attention deficit hyperactivity disorder, a diagnosis that I don't really believe in but cannot deny describes me. The following lists are the qualities outlined in *Mastering Your Adult ADHD: A Cognitive-Behavioral Treatment Program, Client Workbook (Treatments That Work)* that have been given free rein to dictate the literary style of this book:

Symptoms of Poor Attention
distracted easily
difficulty organizing
easily bored
switch from one task to another
difficulty planning
difficulty concentrating
can't do boring or unattractive tasks

Symptoms of Hyperactivity
feel like driven by a motor
restless
can't sit still
always on the go
fidgety

Symptoms of Impulsivity
interrupt often
answer questions before person finishes asking

blurt out inappropriate comments
act before thinking
do things you later regretted
difficulty waiting

Other than the bit about "regrets," the list pretty much represent a fair and reasonable description of my temperament, not to mention the conditions under which my writing style has developed over the years. I concede that these qualities may not be as charming to some as they are to others, but they do put me at an advantage to tell the story of an obsessive, impulsive, and hyperactive political moment, one I saw up close and from many angles in all its dauntless turbulence—good days and bad days both held equal potential for chaos. My ADHD gonzo bricolage may not be your cup of tea, but if you want someone whose neurology perfectly matches the frenetic zeitgeist of a resurgent interest in socialism, I'm made to order.

As such, the millennial or younger reader—those who came of age clicking on Wikipedia articles for a specific piece of information only to find themselves *still* on Wikipedia two hours later, having mired themselves within an endless informational labyrinth of hyperlinks—may find my writing to be a relief. It really is difficult to sit still these days.

For the older reader, it may be a bit frustrating at moments, but perhaps it will also provide a crash course into the frenetic attention spans of the first Extremely Online generation. Even among my peers, I'm a girl of exceptional caprice, but make no mistake, socialism wasn't just a whim or a trend for the millennial Bernie Bro, and certainly not for me; I've been a lot of things in my adult life, but the only thing I've always been is a socialist. If you are of a finer vintage, rest assured that this book is for you too. I appreciate your interest and applaud your patience, as I have never had the luxury of indulging in the suburban petit bourgeois's petulant obsession with generational warfare.

This is not to say there are no limits to my filial piety. There were plenty of mean old bastards in my political "career." Generally though, I cannot overstate the tenderness and gratitude I feel toward the veterans of the movement, particularly those who kept the torch burning against all odds, and in the face of near-universal ridicule, taking the long view, never losing faith despite the state of the world, content in the work they knew was unlikely to bear fruit in their own lifetimes. Odds are I'll be one of them someday, so thank God I never held any particular attachment to youth. It's a fool who doesn't learn from the experiences of their elders, even when they're not always their wisers.

★ ★ ★

This is a book about a millennial socialist's ridiculous adventures in left politics, and what happened when I threw all my weight behind an unlikely insurgent left-wing presidential campaign. Sounds good to a publisher, but it's hardly reinventing the wheel. Hunter S. Thompson's 1973 book *Fear and Loathing: On the Campaign Trail '72* obviously beat me to that one. Like Thompson, I saw an opportunity for a righteous underdog to maybe right some of the wrongs in our country, and I didn't stop carrying water for him until our man was defeated. Also like Thompson, I indulge in florid storytelling (although I don't exaggerate or lie, mostly because I can't dissociate the way that he did). And just like Thompson, I have no regrets. His reflections on the McGovern campaign were without shame or umbrage: "McGovern made some stupid mistakes, but in context they seem almost frivolous compared to the things Richard Nixon does every day of his life, on purpose, as a matter of policy and a perfect expression of everything he stands for."[1]

Damn right. I refuse to throw my candidate, a dedicated champion of the working class, under the bus, and I have little patience for anyone who does. Where is your fucking spine? I don't mean to argue for unqualified loyalty. For example, I am consistently baffled by the Clinton fans who felt no betrayal at all by Hillary's failure to run a winning campaign, despite having all the weight and conspiratorial viciousness of the Democratic Party behind her. To echo Thompson, Bernie made "some stupid mistakes," but he didn't betray us or royally fuck up as a result of his own hubris. Bernie was defeated. Goliath usually wins.

Maybe more than the campaign itself, this book is about failure and defeat. Bernie Sanders was the biggest opportunity of my lifetime so far, and he may remain so until the end. What made his campaigns so uncommonly promising was their appeal outside of the "counterculture left" (as in, the niche of people who will read this book). People who don't care about, or even hate, politics—you know, normal people—love Bernie for his honesty and his indefatigable commitment to them. As a socialist, he was an outsider, but his politics were inclusive yet populist, and his campaigns did not resent, fear, patronize, or hold contempt for squares, normies, or whatever you call them, which is why he had the edge, with a diverse and largely un-edgy electorate.

Thompson's generation learned the hard way the difference between a counterculture and a political movement.

And God help you if you need a "political life" to be wild, or appreciate art, for friendship, adventure, or romance. If anything, the former has been an impediment to the latter for me, though I'd never be able to write a book worth reading if I didn't include at least a little bit of the fun stuff, particularly the romance. And there's precedent for that as well.

Vivian Gornick's 1977 oral history *The Romance of American Communism* was more about the heroic kind of romance than the amorous kind, but it was as much an influence on me as Thompson, though to my perpetual dismay, I lacked the actual party neccessary for a memoir like Gornick's. Her oral history collected the thrilling, inspiring, and heartbreaking accounts of many members of the American Communist Party.

When the book was republished in 2020, she had written a new introduction, now hot with embarrassment for the romanticism with which she had celebrated her interview subjects in 1977. This is likely due in no small part to the heartless reviews it had garnered when it first came out, most notably from Trotskyite and Cold War "leftists" like Democratic Socialists of America cofounder Irving Howe, who wrote of Gornick, "One sometimes has to remind oneself that in her evocation of coziness and warmth she is writing about the CP in the time of Stalin and not about a summer camp."[2] She said the review was so devastating that after reading it she stayed in bed for a week. (Apologies to my would-be Irving Howes: just as you are not obligated to read what I write, I am not obligated to read your opinion of it. And I never do.)

Thoroughly chastened, Gornick's 2020 foreword renounced what she once knew to be true, if not the entire project, saying, "To conceive of the experience of having been a Communist as a romance was, I thought and still think, legitimate; to write about it romantically was not." I think she's being too hard on herself.

Right-wing attacks on the book were predictable, but it was the intimacy of the blows from "fellow leftists" that really hurt. Gornick knew this all too well, and despite the accusations of revisionist nostalgia, she had no compunction about including the ruthless cruelty and political misguidedness that often festered between alleged "comrades." She did not, for example, shy away from the shame and confusion of a man who stood by mutely during the show trial and unjust expulsion of his own mother. I don't think Irving Howe was mad that Gornick also wrote so lovingly about good people and inspiring moments; but he was furious, if not actually jealous, that she had managed to keep the romance alive so long in spite of all the ugly history that she also included.

Gornick also famously derided Sanders's 2020 run, saying she did not find him "inspiring," as he was "old and he's Jewish and he rants and he raves."[3] In the midst of Berniemania, Gornick was honest in her skepticism, even as she was apologetic for her inability to believe in the moment: "I do not find him inspiring and I cannot imagine him as president, and I do think it's because, in my eyes, he is a long-winded old Jewish guy. I know that's terrible, but I can't help it. That's how it strikes me."[4] I kind of get it; you can never hate anyone as much as you hate the mirror.

Many saw her comments as a betrayal of the last hope of a left politics—a hope that had all but burnt out in Gornick's generation, particularly after Khrushchev's "Secret Speech" shook so many of Gornick's comrades' faith in "actually existing communism." But "betrayal" implies the angling for some sort of advantage on her part, and it had been a long time since Gornick had anything to gain by abandoning an opportunity to advance socialist politics; she held out longer than most, and I cannot bring myself to admonish or be disappointed. If anything, my heart breaks for her, and there but for the grace of God goes every comrade. Along with her sense of romance, Vivian Gornick lost hope, maybe not in socialism, but in herself, and the people who reminded her of herself. But how could she have kept the faith after what she'd been through? Lord knows they really beat it out of you.

The loss of faith is among the oldest stories on the left, one that Gornick already knew well, but still succumbed to. Interviews in *The Romance of American Communism* told many of them, as did a myriad of memoirs like *The God That Failed* and Richard Wright's 1944 essay, "I Tried to Be a Communist," which told the heartbreaking story of a former mental patient who wreaked havoc on a chapter by sowing paranoid discord between comrades. When the psychotic history of the would-be witch hunter was revealed, the unjust campaign of persecution against an innocent member horrified Wright, souring him on socialist politics for good: "I was thunderstruck. Was this true? Undoubtedly it was. Then what kind of club did we run that a lunatic could step into it and help run it? Were we all so mad that we could not detect a madman when we saw one?"[5]

Of course I saw viciousness in DSA and on the campaign trail. And of course any honest account of a life in politics will include either witness to or experiences of betrayal, often at the hands of one's closest friends and comrades. Unlike Gornick, Wright, and so many others, I never stopped believing, maybe because I never got it as bad as they did, but at least in some part because I had been inoculated from disappointment and disaffection by reading their memoirs and was thus able to fortify myself. So I am grateful for the painfully honest accounts of the now faithless; they helped me remember that the mercenary tendencies and paranoia are most often matters of organizational dysfunction, rather than failures of people or politics. During Occupy Wall Street, for example, I read and reread Jo Freeman's essay "The Tyranny of Structurelessness" to understand and parse out the fatal defects of anarchist horizontalism we were witnessing but weren't allowed to admit. "This apparent lack of structure too often disguised an informal, unacknowledged and unaccountable leadership that was all the more pernicious because its very existence was denied."[6]

When I or others were being denounced as heretics (if that sounds melodramatic, believe me, it was a melodrama), I turned to Freeman's essay, "On Trashing":

> I was one of the first in the country, perhaps the first in Chicago, to have my character, my commitment, and my very self attacked in such a way by Movement women that it left me torn in little pieces and unable to function. It took me years to recover, and even today the wounds have not entirely healed.[7]

My faith in socialism was also fortified by a number of political failures I personally experienced well before Bernie, even before Occupy, back when I was cutting my teeth on labor, antiausterity, and reproductive freedom in right-wing Indiana. I saw millions of people oppose a war that surged on regardless of popular will. I saw the labor movement kneecapped over and over again as Indiana became a right-to-work state. I saw the Tea Party "movement" move the goalposts of what people were willing to ask for. The decimation of immigrant rights and reproductive autonomy, the violent austerity, and an increasingly punitive legal system that still swells across the country—but for some irrational reason, I have never wavered in my belief that socialism can still win. It's a tall order of course, and one that will require providence, diligence, discipline, dedication, faith, loyalty, vigilance, and, above all, solidarity.

Lately, "solidarity" has been mistranslated into a sort of vaguely affirming neologism—a buzzword like "namaste," or "love and light." But solidarity refers to nothing less than the work and sacrifice necessary to trust and hold on to one another. The late Mark Fisher put it beautifully:

> We need to learn, or re-learn, how to build comradeship and solidarity instead of doing capital's work for it by condemning and abusing each other. This doesn't mean, of course, that we must always agree—on the contrary, we must create conditions where disagreement can take place without fear of exclusion and excommunication.[8]

It's a cliché because the truth is by its very nature a cliché. Maybe nothing can ever really be anything "fresh" about any political memoir of substance. No story about politics can ever be truly novel if it's told well (i.e., honestly); there's just too much historical precedent. This isn't a shortcoming, artistically or politically; I'm continuing a long tradition of lefty memoir, and I am proud to do so.

Like all those other writers, I wrote this book because I was there. Even if I don't have the answers, even if I am wrong, I believe that if I am honest about what I did and what I saw—or what I think I saw—I believe it will be of some value to fellow travelers. Completionism is a misery-maker of an aspiration, so I had to cut myself a little slack; and I'm sure that (like most people) I'm a little bit right, and a little bit wrong. We will always stumble, misjudge, misidentify, and miscalculate. But with history—even this book, my little self-indulgent memoir, is an artifact of history—we have the opportunity to learn from our mistakes, and that means we have to *remember*.

Here is what I remember. . . .

Part I

INDIANA

1

THE SUM OF MY PARTS

I'm from Indiana, which is a place notable for its lack of notability. My friend and gratuitous name-drop Daniel Waters, screenwriter for *Heathers, Demolition Man, Batman Returns,* among others, is a fellow Hoosier, and he told me he set *Heathers* in Ohio because "everyone can imagine themselves living in Ohio. You say Indiana though, and they go blank."

Sometimes someone asks me where I'm from, and when I tell them "Indiana," I watch a barely concealed panic start to glow in their eyes as they mentally grope for a reply—maybe a polite and informed-sounding question about the Hoosier state, or perhaps a memory of driving though it once (was that Indiana?). Wait, didn't they have a friend in college from Indiana? They wrack their brains for something—anything at all—to say about a state they cannot muster a single impression of or comment on. They start to sweat when they keep coming up blank, scrambling to think of a transition that gracefully but vaguely acknowledges that I am indeed from A Place, and that every Place is worthy of honor and respect, when in fact I am from the conversation-smothering, rhythm-disrupting, vibe-killing black box of Indiana.

Two people have actually laughed, apparently under the impression I was pulling their leg, as if I'd said I was from Mayberry or Whoville. It's always good-natured, with a sort of "Sure, pull the other one!" tone that announces to everyone that we're all having a good time here, just joshin' around about silly places. A split second after it dawns on them that I'm not joking, they apologize profusely, mortified as if they had accidentally mispronounced the name of a chieftain from some primitive tribe they think they once saw in a documentary. Did you know that you can smell embarrassment? It's rotten and sweet, like a rodent that died in the wall during a particularly humid summer.

One time a guy flat out refused to believe me, laughing, "No you're not! No one's from Indiana. That's not a real place!"

But I assure you, dear reader [*pauses ominously*], Indiana is very real. [*mysterious and foreboding eye contact*]

Honestly, it's not that big of a deal. Indiana doesn't really care to be noticed. Or at least we decide not to care, given that we don't have a choice in the matter, and we usually succeed in convincing ourselves that it's somehow "better" to be overlooked. Unobtrusive, unpretentious, polite, and dignified.

We like to think that we *could* be noticed, if we wanted to be, but we'd never be so tacky or self-important as to insist upon it ourselves. That way we can beam with the fiery pride of someone who imagines themselves as beatifically humble and quietly judge states with higher profiles for being a bit "showy." Sublimated resentments and delusions of saintly modesty aside, Indiana teaches its sons and daughters that we exist, even though no one is looking.

It's not a terrible way to regard oneself—meaning as little as possible—and it certainly beats endlessly posting into the void in hopes of being "seen," or if you find your fifteen minutes of fame skyrocketing to the reasonable heights of podcast/internet nano-celebrity (reach for the stars, kids!). For better or worse, almost no one is ever seen, so you have to find a way of remembering that you matter, even when no one is looking (which will almost always be most of the time).

Hoosiers are comfortable with going unnoticed, a practiced ease with anonymity one might describe as a facet of our "regional character." One might also describe it as a shade in the shamelessly reductive broad brush of generalizations I am about to dictate to you with authoritative confidence like some J. D.-Vance-middle-American-Horatio-Alger-expat-bullshitter selling myself as the Bumpkin Whisperer to People Who Read (despite not having spent any prolonged time in the Motherland for the last ten years). The latter is more accurate but a little wordy, so let's talk instead about regional character.

I'm a firm believer in the phenomenon of "Midwestern nice." I'd wager the number of reflexive apologies made to furniture that someone has just bumped into is highest per capita in the Midwest. I'd also argue we have the national lead on the number of furious and profane upbraidings of those same inanimate objects, because you cannot be conditioned to be nice so consistently and genuinely without also engendering a latent, pervasive rage. This is, as they say, "the dialectic."

I really do believe we have a preternatural tendency to both possess and value an earnest commitment to kindness and civic duty; my theory is that this social contract was developed to counterbalance our perpetual thrumming anger, some of which I believe is the nervous result of bland isolation and hostile weather. For example, as I am writing this chapter in my hometown, I notice that my sweet, good-humored, and almost *aggressively* hospitable mother has a road rage I have never witnessed outside of the Midwest. She sees one car every ten miles and immediately starts hissing profanity about the "traffic."

Conversely, when my plane arrived at the Indianapolis airport, the cheerful announcement I heard over the loudspeaker could have very well been delivered by the woman who raised me: "If you lost a black, double-insulated women's glove near the Chipotle, we have it at the information desk waiting for you!" I am irrationally proud of where I am from and our attendant Weltanschauung.

So with that duality of temperament in mind, indulge me my biography as an ethnographic survey of political economy (please and thank you, I'm so, so, so sorry, but also fuck you it's my book and I do what I want).

★   ★   ★

In the painfully nice and absolutely furious state of Indiana, which is flat as glass for miles and miles, boils in the summer, and is fraught with floods and tornadoes in the spring and blizzards and ice storms in the winter (but has a perfectly lovely autumn), I was born Amber A'Lee Frost, a name I love to read and hear spoken, particularly by someone sexy. My mother's middle name was also A'Lee, and so was her mother's. And, so was *her* mother's, and—if my great-grandmother recalls correctly—so was *her* mother's. We're not sure if it goes further back than that. No one remembers the first A'Lee, and no one seems to know the origin of the name itself, both facts being the sort of genealogical details deemed unimportant when there is weather to bitch about or jokes to crack, generally at the expense of the people we love the most.

My mother's father was a Korean War veteran who never saw action and grew up on a chicken farm in Southern Indiana. The GI Bill sent him to college, where he was trained as an electrical engineer. If he were born today, I suspect he would be diagnosed both formally and by casual observers as "on the spectrum." He was and is driven, mischievous, prone to bouts of anger, and very, very fun. My mother's mother was the daughter of two union workers who would sit down at the kitchen table and work out the family budget once a week. Strangely, when their daughter (my grandmother) married, she did not have her own bank account, though she worked on and off part-time doing menial secretarial work when she wasn't collapsing into a Friedanian suburban depression for which she was sometimes medicated, and sometimes overmedicated. She was and is artistic, depressive, moony, bohemian in temperament, and incredibly warm and sentimental.

My mother grew up with her parents and older brother in a nice working-class suburb outside of Indianapolis, where a single income could afford you a sleek midcentury three-bedroom ranch house near good public schools, which were sued for segregation in 1968 by the Justice Department.[9] My mother remembers the busing program accelerating when she was in high school but not much of the heated political debate or racist tensions, which tend to be more discreet in the Midwest than they are in, say, the Deep South.

It was a big school with a lot of kids, and now a lot more of them were Black,[10] an observable but unremarkable shift in demographics from her perspective. She has one vivid memory of a recently bused classmate struggling to read a paragraph out loud in a senior art class, which made her decide that busing was necessary for a fair distribution of quality education. This is an example of my mother's approach to social justice and equality. She does not indulge in sanctimony or moral outrage; she simply believes that everyone deserves decent things, that fair is fair, and that opposition to such basic morality and ethics is irrational and/or ignorant.

My mother is friendly, sympathetic, sporty, artistic, literary, intellectual without being pretentious, and very beautiful. As far as I can tell, everyone has always loved her, but no one more than me.

She met my father when she was seventeen, in October of her senior year of high school. "He was five years older than me, had a car and a job, so eighteen-year-old me thought he had made it in life." They married four months later, the following January, and I was conceived in February. She left him in August—in her third trimester—and I was born in October, almost exactly one year after they met. The divorce wasn't finalized until the following January. "It would have been sooner, but there's a law about not getting divorced when you're pregnant. That was frustrating."

I have not researched this stupid fucking law, but I suspect it was to prevent "abandonment," meaning it was also likely a holdover from when Indiana was a "divorce colony" while divorce was illegal (or nearly so) in much of the rest of the country and steps were taken to fight the state's reputation as a "Sodom," festering with "free love," gambling, drink, and all manner of vice.[11]

When my mother was pregnant, she lived with my father's parents: my mamaw, who was one of thirteen children, and my papaw, who was one of nine and quit school to work on the family farm around seventh grade, when he was "old enough to read the Bible." They were highly religious people from Kentucky, stereotypical Appalachian hillbillies who both grew up without electricity or indoor plumbing. They moved to Indiana after their marriage to give a better life to their children. My mamaw had a job with a pension at a paper mill, my papaw started a number of skilled labor businesses—upholstery, roofing, construction, etc.—and made enough to purchase some cheap land for a small, diversified farm, which I loved visiting as a kid.

When I was born, my mother was in the midst of a divorce at the same time as her own parents. After the dust had cleared, she moved back into her idyllic American dream of a childhood home with her brother and divorced father, all in the midst of Reagan's second term.

TOWN #1 (THEN POPULATION: BETWEEN 700,000 AND 730,000)

I loved living in the suburban house, and I loved living with my mother, grandpa, and uncle, when he was home from the Air Force. The house was far more loaded with tension for my mom than it was for me, owing both to the memory of her parents' unhappy marriage and the premature world-weariness that comes from ending up back "home" due to a misstep that had delayed her promising adulthood and thrown her down the economic ladder with a baby in her arms. I also had no sense that the neighborhood was fraught with the dark, oppressive secrets that everyone says lie beneath the respectable spackle of the suburbs. She later told me that she remembered being a kid and hearing manic laughter from across the street, only to realize it was hysterical sobbing. The neighbor, a friendly dentist, had committed suicide by running the car in his garage; his wife had just found his body.

During this time my mother went to college and worked various jobs. I remember her taking me to the sandwich shop where she made meatball subs, and for a while she worked behind bulletproof glass at a liquor store that also cashed checks. She worked a lot of weekends and nights, so I didn't see her very often, and I missed her constantly and wanted to be near her whenever I could. Sometimes after my grandpa had put me to bed, I would sneak into her room and crawl under the covers, knowing I would pass out before she got home and that she wouldn't wake me up to move me, even though apparently I kicked violently in my sleep. I also knew that she would be gone again for work before I woke up, but that didn't matter to me. I knew that I would be physically close to her; it didn't matter if I was conscious.

Once, my uncle came home late, and I woke up when the door opened. He offered to take me to Dairy Queen, and when we got back, my mother was running up and down the lawn in her nightgown, erratic and flailing. When she saw us coming out of the car, she began screaming at her brother, who was mortified and apologetic. She was terrified that I had been kidnapped, possibly by my father, a fear that hovered for years until one day my mamaw reminded her that he wouldn't be inclined to such a heist: "That sounds too much like work for him."

Eventually, she got a full-time job, and we were able to move out.

TOWN #2 (THEN POPULATION: 25,380)

I was five. Our first apartment was located in a town that is now considered "very nice," though it wasn't as nice then, and we certainly didn't live in the nice part of it. The apartment itself was dark, and the complex had a playground of wood that had rotted through—we sometimes heard the biker couple downstairs fighting. I believe my mom called the police a few times when the arguments sounded as if they had escalated to violence. But I liked my kindergarten, and I liked having more time with my mother.

Throughout my childhood, both sets of grandparents were essential fixtures in my care and development, both babysitting and performing the necessary family functions that my mother was far too overextended to provide consistently. My mother's mother would pick me up from school and take me to movies. My mother's father would take me to museums and wilderness parks and encourage an interest in math and science, insisting that I learn how to make a radio, explain a combustion engine, and eventually change my own oil (even though it was $20 at the local mechanics).

I even had close relationships with my great-grandparents— we pop 'em out young, and my family tends to live unreasonably long despite poor health—especially my mother's mother's mother, a bawdy A'Lee who drove a bronze El Camino, reveled in dirty jokes, and praised the union jobs that she and her beloved late husband proudly retired from with full pensions. She loved gay men, including her hairdresser, Paul Lynde on Hollywood Squares, and TV interior decorator Christopher Lowell. Well into her nineties, whenever a picture was taken and she was asked to say "cheese," she would yell "SEX!" I have her wedding dress and it fits me; it's calf-length. And purple.

I was about eight when my great-grandfather was in the hospital dying of cancer. Near the end, when the painkillers were causing hallucinations, he confessed to his son, who had followed in his father's footsteps to become a union railway man, that he saw small, faceless men with round, seemingly hollow heads like basketballs roaming the halls.

"Don't worry dad," my great-uncle said reassuringly, "those are just Republicans."

Years after her husband's death, my great-grandmother saw Dennis Franz's bare ass on the infamous episode of *NYPD Blue* that boasted the first television appearance of male dorsal nudity. She began to cry. It was very uncharacteristic for a woman who preferred to show only her charms and gleeful wit, and when my mother and grandmother asked what was wrong, she replied wistfully, "That man is built just like your father." In actuality, my Great-Grandpa Logan was built nothing like the squat, rotund Franz; he was tall, lean, and muscular. I think this was just the only other male ass she had ever seen, and it left her nostalgic and possibly a little horny.

My mamaw and papaw were the most involved extended family by far, as I spent many weekends during the school year and weeks at a time with them during the summer, either at their house or traveling to see relatives in Appalachia. I liked the mountains, but I was bored to tears by even the most ecstatic Evangelical church services—at least until we got to the music, which was rapturous and soulful. They tried, mostly in vain, to quiet my exceptional fidgeting during the service by giving me chewing gum, and to this day, I can't hold still without something in my mouth (get your mind out of the gutter, or don't, none of my business). My papaw also had a side career as a small-time bluegrass and gospel musician in a few family bands, and I was lucky enough to experience being "on tour" as a little kid, which meant loading up in a motorhome and touring various folk festival circuits across much of the country, where I saw legends like The Osborne Brothers, Bill Monroe, and Ralph Stanley live and up close. I did not appreciate it in the slightest.

Mostly, though, my home was my mother. There is a strange sort of intimacy that develops in a two-person family, even when foundational care comes from the extended family. My mother's parents weren't very affectionate to her growing up, so she took care to extend physical warmth at regular intervals. There were of course the traditional hugs and kisses goodnight or goodbye, but what I remember most was the tactile tenderness of less conventional contact.

When we lived in her childhood home, I would sit on the bed with her while she read or did homework, working toward the degree that my birth had derailed. I would color or flip through a book, or just stare at her vanity with all its magical jewelry boxes, makeup, and perfume. When she had a break, she would put on the radio and draw a smiley face on every one of my fingers and toes with a ballpoint pen. I loved when she cut my hair or when I put my head in her lap for her to clean out my ears with Q-tips. Once when she was picking me up from a weekend at her mother's, we stopped at a McDonald's (which she usually opposed on health grounds), and I got a milkshake. I was sitting at the table, sipping sleepily, when she made an over-the-top slurping noise as a gag. I laughed, spitting a mouthful of milkshake across the table. She guffawed, then peeled into breathless giggles, and hissed a conspiratorial, *"Run."* We left the mess behind, dashing to the car like we had just robbed a bank.

We would take turns putting our ears on top of one another's heads, then necks, then stomachs while the other chewed and swallowed bites of their dinner, howling until we couldn't catch our breath over observable evidence of not only mechanical digestion but also the invisible mysteries of peristalsis itself. I can't remember if we ever found and employed a toy stethoscope or if it was just an idea I fixated on.

One time I was rifling through an old sewing kit and found the sort of soft tape measure I knew from old movies, the one used in scenes where a beautiful woman would get sized for a gown. We then proceeded to measure each other's heads, limbs, fingers, and toes, forehead width and height, and philtrums (the basin plateau between the nostrils running from the nose to the upper lip). I recorded our results in a notebook with a unicorn on it. Love is deeply weird.

I don't remember very much about the first apartment except that one Christmas morning I was surprised with a perfect little black kitten that I loved obsessively and a Teenage Mutant Ninja Turtles tent and matching sleeping bag, both of which replaced my bed for years. I remember my mom's bedroom more than my own; hers was sparsely furnished, with the old dresser and vanity and matching bed from her teenage bedroom and a rocking chair that had used to be in my baby room. On the wall was a massive black and white poster of Virginia Woolf, who, my mother told me, said that people need time and space and a little bit of financial security to make art or create things, which is why most of the art and literature we've heard of was made by men.

I wanted her to decorate the bedroom, add some warm 1970s earth tones that might remind me of our old midcentury ranch house we shared with my grandpa and uncle, and her old room in particular, with its faux-wood-paneled walls and louvered closet doors, all of which made me feel warm and golden, like a forest clearing at sunset. Being too young to understand that bohemian minimalism was an aesthetic choice that my Shakespeare- and Nirvana-loving mother had made consciously, I found the austerity very cold and the face of Virginia Woolf "depressing."

We had a faux-wood-finished television with push buttons that only got a few channels, and television was usually limited to what we both enjoyed, especially if she believed it would enrich my intellectual and artistic development: mostly *Mystery Science Theater 3000* somehow pirated onto a local cable access station, nature documentaries, and whatever vintage BBC was on PBS—Shakespeare, operas, ballet, *Masterpiece Theatre, Mystery!,* and Monty Python. I saw and loved the "Parrot Sketch," and quickly became that annoying kid who would memorize and perform every part of any Python routine to anyone too polite to tell me to shut up.

TOWN #3 (THEN POPULATION: ABOUT 17,600)

I was six when we moved to where I would attend elementary school; the apartment was a massive improvement, obvious even to me. The town itself was sprawling and still largely agrarian at the time, but there was a picturesque square with a courthouse and little shops—hardware, antiques, and an ice cream parlor I loved. It was the kind of wholesome, idyllic town that zombies or aliens come to destroy in horror movies.

During this time, my mom still took college classes at the "commuter campus" shared by two major Indiana universities, which had been set up as a cost-effective alternative for "nontraditional students" ("Troops, ex-cons, and single moms, GO JAGS!"), requiring neither dorm residency nor the myriad of fees associated with "campus life."

She also worked a full-time job and took me to both when she couldn't find childcare. She was often depressed and constantly anxious, and I began to understand that this was all related to money, eventually figuring out from my grandparents that my father did not pay child support but that he could and he should. My mother still managed to pay for ballet classes. (Unlike everyone else in my family, I was incredibly bad at sports and hated playing any of them except basketball, which is basically a religion in Indiana, but one I was woefully too short to be any good at.)

It also became clear at this point that I was good at school, when I was able to hold still. I was put in "Gifted and Talented" classes, a euphemism for kids who read for fun and figured out how to take standardized tests very quickly so they could go to recess early—or, as I later figured out, for kids with particularly ambitious parents.

This was around the time I remember meeting my father for the first time, in secret, through a clandestine plan of my mamaw, who said that if I told anyone, "they'll send him to jail." When I arrived at the run-down rental house where he was staying, he was asleep on the couch in boxer shorts, covered in roofing tar. When he woke up, I didn't know what to say to this filthy, half-naked stranger. Later, back with my mom, the secret weighing on my tiny conscience, I broke down in tears and confessed. She said that she was glad I had told her, that she wouldn't get him in trouble and that she was happy I had met him. Afterward, she told my mamaw that in the future she wanted to be informed of when I was seeing him. I don't remember visiting him after that until almost a year later.

I liked this period of my childhood. I was doing well at school and had good friends. I did not want to move again.

TOWN #4 (THEN POPULATION: BETWEEN 6,000 AND 8,000)

I was twelve. Despite my attachment to what I had finally come to think of as my hometown after years of fantasizing about moving back to the ranch home in Indianapolis, I was able to muster some excitement for the next move. My grandpa lived there, in what I thought was an enormous house, with his second wife. The town itself was very, very pretty, with parks and sidewalks and a big library that I loved. I soon came to understand that this was because the town had recently experienced an influx of monied residents, and that my junior high school was full of "rich kids," none of whom lived in apartments. When they first asked where I lived, one girl replied, "Oh, our maid lives there!" She was trying to be nice, so I just smiled.

A small number of kids, however, exhibited actual hostility, which I eventually returned tenfold. A popular girl threw my sports bra into the running showers before gym class, joking, "Oh, whatever, you don't even need one." (I was extremely small and skinny, and a preternaturally "late bloomer.") After a few days of simmering and fantasizing about the devastating things I wished I could say to humiliate her, she was in the seat next to me in home economics. At one point, she stood up with her pencil as if to sharpen it, and with a deft swipe slid my books from the table to the floor. The teacher had just left the classroom, and without thinking, I jumped up to wrap my arm around her neck in a headlock, dragged her down with my body weight, knocking her skull into the stationary table-mounted sewing machine before bouncing it a little too hard off the carpeted floor. When she shouted, "My HEAD!" I said, coldly, "Oh whatever, you don't even use it." It got a laugh, and no one tattled—least of all the girl, who knew that it would be mutually assured destruction.

Look, I've seethed with *l'esprit de l'escalier* in the shower. I have formative experiences of humiliation and powerlessness, just like everyone else. But those aren't the only stories worth telling. "One time, I was nailed to a cross" isn't any more honest than "one time, I did a perfect kick flip," if you actually did it. It's not even more relatable. There are enough cynical writers out there, leaning on dime-store self-deprecation to ingratiate themselves to readers. I'm not censoring my kick flips, and you shouldn't either. Confess and honor the moments in your life when you were cool and you knew it, especially when there was a crowd who agreed.

I beat the shit out of that poor girl. And it was awesome. And no one ever bullied me again.

I still failed home ec for refusing to complete a sewing assignment, which upset and confused my mom, who was unable to understand why her previously happy and studious daughter was suddenly sullen and failing classes.

Flunking a class that we both believed to be sexist began the first of many massive mother-daughter fights that would periodically erupt until I had safely and unpregnantly graduated high school. I said that sewing was stupid and I wasn't going to be a housewife anyway. (I have since been a housewife and currently own a very nice sewing machine.) If I had been quicker, I would have reminded her of Virginia Woolf, but I merely resorted to denouncing the town and my classmates, who I said were snobby assholes. (Swearing was allowed so long as I didn't lean on it.)

She calmed down and admitted that she had hated junior high, too, and said that "someday this will be over," but sometimes you just need to slog through the assholes because real life was waiting on the other side. This was a "stupid little place with a lot of stupid little people in it," but they were mostly good, and I would make friends here and one day move on to a much bigger world, while the stupid little people would be stuck in their stupid little mindsets forever.

I insisted that this was all well and good "someday" but that it was cold comfort at the moment, when everyone in school hated me.

"Oh Amber," she said, genuinely moved by her own sympathy for me, "no one hates you."

She added brightly. "Most of the time, no one even notices you!"

That stung for a minute. But this very Midwestern ethos is still the best, most liberating reassurance I have ever received. Awareness of your own insignificance really takes the pressure off. I became more confident, made good friends, got into punk rock, and switched from ballet to guitar lessons, which pleased my papaw to no end. I never practiced, but I was a good singer, so no one could tell. I spent enough time on schoolwork to keep my mom happy, meaning the bare minimum to stay in advanced placement classes, and I got solo parts in the choir programs, one of which I sang right next to the girl I had dragged down into a headlock.

I still found the town stifling, but going to a rich school had a lot of perks that my mother wouldn't have been able to afford herself, such as a three-week student exchange program in Aix-en-Provence, France, that proved her right about the size of the world. It reminded me that junior high was a pit stop just in time for the next move to an even smaller town.

By this time I had grown used to moving, got good at making new friends quickly, and leaving them behind without looking back. I developed a talent for "leaving," and I'm still pretty good at cutting ties, quitting jobs, skipping town, breaking up with people, abandoning projects, etc. For example, I nearly didn't finish writing this book, which was derailed by anxious avoidance and a somewhat impulsive move to Los Angeles. The way I see it, you're only tied down to something you belong to; the moment the Bernie campaign ended, I didn't belong to anyone or anything.

TOWN #5 (THEN POPULATION: 1,588)

I was fourteen. A modest single income and a pile of student debt landed my mother an adjustable rate (subprime) mortgage for a new home. This was before everyone knew that the banks were not, in fact, "too big to fail," a phrase popularized by Princeton- and Yale-educated congressman Stewart McKinney the very year I was born. By the time the financial collapse had set in, my mom had just refinanced, narrowly avoiding the royal screwing that would soon befall millions of people all over the world (including recent college graduate Amber A'Lee Frost).

Despite its smallness, I liked this new town. For one thing, no one else had any money either, so snobbery was considered nothing short of a sin. The richest girls in school lived on a family dairy farm that employed two people and generated about $100,000 in annual revenue. And they were nice to me. They were nice to everyone, if a bit churchy. Second, we now had a house and a yard in what I later learned was called an "exurb," or a housing development constructed in a rural area, with no actual "urb" proximal enough to make it a proper suburb. When we first moved in, very few other houses had been built yet, leaving the ones that stood starkly in the former cornfield look as if they had been transported from a real town onto the surface of the moon. The school was also very small, with a student body composed of a few kids from the rural parts of two or three bordering towns and at least two "unincorporated communities." I think my graduating class ended up with eighty-one students, after a few had dropped out due to pregnancy (one girl in my class was already in her second trimester on the first day of school) or the usual "fuck this" reasons. Academically though, it was well ranked, with a lot of good teachers, though I did notice all the maps still showed the USSR, except the one for the geography class. (Geography is not a requirement for graduation from an Indiana public school.) My type A professional-track hyperachiever junior high had put me a little bit ahead of my new high school classmates academically, so I got a fresh start and skipped a grade in a few classes, reinventing myself as an excellent student.

The common refrain of the rural teen is that "there's nothing to do in this town," and there is some truth to that. Houses were very far apart, and my school, which consisted of grades 7–12, was surrounded by cornfields on all sides. Internet connection of any reasonable speed came very late to us, and an older computer plus dial-up meant that it was rarely worth the time and trouble to log on to whatever music message board I was posting on at the time. Even the computers at school weren't much faster. Once I was daydreaming during French class, and a massive dairy cow ambled by the window, having evidently made a jailbreak over a downed fence from the farm across the street. "I have to get out of this town," I thought. Having to park your car in the middle of a rural road to approach and gently push a Holstein out of traffic's way was not an uncommon occurrence.

Rural life does afford some luxuries, a few of which are very appealing to a teen girl. Many things that are expensive in a bigger town or city are incredibly cheap in the country.

We bought a beautiful, dressage-trained thoroughbred horse, and she cost less than my first car, a Ford Tempo with more miles on it than it had any right to rack up. Her monthly board at a farm near our house cost a little more than cable television.

Another defense of small-town life: it's much easier to be "bad" in a rural place without anyone knowing. Driving was the best; you could drive and drive, as fast as the car would allow, radio blasting, on flat expanses of road, without another vehicle in sight for miles. I was volunteered into the labor force at the age of fifteen when I worked the drive-thru at the Taco Bell in the nearest "real" town. I would estimate that my own had about five hundred churches, a liquor store, a convenience store next to the high school, a truck stop that burned down in a fire everyone suspected was an insurance-arson job, a seasonal ice cream drive-thru, and a diner famous for its catfish—the last two you could work for at the age of fourteen for less than minimum wage due to agriculture law loopholes written to protect child labor on family farms. I wanted to work at the diner. My mother: "Amber, you're not working for less than minimum wage to gut catfish. You'd hate the smell anyway."

My leisure time was spent on "artsy" extracurriculars, plus a wholesome clandestine youth of moderate drinking, smoking very weak pot, and a secret older boyfriend—a high school dropout on probation who sold the aforementioned weak pot, and whom I was forbidden to see by my mother. Terrified that I would follow in her footsteps, she took my bedroom door off the hinges when she discovered I had been talking to him on the phone. (Sorry, Mom, he had a job and a van, and he was a drummer.) Mostly I liked driving alone with a weak joint and good music, and going

to "shows," meaning live music, at all-ages clubs or somewhere the doorman wouldn't check my ID.

This was around the time that I began to understand
why no one in town had any money. Many of my school-
mates were farmers' kids, but the consolidation of big agriculture meant that multigenerational family farms could no
longer turn a profit. In an attempt to attract industry, the
county and state successfully wooed a company called Quali-
Tech with giant tax breaks, and a steel mill was constructed.
It opened in 1997, just three years after the North American Free Trade Agreement, signed into law by Bill Clinton,
flooded the American market with cheap foreign steel, devastating American steelworkers and their union. The factory
declared bankruptcy and closed in early 2001—my sopho-
more year—after layoffs had already reduced the workforce
to 125 people.[12] The president of the company called it "a
very responsible move," since "the steel business is not in
very good shape."

In the end, sixty workers were retained to sell off what
was left, and the factory sat dormant in the center of town,
unmanned and inoperative, massive, blinding, and silent, a
bleached skeleton in the middle of the cornfield that I drove
by every day on the way to school.

In 2002, another company, Steel Dynamics, bought
the mill for $45 million. It opened two years later, by
which time the company had invested about $100 million
into it. By 2012, the mill employed around five hundred
workers just as Indiana became a right-to-work state, alle-
viating the threat of a totally unionized workforce to their
profits. Now, the politicians had said, jobs were coming
back, and workers had a "choice" in whether or not to join
the union.

That same year, Barry Schneider, vice president of Steel Dynamics, extolled the Indiana legislature for its attack on labor and accommodation of corporate interests:

> We are appreciative that Indiana continues to be a state where Steel Dynamics can expand our product offering and increase our productivity while further establishing our future in our ███████████ home. . . . The recent enactment of the right-to-work legislation is further evidence of Indiana's commitment to providing the most competitive business environment possible for global companies like us to grow.[13]

In addition to a desperate and ununionized workforce, Steel Dynamics was offered up to $600,000 in conditional tax credits through something called the Indiana Economic Development Corporation, and the county "supported the project through additional incentives."

After 9/11, the military looked like the best opportunity for a career to a lot of kids I went to school with. Fearing my mom's student debt, I went as far as looking into the National Guard, but despite the convictions of *literally* every single person I knew (even the local diner had started serving "Freedom Fries"), I suspected the invasion of Iraq was unjustified, possibly immoral, and perhaps even potentially dangerous. I was not, however, "radicalized" by the war. I was gradually coming to the conclusion that politics was about money, money was about power, and my life and future had been and were being shaped by the lack of both. I also liked the idea of freedom, but I couldn't decide exactly what it was.

My father was in and out of my life throughout my childhood; if someone were inclined to armchair diagnosis—

not that I'm encouraging irresponsible speculation—they'd likely bet their life savings on a pretty classic case of bipolar disorder. Sometimes a manic swing would leave him consumed by a single-minded paternal drive. He once picked me up from high school on the Harley with his fellow bikers in roaring procession, very much impressing my classmates. By then the outlaw biker gang occupied most of his time. I thought that looked a little like freedom, but decided that freedom didn't mean absolution of all responsibility to any person or institution outside of your little club. When he missed my high school graduation (I learned from my mamaw it was for something gang related), I decided that his frenetic participation in my life was more effort than it was worth, and I knew that if I stopped making the effort he'd be out of my life. So I stopped.

Graduation was, however, largely a positive experience, and I was even excited to drive forty-five minutes to an hour to the same "discount" college my mother had attended, despite being accepted to IU Bloomington, which cost much more. Regardless of my frugality and relatively consistent part-time employment during school, I ended up incurring about the same amount of student debt that my mother had, as evidently the cuts to grants for low-income students left me in about the same position in the early 2000s as my mom was in after having a kid in the 1980s. Just before I started classes, I did the math of how much I would owe, and tearfully told my mom I didn't want to go to college, that it seemed like a trap. "Don't worry," she said, "everyone does it. You graduate, you get a job, and you pay it off."

I worked as a hotel maid, as a nanny. I worked at a dog kennel and a day care. I worked at a Starbucks and a Subway.

I worked stoned, at an *Andy Griffith Show* theme restaurant. These manifold careers did not cover my expenses.

TOWN #6 (THEN POPULATION: ABOUT 80,000)

I was twenty-one. I have never found any truth in the common wisdom that hangovers get worse with age; mine have always been terrible. I think it's because I never vomit while drunk, my organs marinating in the poison until the next morning—or afternoon—which will inevitably be spent with my head hanging over the toilet. This does not stop me. Once, wasted off Old Crow, a "bourbon" that should be outlawed, I took a man back to an apartment where I was housesitting for a friend. Unable to find the light switch, we nonetheless managed to find the twin bed. In the morning sun, it became apparent that my friend had left out a large bowl of oranges for weeks, which had rotted and gestated an entire South American country's worth of fruit flies. I of course took to the bathroom to retch violently. I am an extremely vocal vomiter. Awakened by the sounds of my distress, the gentleman fetched me a Coca-Cola spiked with a bit of the hair of the dog. We were married for four years.

I had met him at a party. I was visiting the aforementioned friend in Bloomington, Indiana, where she attended the state college. He was a townie and had moved from nearby nowhere for work, first in a factory that downsized, then a grocery store that downsized, then for a university dining hall.

He grew up in a two-bedroom parish trailer next to the Assemblies of God Church where his father preached. He and his year-younger brother had shared bunk beds until the former left home, reuniting a year later as roommates (separate bedrooms this time). They were both homeschooled via correspondence with materials from Bob Jones University. He was a skinhead (the fashionable, working-class punk kind), and he was in a band and a (relatively) nonviolent gang that sometimes scrapped with the racist skinheads but mainly dealt in scalping (no pun intended) tickets and offloading merchandise that "fell off the truck." Best of all, he had also been a shop steward in the UCFW (the grocery union), which was eventually busted, leaving him bitter, angry, and militant. He was at the time very sweet, and he wasn't scared of me, which is my favorite quality in a man. He was gentlemanly but extremely assertive, and he displayed a strong confidence that I later learned was contingent upon inebriation. He was a twenty-four-year-old alcoholic when I met him, but the fun kind. By the time he turned twenty-seven, he was the not-as-fun kind.

Our meeting was an ideal romantic interaction for me, as I am a sexual coward who prefers to be pursued (i.e., a woman). I learned how to flirt by feigning minor misfortune or petty inconvenience. I used to travel with a spent lighter so that the object of my interest might see me struggling with it and use the opportunity to provide me with fire, something men seem to get an atavistic and virility-enhancing thrill from. It's a cheap trick, but why spend when you can save (by being saved)? I didn't even smoke back then.

Beyond this louche pantomime of heteronormativity, I could make people laugh, which also allowed plausible deniability of my romantic interest. My first "line" was cribbed from Tallulah Bankhead, and I only deployed it when I was drunk and absolutely sure I had caught an attractive stranger looking at me no less than three times. I would wait until they walked behind me, look over my shoulder, and sigh with terse exasperation:

"I thought I told you to wait in the car."

If they wanted to talk to me, this was an invitation to flirt. If they did not, I was just joking. If they thought it was funny and hot, they were the sort who would rise to the occasion—"victory favors the bold" and all that. If they found it rude or intimidating, they were prissy, or just pussies who couldn't take a joke, and were perceived as such by onlookers (at least this is what I told myself). Either way, I won, sacrificing no dignity, risking no rejection.

I only recognized this pattern many years later. I was in Berlin on tour with my podcast doing an event for American expats who were phone banking abroad for Bernie Sanders, and I had met a Greek economist who had excellent cocaine. He was a married father of two, and he was excited by my antagonistic questions about whether or not unindustrialized Southern European countries could possibly resist the finance capital of German economic hegemony known as the European Union. He laughed at my jokes, even the ones at his expense. I shoot for "smart, funny, and the kind of bitchy that gets smart guys hard." His family was on vacation, but I slept alone, on the bottom bunk of his kids' bed. I only go where I'm wanted, but sometimes you just want the invite so you can turn it down.

But before all that, I got married at twenty-three. We were madly in love. We formed a (not very good) punk band and even toured a little. We had lots of friends who almost all made some kind of art or played in some band, and in the beginning we could afford a fun little life in a college town. Rents rose though, and I graduated into the economic meltdown with debt. He struggled to find work and eventually enrolled at Indiana University, where his redneck bona fides and admittedly brilliant mind earned him a scholarship for "nontraditional students." He was great at school, much better than me. He worked with focus, whereas I was and still am textbook ADHD, which, again, is a diagnosis I still do not believe in, even as I'm obviously afflicted by it.

Despite his working-class identification, aesthetic, and resentments, my ex wasn't always the class warrior I had dreamed of. To this day, I've never seen the last eight minutes of the movie *Hoffa* due to a screaming match we got into over whether or not the Teamsters were morally justified in working with the mob to crack down on scabs. I'll let you guess which side I landed on, but long story short, I called him "bourgeois," he called me a "moral relativist," and I stormed off drunk into the night, coming back from a friend's place even drunker a few hours later.

I refused to speak to him for two days and made him sleep on the couch for two nights. I think he eventually came around, though not before getting screwed over by bosses a few more times.

I googled "socialism." I started a chapter of Democratic Socialists of America. In Indiana. I made him vice president.

At one event no one came. At another, two anarcho-primitivists showed up and ranted about the state.

It was slow going, but we believed we were militant. Together.

2

MEN WITH SHOVELS AND PERVERTS OF INTEREST

On December 12, 2019, I watched the UK election returns at a bar that was more club than pub, with massive televisions and blaring music. It was a stressful and incongruous environment for an ambivalent atmosphere of both careful hope and half-denied dread. I saw a friend of mine, an NHS doctor whom I had interviewed as part of a series of short films for Labor Campaign for Single Payer Healthcare, an American organization of trade unions that was pushing for universal healthcare in the United States. During the segment, I asked him to guess the cost of different health procedures, services, medications, and care in the land of the free; we filmed his guesses and his horrified reactions and responses to the actual costs. He had worn the stethoscope he received as a graduation present on camera, but with the hammer and sickle that was custom-engraved upon it turned discreetly inward against his shirt, like a coy inside joke or a secret little charm. He was always funny and always sweet, and I was glad to see an unexpected but familiar face.

Earlier in the week, members of my podcast and I had

gone canvassing for Jeremy Corbyn with a trade unionist friend of mine in Barking and Dagenham, an East London borough with an auto plant that in 2008 had made more Ford diesel engines than anywhere else in the world, and which had been shut down in 2013. "A bleak, postindustrial former auto-manufacturing town? It'll be like going back to the Midwest!" I had joked to my Wisconsinite cohost with hammy enthusiasm.

That night at the bar, Dr. Friend was warm as always, but openly nervous. He said he wished he was at home and that this was the first time he hadn't watched the returns with his father. When the results were announced—very suddenly and all at once, because the UK doesn't take days to tally them—his face fell. He apologized and said he had to go.

When I got back to the states, I cowrote a postmortem of the Corbyn campaign with my friend Anton Jäger.[14] The introduction was all me though, and I was compelled to reflect on the two very different Durham Miners' Galas I had attended, and the little hints that I had seen and perhaps tried not to see that portended Labour's loss, parallels of which had already begun to worry me in the Bernie campaign:

> The Durham Miners' Gala is the strangest and biggest anachronism of the British workers' movement—a massive celebration of the workers of an industry long since felled by Thatcher and capital, it still attracts hundreds of thousands of people to the North of England to honor those who built the world.
>
> Last year, the Gala was serious-minded but joyous and truly optimistic. Corbyn took the stage to give his address and was met with wild cheers. This

year, the mood was different—a bit tired, a bit appre-
hensive. The crowd looked nearly the same, save for
one notable increase in a previously rare specimen,
the bellowing European Union activist. As if out of
nowhere, Durham had broken out in a suspicious rash
of EU flags, conspicuously out of place in the heavily
pro-Brexit city (particularly given [the proto-EU's]
indirect role in crushing the 1980s Miners' Strike).

Among Thursday's more shocking upsets
this election was [Corbyn supporter] North West
Durham's Laura Pidcock, who, after referring to the
Leave/Remain conflict as an "arbitrary division,"
lost her seat to a pro-Brexit Tory.

It turns out that the division wasn't so arbitrary and
that reindustrialization was in fact a major priority for
working-class voters, particularly in postindustrial re-
gions, a number of which had voted Tory for the first time,
mirroring the Hillary Clinton campaign's assumption that
Democrats would always remain loyal to a party that not
only hadn't done much for them lately but also had actively
participated in constructing some of the policies that immiserated them.

The digital ink the media spilled arguing over Corbyn's
alleged antisemitism could have lit up Paris on Christmas,
and the bourgeois press had frenzied like sharks in chum
when the highest-profile Jewish journalist in the UK to
speak out in defense of Corbyn had been anonymously and,
as it turns out largely spuriously, #MeToo'd. I tried to warn
him, six minutes before he posted a public apology, which is
never received by the public as anything beyond an admis-

sion of guilt: "Don't say a fucking word." But he panicked, and sealed his fate.

Throughout the debates over "antisemitism in the Labour Party," similar concessions were made to bad actors, as if political enemies could be placated with formal statements of contrition and pledges to purify one's ranks. Now on the back foot, many of the most high-profile Corbyn supporters spent a lot of time conceding moral authority to their political enemies, apologizing to a mob that didn't actually care about, or really even believe, their own accusations. I still maintain that, to the extent that the antisemitism "scandal" may have influenced Labour voters, it was not in convincing any sizable number of them that the party was racist; if the smears had any effect on turnout for Labour, it was due to the moral and intellectual insecurity of suckers who didn't know the game, and a not insignificant number of sanctimonious subversives within the party who maintained they were merely "very concerned" that Corbyn's support for Palestine had "allowed" bigotry to fester. The pathetic inability of the Corbynista chattering classes to just say "Fuck you, that's a lie and you know it," likely did not inspire confidence in voters.

And of course, after so many internal leaks have been made public, it is at this point impossible to deny that Corbyn was, just as Bernie would later be, repeatedly sabotaged by the resentful and devious right wing of his own party, again and again. The libs will always prefer Boris to Jezza and Trump to Bernie.

Still though, the former Labour strongholds in the postindustrial North of England, where Brexit was perceived as the only path back to a powerful industrial workers' movement, all but prove outright that those voters remember. They want it back, as well they should.

★ ★ ★

In both the UK and the US, there's been frantic campaigning by many would-be socialist politicos to insist that the industrial worker is no longer necessary for social democracy and that there must be some new agent of history to take their place. It's important here to note that these politically unambitious cynics, usually smack-dab in the center of the media/activist/academic Venn diagram, are not *merely* faddists scrambling for a fresh, new, and perhaps more "woke" substitute for the blue-collar workers whose putative, anti-elitist resentments make them so nervous (though many most certainly are). They are also, more often than not, something far more pernicious.

These people are perverts.

Specifically, they tend to fall into one or more of three broad categories of pervert: masochists, pedophiles, or necrophiliacs.

I would add that, in addition to the fetishes they have mistaken for political strategy, they all repeat the failure of foresight and providence that my friend Jed once put so perfectly when he said, "The left can't count." As the meaning of my diagnosis and classification may not be immediately apparent, I will provide the reader a brief ethnography of these deviants.

Let's start with the masochists. These are usually guilt-ridden, progressive, liberal, college-educated professionals who have internalized the idea that the socialist movement can and/or should look to "marginalized people"—the fuzzy neologism now generally employed as a euphemism for "minorities" and women—to lead the way to victory. In the masochistic mind, this total abdication of responsibility to the people *least* in a position to exercise political agency is an act of atonement for the "privileges" enjoyed by the un-marginal, largely because the masochist believes that "privileges" exist as the undeserved spoils of ostensibly transhistorical sins such as racism, sexism, xenophobia, etc. The left masochist imagines that he, being the beneficiary of these sins, has been very, very bad. He wants to be punished for his ill-gotten (though often very relative) "success," which explains why he so often appears so titillated, if not ravished, when the right wins, which they do, over and over again.

So what's wrong with centering the margins, besides the obviously too-cute-by-half oxymoron? For one, the identitarian categories that are so often conflated with abjection contain many individuals whose priorities run counter to the working class. To possess (or to be possessed by? the relationship is never clear) a "marginalized identity" does not mean one is abject, disenfranchised, or even particularly hard up. So obviously, masochists attract dominatrices, or in this case opportunistic self-appointed "representatives" of the margins, who of course can benefit politically, socially, and financially from leveraging their identities and whipping their eager supplicants.

But what of the *authentically* marginalized? Those who have *truly* suffered in ways we can confirm? Well, those people can be chancers too, and frankly they have more moral justification and incentive to pick up the paddle, much to the delight of a whimpering pervert desiring punishment. "Marginality" as social or political currency is simply not an economy any social movement should be engaging in.

In my own experience in activist circles, there have been many, many times when I could have exploited my own lack of "privilege" (again, relative to others in the room) as the only woman and/or working-class person—plus a number of cultural signifiers that are conflated with actual class position (the young marriage, the single teen mom, the middle-American background, etc.)—in order to dominate the proceedings, if not the group itself.

As luck would have it, I prefer to reserve my perversions for actual sex and my aggressions for actual animosities (or at least for the beloved pastime of bullying). Moreover, when it comes to organizing or discussion, I prefer to be valued for my contributions and my commitment rather than what I represent in the masochist imaginary. However . . . if I was perhaps a little more ruthless, perhaps a little more ambitious, or merely the sort to get off on intra-social, pseudo-political BDSM . . . well, I could have been a tyrant. I won't say I have never been tempted.

And those piggies would have *loved* it.

Even if there *were* a vetting process for the true-blue comrades among the most wretched of the earth that could reliably identify those who possess a saint-like ability to resist the temptation to opportunistically wield the whip, there is nothing to suggest that there is some superior wisdom, virtue, or skill inherent in them merely by virtue of their marginality. To assume otherwise is to fall prey to the over-simplified logic of standpoint theory, which assumes that subjectivity is the key to objectivity. Experiences of marginality, just like experiences of successful social and political integration, give you information; but experiences do not automatically give you the ability to interpret or the insight into that information, and the marginal certainly aren't any more free of attendant ideologies. Or, to put it more plainly: a shitty life doesn't make you better than anyone else. (I'll admit, this is something that took me a while to figure out after coming to New York and meeting more than a few rich, radical-chic assholes who seemed to think of politics the same way I might think of a fun, slightly slutty dress. Don't get me wrong; I *am* better than them, but not because of that.)

Then there is what should be the most obvious practical objection to fetishizing the margins: marginal people are usually pretty busy trying to get out of the margins, as it is a condition defined by a lack of power.

This is why for Marxists, the category is "the workers" rather than "the margins," or as the masochist imagines them, "the tragic."

Vivek Chibber said it best in "Why We Still Talk About the Working Class":

> The working class is unlike any other social grouping in the noncapitalist section of modern society. However penurious it is, however dominated it is, however atomized it is, it is the goose that lays the golden egg. It is the source of profits, because unless workers show up to do their work every day and create profits for their employers, that principle of profit maximization cannot be carried out. It remains a dead letter.
>
> Workers, therefore, have an opportunity, if they can take advantage of it: they hold the lever to the stream of profits that keeps the system going. Capitalists have the authority over them, but unless

they agree to do what their employers say, the employers are left simply holding the bag—no profits for them.

Workers, therefore, are important for a strategic reason, which is that they are the agent, and the only agent, that has a structural place within the society that can bring the power centers to their knees.[15]

When the working class is strong, it "brings the margins in." Conversely, when the working class is weak, the margins expand, both to make room for more people and to distance those people from power. The workers' movement is the only thing that can reliably correct (and prevent) marginalization in the first place, which is why the political strength of blue-collar factory workers was so instrumental to the social democratic advances and political victories of the working class, and why the decline of that power has immiserated far more people than just the laid-off auto worker.

Deindustrialization in the developed world has devastated minorities and women across the planet; capitalists didn't "send jobs" to the Global South out of the goodness of their hearts, they did it to set up colonies, where it was much easier to maximize profits by controlling and disciplining workers. The outsourcing of manufacturing has retarded these countries' organic economic development with the express purpose of *keeping* them underdeveloped, a permanent source of desperate labor. It wasn't too long ago that immigrant rights activists marched alongside US labor leaders to stop the mutually destructive policies of free trade that both scattered sweatshops across the world and devastated American workers.

For "marginal people," deindustrialization was, and is,

a shrapnel grenade in perpetual detonation, sending more and more people sailing from the very ground beneath their feet and further into the margins. But even as the margins crowd, a minoritarian army of the most disenfranchised is still a minoritarian army of the most disenfranchised, and way out there on the margins they're not going to win by themselves.

Masochists, however, don't *want* to win. They want to be spanked (metaphorically speaking).

But moving on . . .

Also among the political perverts are the pedophiles, who believe that the *youth* will be the new agent of history. These pedos' conceptions of young people often echo the middle-class Victorian's belief in childhood innocence and purity, and the pedophile is left breathless at what they believe to be primitive wisdom emerging from the mouths of babes. A lack of experience, for that is what youth is by its very definition, seems to them a sort of grace, and perhaps the only thing that will save us from damnation. Of course, operating as they do in a child-worshipping cult, it should be clear that they don't actually like kids, they just "*like kids.*"

Currently, anyone with any exposure to leftists or liberals is forced to witness such political pedophilia in the ecstatic glorification of Malala Yousafzai, the Sunrise Movement, the youth surge in Democratic Socialists of America, and that walking, talking umlaut, Greta Thunberg. However, such Humberts and their unwitting Lolitas have been around since the postwar period, when the concept of the teenager was invented by marketers, who had recently found themselves blessed by a baby boom of new potential consumers. More recently, the pedos placed their hopes on the downwardly mobile millennials who came after the post-2008 financial collapse to Occupy Wall Street (alas). Before that, though a bit more diffuse, the kiddies of interest were the Gen-X Adbuster anarchists who stormed Seattle for a last stand against free trade (again, alas).

And of course, there was the biggest youth movement in modern history, the counterculture boomers, who *really* thought they were going to change the world until they hit the wall, adjusted their expectations, and cut their losses to work on their stock portfolios and reminisce about free love and free drugs as they eased us into a world of free trade.

The failure of the New Left is why so many political pedos are baby boomers; having declared age an affliction, they inadvertently set their own self-destruct sequences, and now they don't know what to do with themselves. They're ashamed of the world they failed to revolutionize, remorseful of their hubris, and fearful of the encroaching irrelevance they assigned themselves long ago, when they somehow failed to consider that establishing a political currency so fleeting as youth might come back to bite them in their wrinkled old asses one day.

Still, I caution against anything as petulant and middle-class as generational warfare. The Old Left seemed out of touch at the time, and it's understandable that the hippies didn't know what they were doing, or, rather, not doing. From where and when they stood, the chaos and hostility of the era looked very much like the death rattle of the old order. As Hunter S. Thompson said, "There was a fantastic universal sense that whatever we were doing was right, that we were winning."[16] Alas.

When veterans of the New Left and the counterculture feel guilty or somehow responsible for the state of the world, it's almost always only because they continue to operate under the individualist delusions that defined their generation. This is not to say they didn't expend a lot of energy on political dead ends, it's just that, unless they were in the halls of power, they're overestimating their influence and how close they ever really got. Their disappointments, anxieties, and pain, however, do not excuse the pedophilia, which is not only creepy but also a grave tactical error.

Much like the masochist, the pedophile paints their fetish objects with a broad brush, always imagining some sort of progressive uniformity among a diverse demographic that is sometimes apolitical, sometimes right-wing, sometimes left-wing, and sometimes, oftentimes, a curious hodgepodge of political and social idiosyncrasies: young people.

Also like the masochists, the pedos use their fetish to justify passing the buck, indulging in another total abdication of responsibility to keep fighting, to work intergenerationally, and in particular, to honestly and dutifully recount, and try to explain, their successes and failures to fledgling activists who should be learning from their experience. As with the marginalism of the masochist, what first appears to be handing over the reins is later revealed to be leaving them with the bill, sending them into battle on your behalf, and all manner of other terribly mixed metaphors that I refuse to smooth out, possibly due to my petulant millennial sense of entitlement.

What's worse, the pedos appear to be accelerating; we see the kids that are supposed to save the world getting younger and younger, meaning *actual* children, who have very little agency, as they are generally too young to even be on the labor market much less develop a class consciousness. This is not to say that the inexperience of youth leaves them without convictions or instincts, but Children's Crusades have a tendency to turn out pretty tragically.

And what do kids learn from being thrust into activism at an earlier and earlier age? Mostly that, yes, they *are* powerless, and that popular will has less influence over elites than it has in a very long time. A dispiriting failure endured too young can really burn a kid out for the long run; it saps you of the sort of energy and passion that has to be developed, maintained, and periodically rejuvenated. To foist such urgent burdens like climate change on the young, to wash your hands of your responsibility to be older and wiser, is to send them into war alone, unprepared, without even warning them about the one thing you're most familiar with: failure. People who care about kids don't leave them fucked, so to speak.

The liberal media does much to perpetuate this toxic cycle by basically turning out political kiddie porn. In 2017, I went to Canterbury, which had just gone Labour in the general election off of the Corbyn energy after decades of Tory rule. Triumphant article after triumphant article celebrated the swing and congratulated the "youth vote." When I arrived and interviewed Canterbury Momentum members, however, they informed me that there was one problem: none of it was true. Their canvassing strategy had been to go outside the posh areas and speak to the people normally ignored in elections, in particular the people who didn't tend to vote. While they did get students from the nearby universities to canvass for Corbyn, I was informed that the majority of students who end up voting do not register in Canterbury but rather where they came from.

"Also," said my contact, "it was summer. Most of the

students had already gone home!" This massive oversight is not surprising, especially given how London-centric the UK media tends to be, but the fact that no one in the left-leaning media had thought to even *ask* Corbyn campaigners how they had turned out the vote in Canterbury, and that the media had just rushed to declare the then-largely-absent students the saviors of the party, well, that's a pervert for you.

The thing about youth is that, if you're lucky, you grow out of it (sure beats the alternative). This brings us back to basic numeracy: the left can't count. Not only do the young comprise a very temporary category for individuals, but their demographic is also diminishing in number. The baby boom is over. Even if "the youth" shared a political hive mind (again, they do not), the "wave" of young'uns of the postwar era hasn't been repeated. The kids are fewer than they once were, and they have less power than they once did; they can't win.

The pedophiles don't really want to win either. They want to fuck kids (metaphorically speaking).

Finally, you have the necrophiliacs, who, while seemingly harmless, are the most insidious perverts of them all.

In March of 2021, a second-generation college professor at the University of Chicago ran an op-ed in *The New York Times* under the headline, "Manufacturing Isn't Coming Back. Let's Improve These Jobs Instead."[17] The thesis was that "care work"—which he defined rather broadly via Ohio State sociologist Rachel Dwyer as "jobs tending to young, old, disabled and sick people, along with housekeeping, food service and domestic work"—should become the primary focus of organizing.

He correctly observes that care needs are increasing, specifically because union manufacturing work has been so decimated and disciplined, reducing a formerly thriving, powerful labor movement into a deracinated and alienated ex–working class that is increasingly miserable, sick, and dying: "As industrial employment contracted, it left behind populations that were poorer, sicker and older." No argu ment there. However, not only does the author view this suffering and decline as a foregone conclusion (*why* exactly "manufacturing isn't coming back" is never really explained) but he also sees the healthcare crisis of deindustrialization as *actually* an opportunity, since now "we" (the "we" here is not defined) can simply organize all the people required to tend to an ever-expanding misery.

(In the interest of full disclosure, I will concede that the author in question has called me a "fascist" on Twitter. However, ladies and gentlemen of the jury, I will take the high road, and rather than malign him with fallacious and sensational insults, I will engage with the argument pre- sented before illustrating beyond a shadow of a doubt that this man is—and I cannot stress this enough—a necrophil- iac . . . metaphorically speaking.)

The first obstacle with this approach is that what the au- thor is suggesting is, in fact, unappealing to most people, especially the remaining industrial working class, the former industrial working class, and, indeed, anyone with a mem- ory of a strong industrial labor movement. I would hazard to guess that they would consider such a "plan" pretty ghoulish; the suggestion that everyone left in the wake of deindustri- alization should merely feed off their own dead and dying ignores the fact that they'd prefer not to need such dire care in the first place. Additionally, this plan actually depends on senseless suffering. Taken to its logical conclusion, one would have to argue that making people healthier by increasing their standard of living is bad for (care) workers, since it would decrease demand. Business is booming, folks, we have to protect the industry. Forget the means of production and the wealth of the world, your own dead and dying are enough to sustain you!

I'd also argue that this concession to the allegedly inevitable and permanent death of the factory worker lines right up with the worldview of "mugged by reality" liberals, and it is so repellent to the working class that it motivates them to vote for anyone who refuses to accept the destitution and powerlessness of neoliberal capitalism. Remember that both Trump and Johnson were elected—at least in part—due to vehement anti-deindustrialization sentiment.

Or perhaps I'm wrong. Perhaps these ideas will be the topic of discussion in postindustrial towns across America. Perhaps the author could do a speaking tour of union lodges all over the former steel belt, where his argument would be extremely well received. Maybe they'll slap him on the back, say, "Gee buddy, I never thought of it that way," and buy him a beer. Still, even if this vision was celebrated throughout the land, there are other practical objections to both the position and his reasoning.

Aneurin Bevan, architect of the UK's National Health Service, was correct when he said, "The language of priorities is the religion of socialism." However, there is nothing to suggest that "care work" should be an "instead" or that public investment in manufacturing is somehow in competition with care work for resources or attention (unless you subscribe to the aforementioned ghoulish conclusion that suffering is our new industry).

Additionally, "care work" is a fuzzy category at best, and one that lumps in public hospital nurses with private in-home care workers. Insofar as care workers could be considered a coherent workforce, much of the growth within this industry comes from the private sector, which is devouring what little public care work remains. To his credit, the aforementioned author tacks this inconvenient little detail on at the end, saying, "In the long term, it may not be possible to rebuild mass prosperity around care work without converting the industry to a nonprofit and even public basis." It seems then that his argument is predicated on putting the cart before the horse.

In response to that pesky little issue of care work privatization, the author suggests that "the federal government could require increased nurse staffing levels, which would drive up pay and limit overwork. It could mandate higher wages and stronger labor protections for all care workers. It could put home and community-based services on equal footing with care in nursing homes under Medicaid, or even move toward a public insurance program for universal family care." They could. And I could grow wings and shit on the University of Chicago from five hundred feet in the air (all things are possible through Christ). But since my personal Lord and Savior is conspicuously absent from federal policy, I would suggest that workers seizing the means of production is a surer path to a more egalitarian and humane world.

Another immediate advantage of most manufacturing, trucking, or building work is that you don't have to pay to play; you may require training, but it's usually on the job, and (most importantly) you get paid. You don't need a college degree to build engines or to be a carpenter. Nursing, however, is a profession requiring years of very costly education and often unbelievable debt. Obviously, this is a barrier to entry for most Americans.

Furthermore, I have, perhaps inaccurately, always assumed the academic, left-liberal, anti–hard hat set to be very concerned about "the environment," something they often view as a once-Rousseauian paradise now polluted by human beings. I've been under the impression that they are greatly worried by climate change, something they imagine eschatologically and warn us of with cinematic sermons reminiscent of a fire-and-brimstone apocalypse. In doing so, they often appear not only hysterical but also inaccurate, overdramatizing a very real threat by describing something that in no way resembles the gradual increase of instability marked by intermittent catastrophes that defines actually existing climate change (which is scary enough as it is). It's difficult to hold it against anyone who would write them off and subsequently doubt the urgency of the issue itself.

This hysteria, however, begs the question; what do they think the carbon footprint of shipping steel from China to Detroit is? How are we going to get all that badly needed public transportation? Broadly put, we need a new, green infrastructure, and even more broadly, we need to restore and expand our regular infrastructure. I have often said that when historians look back on this time in America, they will comment in bafflement at the hypernormalization of physical decay; it didn't take too long before we all just took for granted that buildings burn down, bridges collapse, and sometimes the Amtrak just sort of . . . flies off the rails.

We need a Green New Deal. Hell, we need another, *regular* New Deal, but we can't do any of that without hard hats.

Challenging capital is also much trickier and more difficult for care workers than industrial workers precisely because care work is so essential. Nurses usually can't all walk off the emergency room floor in a wildcat strike without putting patients at risk, which is why they generally don't.

If the pedophiles and masochists can't count voters, then the necrophiliacs can't count dollars; the choke points of healthcare profits simply aren't in the care sector. The big profits are in insurance companies, pharmaceuticals, and medical supplies (the latter of which, I might add, are goods that must be manufactured).

As for manufacturing not "coming back" to the United States, it's worth pointing out that it didn't ever exactly "leave," at least not totally.

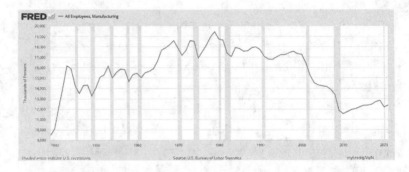

American manufacturing reached peak employment in 1979 with 19.428 million workers.[18] In 2019, it was at a dismal 12.817 million, but it's important to note that the decline itself hasn't been a steady descent. There was minor growth in 1984, and again from 1988 to 1989, and a relatively steady increase from 1993 to 1998 to levels commensurate with the low dips of the 1970s, and often with levels above— sometimes considerably above—that supposedly golden era of manufacturing from the 1950s to the mid-1960s. Since the all-time low of 11.529 million in 2010, manufacturing jobs have been slowly but steadily increasing (until they dipped again in 2020). Even that hero of the working class, President Donald Trump, saw an increase of more than 450,000 manufacturing jobs.

Clearly, there's still manufacturing in America. And clearly, it's possible to open a new factory in America that turns a profit. As for the ones that "leave," they can certainly be compelled to stay; even tepid liberals don't mind tinkering with taxes here and there to discourage American companies from offshoring. It's hardly a leap to believe that if we were ever able to tinker *real hard*, we could get 'em to *on*shore. (I still hold the old-school socialist position that we could nationalize entire industries, but hey, one step at a time.)

I am not saying that any of this will be easy—merely that it's clearly possible, which we know, because we've already done it on a small scale. I don't have a road map, but I suspect that increased unionization and labor militancy in the actually existing manufacturing workplace would certainly give it a shot in the arm. Slowing the free movement of capital from state to state and country to country wouldn't hurt either.

The author of this little misery industry manifesto says industrial workers were "left behind"[19]; but make no mistake, they weren't left behind—they were evicted, because they were strong enough to pose a threat to capital. This means that not only are there *fewer* manufacturing jobs, but the ones we have left are far shittier. The relentless shock of mass layoffs and high unemployment means that workers usually take what they can get. But we still make things in America, things besides misery. We even still build new factories, but when capitalists can bust unions and get cheap materials and labor from other countries, the new factories they open in the United States give them a chance to hire a new crop of workers (which of course, saves them money on shipping), but at lower wages, and without a union. These are all obstacles, but they're not dead ends.

And yes, there are also technological advances that reduce the number of workers needed to produce materials
and products. Luckily enough, we need *way* more things in
this country. For all the talk of American consumerism and
waste, we don't seem to be gluttons for the bigger, more
important things that are essential to a thriving society—
railroads, schools, hospitals, etc., come to mind.

Most important of all, manufacturing not only still
employs people in America, it also still creates billions and
billions of dollars in wealth, which is the other major advantage it has over care work.[20] It's leverage, not social value,
that makes care work less weaponizable against capital: the
dollar value that workers are capable of threatening by withholding their labor.

Unfortunately, the care labor involved in the management
of those who are suffering the most isn't particularly lucrative, since the very wealthy are content to pay out of pocket,
and hospitals are increasingly privatized, if not shut down
entirely. With cuts to healthcare benefits, hospitals, Medicare, and Medicaid, impoverished patients will be increasingly relegated to a lower tier of healthcare, where they can
only pay poor nurses poor wages, while the healthcare the
wealthy purchase is safe from downward redistribution. The
capitalists can afford private healthcare, childcare, schools,
and more; but they cannot turn their wealth into more
wealth without manufacturing, trucking, and construction.

But how does all of this make this author a necrophiliac?

At first glance, it would be easy to mistake him for a
necrophagiac—someone who fantasizes about eating the dead.
But the author doesn't actually want to eat them *himself,* he
merely suggests that the working class consume the suffering

of *one another*. What thrills him is observing the expired, even watching them defiled or devoured by others (zombies eating the living and the dead, the latter of whom sometimes get away only to become zombies themselves; you know, Romero rules), but actually sampling the sickly cuisine himself? There's not enough hand sanitizer in the world.

The book on which his op-ed was based is a hagiographic history of steel manufacturing and the heroic workers who fought to preserve it. The cover features a modernist, WPA-style image of a factory, newly stamped with the red cross. It immediately reminded me of another cover, Stuart Holland's *The State as Entrepreneur*, which also features an image of a factory in the very same style, except Holland's factory is held by a human hand. While the latter cover portrays a world where workers literally "hold" the means of production, the former reimagines the factory as a hospital—or possibly hospice—where workers apparently go to be ill, age, and die. One cannot argue that the pervert has no love for the working class, but he, like so many liberals, prefers them in hindsight, preferably safe in their coffins, or at least wandering around the graveyard in a famished stupor.

The psychosexual appeal of political necrophilia is threefold.

The first is simply material. Unlike the masochists, the necrophiliacs aren't looking for self-flagellation so much as professional recognition and career advancement; there is social and literal capital to be mined from an increasingly smaller pot of funding for scholarship, and the university now favors novelty and hyperspecialization rather than "grand narratives" like Marxism. There are more PhD spots in constructing an often-specious dichotomy of "pink collar" versus blue collar, or "white working class" against POC, and you're more likely to get tenure if you manipulate a veneer of feminism or antiracism to score liberal brownie points.

The second reason the labor necrophiliacs thrill at the decline of hard hats with union cards? Fear.

It is important here to clarify something about necrophilia.

As death activists go, I'm partial to a pretty millennial woman named Caitlin Doughty, the mortician, author, and YouTube personality who made her name with her video series, *Ask a Mortician*.[21] Doughty's tone is easygoing and lighthearted, but she takes her mission, which is one of education, kindness, and comfort, very seriously. She has developed a real fanbase with her frank (but gentle) demystification of that which comes for us all. Similar to any good sex ed teacher (the Thanatos to their Eros, if you will), she answers the sort of questions people often prefer to ask anonymously; obviously, necrophilia comes up.

In March of 2014, Doughty made a video to answer a question about the prevalence of necrophilia in the industry. Never one to shy from taboo, she gave some history of the term, and a little rundown of what we "know," given the somewhat understandably limited number of studies on the subject: "necrophiles" are usually men, there's no proof it's genetic, and most fascinatingly, *only about 15 percent of necrophiles are actually fetishistically attracted to dead bodies.* For the other 85 percent, "the desire is to obtain an unrejecting, unresisting partner."

She suggests, as an example, the condition of impotence, a potentially humiliating experience where performance anxiety might be alleviated by sex with a human body that is no longer capable of reacting, much less responding to your inadequacies. "Dead bodies are emotionally safe, and [necrophiles] are able to project their desires onto what is essentially a blank canvas."

A corpse can't laugh at your soft dick or look at your soft belly with disgust . . . or call you a pussy-ass little college-boy bitch. Someone with a paralyzing fear of the living might very well find safe refuge in that.

So maybe the author of "Manufacturing Isn't Coming Back" doesn't love the nurses so much as he fears a hard hat with a union card and a pulse, those scary men and their blue collars who remember NAFTA and who might reject him and his ideas.

Maybe he just can't get it up . . . metaphorically speaking.

Doughty also goes on to clarify that corpse fucking isn't a victimless crime; for the loved ones of the departed, the very idea of some pervert molesting the remains of someone they care about—someone who may be gone from this world but lives on in our hearts—is an extreme violation of something "sacred." I know the phrase "lives on in our hearts" sounds like Hallmark card pablum, but for the grieving it's often very, very real.

For the petrified political necrophiliacs, it's not only rejection they fear, but potential harm at the hands of the dangerously alive. To them, a construction union's endorsement of Trump is not evidence that manufacturing and organized blue-collar workers have a political agenda that has gone unaddressed or even opposed by the Democratic Party—say continued work for its members—but that those savage union members (read: men) are merely inherently stupid, bigoted, and corrupt. They're scary.

After Trump was elected, a senior editor at a high-profile progressive news site made a public Facebook post:

> Wanted to share an experience from earlier today. This afternoon, I had a plumber come to my apartment to fix a clogged drain. He was a perfectly nice guy and a consummate professional. But he was also a middle-aged white man with a southern accent who seemed unperturbed by this week's news. And while I had him in the apartment, I couldn't stop thinking about whether he had voted for Trump, whether he knew my last name is Jewish, and how that knowledge might change the interaction we were having inside my own home. I have no real reason to believe he was a Trump supporter or an anti-Semite, but in my uncertainty I couldn't shake the sense of potential danger. I was rattled for some time after he left.
>
> I'm very privileged in so far [sic] as this sense of danger is unfamiliar to me. And I know I feel it much less acutely than a lot of other people right now. I'm still a straight, white guy who can phenotypically pass for gentile. Plus my first name is pretty WASP-y.

> But today was a reminder that ambiguous social interactions now feel unsafe and unpredictable in a way that they never did before. And even if Trump is gone in four years, I don't expect to ever reclaim that feeling of security. That's just one more thing you voted for, if you voted for him.[22]

After my initial scoff at his sign-off (as if he had any Trump-voting friends, Facebook or otherwise), I realized that not only are so many middle-class liberal professionals, particularly those who make up the liberal media, absolutely fucking insane, but their politics operate according to a delusional fear of working-class people that rises to the level of psychosis. They are terrorized by narcissistic fantasies of persecution at the hands of the unwashed proles, as if the "perfectly nice guy and consummate professional" who unclogs your disgusting drain (because you don't know how) doesn't merely disdain you but actively despises you with a single-minded hatred and malice that poses a real physical threat to these genteel heroes of progressivism. ("Amber, they don't hate you—most of the time they don't even notice you!")

Later I wrote an article about how to responsibly and ethically cover far-right-wing movements, and I had to mention that it was not in fact good journalism to "ruminate and fantasize from the safety of your middle-class New York City professional media life that you are some kind of millennial Anne Frank just because you're petrified of blue collar workers."[23]

Liberals *want* to like the workers, but they fundamentally perceive them as wild animals; thus, they can only find them sympathetic when they are domesticated, endangered, or— even better—extinct.

There is still a third aspect of necrophilia that titillates those who lust for the dead: it flatters their sense of professional superiority.

Returning to the pervert's monograph, it's notable that he chose for his hero one Eddie Sadlowski, a third-generation Chicago steelworker and labor militant. Sadlowski was funny, bold, and tough, and looked as if he had been plucked straight out of central casting. To the delight of many, his union thug persona belied a social liberalism in step with the New Left of the time. At first glance, liberals might assume an Archie Bunker, but Sadlowski's cultural politics were closer to Meathead's. He was hated by his enemies and even more beloved by his comrades. But he was *extra-appealing* to the professional set, not only because he did funny interviews with *Penthouse* and *Rolling Stone* where he denounced the Vietnam War and racism within and without the union movement, and not *only* for having lost a militant and righteous battle against capital and the sclerotic and corrupt elements within his own union.

They loved Eddie Sadlowski because Eddie Sadlowski didn't like his job.

★   ★   ★

January 10, 2021, from Mark Dudzic, president of the Labor Campaign for Single Payer Healthcare:

Funny how "high culture" reaches into the working class in ways that are unnoticed by the bourgeois gatekeepers. I don't know much about your background but the picture of a young working class Holy Roller ballet-loving girl put me in mind of my mother, who raised 5 kids while working midnights as a nurses' aide in a hospital. She loved Broadway show tunes and used to blast the Metropolitan Opera's Saturday matinee broadcast every weekend as she cleaned the house. (My father, on the other hand, had almost no cultural interests. When he wasn't whacking us around or blowing his paycheck in the bars, he would watch nature shows on tv to reinforce his darkly Darwinian and essen-

*tialist view of human nature . . .). She instilled in me a
lifelong love for opera. A few years back, the chief steward
of the stagehands union at Lincoln Center (a big supporter
of M4A) took me and my wife on a backstage tour of the
Opera House as they were getting ready to broadcast the
Saturday matinee. One of the peak experiences of my
organizing life. My mom would have been so pleased to
hear it. Really evokes the "soul of a soulless world" that
the old bearded one talked about.*

January 14, 2021

*Your mother sounds like a woman after my own
heart. And your lovely story reminds me of my writing
partner* ▮▮▮▮▮▮▮▮▮ *father, an electrical supply sales-
man from Bensonhurst whose small business has always
vacillated between booming and failing. The best contracts
during a boom year however, were with Lincoln Center,
which of course has incredible perks. This Ostjuden
Brooklynite who attended Brooklyn College (the first in
his family to do so) in the 1970s, has a natural inclination
toward the sublime, and he was very serious about exposing his children to the arts. He took them to opera, plays,
and symphonies all throughout their childhood, whether
times were lean or plentiful. As kids they didn't realize
how exceptional those experiences were, but as adults,*
▮▮▮▮ *and his sisters understand they lucked out, for
the free tickets of course, but even more so for their father's
good taste.*

*And you make my upbringing sound so cinematic! As
a kid I would have probably usually described it as "boring, surrounded by nothing but cornfields, can't wait to
get out."*

Funnily enough, growing up I was always under the impression that my mother—who is responsible for encouraging my interests in/pursuit of everything from ballet and opera to punk rock—came by her appreciation of the arts via the "middle class values" instilled in her by her own parents (before she got knocked up in high school and plummeted down the economic ladder as a single mom in the Reagan's '80s, of course).

At some point I realized that actually, both of her parents were more similar to your father; my grandpa and grandma were both very angry and depressed, respectively, and both were generally either emotionally or physically absent—or too hostile—to really share culture or interests with their kids. Talking to my mom, her brother, and my grandma and grandpa, I eventually pieced together that she had discovered her own "middle class" interests in the arts—painting, Shakespeare, the symphony—entirely from the then-decently-funded (and recently bussed) Indianapolis public schools, plus all the "fancy stuff" (my uncle's phrase) on PBS.

Apparently, when the arts are integrated into public life, people don't really need specialized training (or even decent parenting) to appreciate them; go figure!

Solidarity,
Amber A'Lee

★   ★   ★

In January of 1977, when steel employment and union membership was flying high, "Oilcan" Eddie Sadlowski gave a now-famous (or infamous, depending on who you ask) interview to *Penthouse* magazine during his campaign for president of United Steelworkers of America. He was described on the cover as "America's Ballsiest Labor Leader," and he did not disappoint. He denounced his opponent for "tuxedo unionism" and concessions to management. He was funny but serious-minded. He radiated a brazen charm, the kind of self-assuredness that could come off as cocky from a lesser man. Moreover, he was fearless and principled, a true union man whose loyalty was to the workers.

But he shocked many when he said that nobody should work in a steel mill:

> Working forty hours a week in a steel mill drains the lifeblood of a man. There are workers there right now who are full of poems and doctors who are operating cranes. We've run the workers into the ground. Ultimately, society has nothing to show for it but waste. A doctor is more useful than a man with a capacity to be a doctor spending his life on the crane. Such men are kept from functioning at their best, not only by U.S. Steel but by doctors themselves. I advocate putting people who work in the steel mills into medical professions. They have the brainpower to become scientists, yet the system sells them short.[24]

Judith Stein's groundbreaking history *Running Steel, Running America: Race, Economic Policy, and the Decline of Liberalism,* opens with an anecdote. After completing her research on the steel industry in Birmingham, Alabama, Stein dropped off her rental car at Alamo, where an employee drove her to the airport. He was a young Black man whom she estimated was about nineteen or twenty years old, and they struck up a conversation. When the steel ore mines had shut down (in favor of cheaper ore from Venezuela), his miner grandfather had been transferred to the Fairfield Steel Mill. His father worked at the pipe mill. The young man had been enrolled in community college, but he quit; what he really wanted to do was work at the mill. The minimum wage job at a rental car service was what he was doing in the meantime. When Stein asked him what he thought his prospects were, he was "pensive," and replied merely, "Well, there are a lot of men on layoff."[25]

Plenty of blue-collar workers wanted to be blue-collar workers. Plenty of blue-collar workers like or even love their jobs—yes, even in steel mills—especially if they're working under decent conditions for decent pay. It doesn't mean they like every day at work, or even every week, or that there aren't aspects of their job they hate, but unless you're a Stockholm Syndrome–afflicted tech guy, everyone hates their job some days.

It's true that work at a steel mill can be unbearable, but many people disagree that it necessarily has to be, and many would counter Sadlowski's line that "No man wants to wake up every day and face the blast furnace" with "Well, of course not *every* day." Americans work too much, and even if you don't, sometimes work just sucks.

As for poems, music, literature, etc., the obstacles to the creation and appreciation of the arts for people is not blue-collar work. The working class have not only always made and enjoyed art, but when they're strong, they've also organized their own arts and culture institutions and programs. The brass bands of Durham or the Labor Day marches in the United States are the more obvious examples, but Labour and Communist Parties have built public theaters and funded community classes in painting and literature. They demanded and won public funding for instruments in public schools, museums, orchestras, operas, and all the "high art" that was formerly the domain of the elites. I saw my first play from Shakespeare, *Macbeth*, on PBS. I saw my second in a park, where a community theater put on *The Taming of the Shrew* for free. (That I was rooting for both Lady Macbeth and Katherina, the titular shrew, may have portended some of my future virtues.)

Even without community, family, or educational support—even without permission—kids still paint murals on the sides of buildings, distribute music they record from home on the internet, draw comics, and make zines. Hell, even on food stamps I was in a (not very good) punk band. The enrichment of mankind's further creativity and appreciation for the arts is fostered by financial security, leisure time, and public funding and programs, not the cultivation of some professionalized or liberal arts–oriented workforce.

And as for the perception of care work as somehow less grueling than factory work, I can't say I ever worked in manufacturing (though I did drive a forklift in both a garden center and a cocoa warehouse, which I very much enjoyed and likened to playing a giant, mechanized game of *Tetris* all day), but I did work at a daycare that catered largely to parents who paid with vouchers for low-income households, many of them very recent immigrants. I also spent two years as a "DSP" (direct service provider) for people with moderate to severe intellectual and physical disabilities, most with comorbid mental illnesses, in Spencer, Indiana.

I actually loved those jobs (though not the pay), but I'm not sure that a lot of people understand how much of "care work" is changing adult diapers or being smacked in the head by schizophrenics or trying to comfort a small child whose mother beat them or whose father died in a war. I loved those jobs, at least in part because I like working with other people, but also because I always knew the intrinsic social value of what I was doing. I was proud of my work. It was rewarding and challenging, and not everyone can do it, or at least do it well. There is pride in having (and further developing) the patience and sensibility for jobs like that. I'm nothing close to saintly, and I certainly bitched about work. It was incredibly stressful and exhausting, I had no benefits, and the pay was shit. And a lot of my coworkers hated their jobs, not because they were bad at them, or because they didn't feel the same pride and satisfaction I did, but because it was just harder for some of them than it was for me. And it was easier for some of them than it was for me.

The truth is that even under the best conditions, a job that might be utter hell for one person can be perfect—or at least worth all the bullshit—for another person.

Once, when I was taking the Megabus to God-knows-where, I messaged my friend Jed—the one who noticed that "the left can't count"—with a picture of a bridge in Trenton, New Jersey, that famously reads, "Trenton makes, the world takes." Jed's father worked for the Fisher Body Plant in Trenton, and when I said I loved how bitter it sounded given Trenton's industrial decline, he replied, "I never read it that way, but maybe because my dad always says it with pride."

And, after a beat, he joked, "I don't think postwar Trentonians were smart enough to have pathos."

As much as professionals and "creatives" like to imagine their jobs as the envy of the world, the truth is that not everyone *wants* to be a doctor or a poet or a podcaster (a frankly ridiculous "job" that would most likely be eliminated in any civilized society with any semblance of reasonable economic planning). Most people don't even want to be a professor at the University of Chicago; I sure as shit don't (talk about "draining lifeblood," you couldn't pay me enough). There are plenty of happy hard hats, many of whom even wanted to be hard hats when they grew up. And that's a good thing, because we still need the Makers, and the Movers, not only to make and move, but to get the bosses by the balls. For all the tech bubbles and FIRE economy nonsense, it's still "things" that comprise the foundation of wealth. The people who build those things and transport those things, they're the ones most advantageously situated in proximity to the bull's testicles (metaphorically, I'm sure).

Manufacturing is in decline, yes, but it doesn't have to be, and there are other major choke points in blue-collar work. Self-driving cars *may* be coming one day, but for now, you still can't mechanize—or, for that matter, outsource—truckers. What about the people who load and unload those trucks, and ships, and planes? And what about those new Satanic mills, the Amazon warehouses? What about the people who build all those buildings where the capitalists shop, live, luxuriate, and "do business"? Of course care workers should organize, especially those workers with potential for serious leverage in the workplace, but the most potentially powerful workers' movements come from industries that can ruin a rich man's day, with large, lucrative, and geographically concentrated workforces.

So then why would any sane labor strategy dismiss not only the possibility of invigorated domestic manufacturing but even organized hard hats, much less present that dismissal as the pragmatic choice between factories and a specious labor category like "care work" that is only coherent insofar as it describes the people charged with managing the morbid symptoms of deindustrialization? They might as well demand we organize the gravediggers (though the presence of men with shovels might be a little too blue collar for their tastes).

Of course these necrophiliacs would tell the working class—or rather the colleagues with whom they discuss the working class—what workers should want instead of power and the means of production. A cubicle, or a nice hospice of the damned, perhaps? And of course they're light on strategy beyond instructing them to ask the bosses or the unaccountable federal government for favors, implying that the expulsion of the working class from the reins of power was merely neglect.

None of this is to suggest, by the way, that Sadlowski was way off the mark, or even that he believed everything he said.

Interviewer: "Do you envision ultimate ownership of the industry by the people who work in the industry?"

Sadlowski: "No. That might work in Western Europe, to some degree, but it doesn't seem likely here."

He may have meant that he believed that steel wouldn't ever be socialized, or he may have been playing close to the vest: he was, of course, considered a major threat to the steel magnates, and it wouldn't have been particularly wise to announce his plan to expropriate the industry.

He was wrong about some things, of course. As are we all. The truth is that in some ways he just jumped the gun; in other ways, he was too late.

Sadlowski: We have already benefited from what our brains have produced technologically. We've reduced labor forces from 510,000 fifteen years ago to 400,000 today. Let's reduce them to 100,000. The coal miners went from 400,000 to 68,000.

Interviewer: But what happens to the guys who get laid off?

Sadlowski: In the present structure, they find employment somewhere else. Society absorbs it.

To Sadlowski, who was working during a time of high employment and strong unions, it probably looked like society was going to absorb the laid-off workers and labor would remain powerful enough to benefit from the advances in technology made possible by the profits of manufacturing. The auto workers came very close to establishing a four-day work week, for example. Instead, the capitalists out-organized them.

Sadlowski cannot be blamed for his strategy; no one can know the future. But a historian should at least know the past, particularly when the hero he claims to celebrate developed his strategy with a labor force size, militancy, and power that we have lost entirely. If steel workers were felled with their army of wealth producers, we will not be in good shape if the only shop floor is a mortuary.

And herein lies the danger of the political necrophiliacs; sometimes, when they get ahold of the reins of policy, they can get a little too excited, and they start making the bodies themselves. They may, at first, appear as reverent mourners of the labor movement, but the truth of the matter is they're simply getting off to something they have decided is "doomed." Thus, their interests run counter to the interests of a living, breathing working class, whom they always seem fonder of after they're gone.

For those with morbid fetishes, business is booming. They insist everyone just forget about the means of production and the wealth of the world; that ship has sailed, and the future is in the new economy of agony! Still though, the necrophiliac author cannot resist a wistful reflection: "Eddie Sadlowski is a fascinating figure. A real heroic, doomed figure of the labor movement."

It's the word "doomed" that irritates. I dislike this word, "doomed," particularly after the word "heroic," a combination that hints at a romanticized notion of defeat, as if labor militants have to die for their sins to be proven honorable. Also, the word "doom" suggests not only the inevitability of defeat but also its permanence. That permanence, that despair, doesn't make sense to anyone who considers the labor movement something that doesn't end with one "heroic" man; they consider the labor movement a multigenerational war in which we're going to lose a lot of the battles, something that started before you were born and something that will continue well after your death. I don't think Sadlowski was doomed. I think, like most working-class heroes, at least most of the time, he just lost. But what he did isn't dead: the conviction, the tenacity, the dedication, and the people he kept going. Even the mistakes are contributions, something for future generations to learn from.

In Chicago, after Sadlowski died in 2018, they changed the name of the Friends of Labor Fest to "Eddie Fest." Hallmark card or not, I don't know what else to call that except proof that a person and their fight can live on in our still-beating hearts.

3

GET SOME ACTION

My ex-husband had been a shop steward for his grocers' local union before he and many others were replaced by self-checkout machines. We continued to patronize the grocery store that busted his union; it was the only one close to us, and it had the lowest prices. We did not use the self-checkout machines, though.

I cannot remember if we were on food stamps at the time, but we must have already been on them once before, because I remember my resentment when eyeing the premade food. I have found that for many people who have been on food stamps, you never again go grocery shopping without remembering the things you could or could not buy with food stamps. No alcohol, obviously. No toothpaste, deodorant, or toilet paper; we were apparently expected to wipe our asses with our hands. The other one was no prepared food, I assume because we are supposed to spend our days cooking, as we clearly had the time, what with not working and all.

I can't remember if we were on SNAP the day we got something from the refrigerated bin of prepared food, the kind that holds sandwiches, deli plates, potato salad, etc., things for picnics and whatnot. I can't even remember what we got, if it was grocery store sushi, or a cake, or buffalo wings. I'm pretty sure it was buffalo wings, because that was something he liked and something I didn't. Let's say, for the sake of the parable, it was buffalo wings. The line was extremely long for the checkouts manned by human beings but extremely short for self-checkout. My ex-husband looked at the line before saying with a resigned sigh, "Whatever. We lost, and I had a long day, and I wanna go home."

So we went to the machines that had replaced my husband. But when he took the wings out of the cart, he didn't scan them. He put them straight into the bag and muttered, "this is ours now." I knew he wasn't being reckless. Having worked at the store before, he knew and had told me how the security cameras were not only unmanned but totally inoperative, connected to no screens or recording devices. Cutting down on labor costs already, there was no way the company would pay a security guard to make sure we didn't steal. What appeared to be a massive surveillance system was nothing more than a bunch of disembodied little dummies. Not even real robots, just conspicuous little glass eyes meant to give shoppers the impression they were being watched.

Again, I don't really remember what we stole that day, or if we were on SNAP at the time, or if we were merely haunted by the memory of it, anxious and knowing full well that we'd be on food stamps again soon enough. I do not remember if he was attending college at the time, where professors were thrilled by his "nontraditional" enrollment, and asked if he had read Jim Goad. I don't remember if he was working in food service, or cleaning offices, or both.

I *do* remember sucking his dick that night.

Of all the socialists I know, a few are strategic, situational Luddites, but none are ideological Luddites. If there are technological advances in the industry, if someone invented a time-saving machine that could replace my husband and leave him on food stamps, sure, fine. We all have long days. And we all want to get home. But the only reason that machine got made is because some grocery store CEO stole wages from people like him so they can send their soft-handed sons to some university that neither of us could afford without signing away our firstborn, because that is where those soft-handed sons would invent the technology to replace human beings with machines and fill their fathers' wallets with even more ill-gotten cash. My husband made that fucking machine possible, so where was his cut?

When our marriage collapsed under the weight of cliché resentments, the sort that always seem to result in an amnesia for why we even wanted each other in the first place, I finally called it and filed for divorce. I only wasted a little time resenting him for his drinking, his anger, and what I perceived as his self-pity, before remembering that he never really had a chance. *We* never really had a chance. He deserved a lot more than he got. He deserved dignified work and some control over the profits he made for other people, he deserved healthcare and a pension. He never got a fraction of what he deserved, but that night, at least he got some fucking buffalo wings. And a blow job.

In the interest of full disclosure, I admit that, during that period of our marriage at least, I was a pretty soft touch. But the sexual thrill you get from committing a righteous crime with someone you love certainly added to my enthusiasm.

I don't even *like* buffalo wings.

But I do love a working man.

★ ★ ★

"They give your blood back," said R. He played Moog and keytar in a very new wave synth-punk band—think Devo, if they huffed paint and got pussy. I first met him at a house party where he wore a bathrobe and slippers because a girl had just broken up with him and he was depressed. I had a crush on him, and he was Catholic, which seemed to suit his terry-cloth monk's cowl and explain the lack of shame he felt about not having money. He was only ashamed when he felt he had been a dick to someone (then he felt extremely ashamed). I thought that was noble.

When unemployment, food stamps, student loans, and under-the-table work weren't enough to get by, my ex and I would go to a facility called BioLife to sell our plasma. You create an account online, set an appointment for an initial physical to determine if you're healthy enough to "donate" (a euphemism for "selling" plasma, which is illegal, which is why our "donations" were paid in "donation fees"), and if you pass that you can sell that day. You can sell twice a week. As of writing this, BioLife's website advertises "donating" as "part-time that pays well."[26]

We were usually in adjacent medical cots hooked up to IVs, and machinery would remove our blood, separate the plasma, then transfuse the blood back into our bodies. They *do* give your blood back. Many (if not most) of my friends had already done it, and they assured us that the process was simple and painless. You get bonuses for recommending friends, and at the time you got ten dollars more for the second appointment in a week. Easy money.

If you were a man, they would ask you if you have sex with men. If you were a woman, they asked you if you have sex with men who have sex with men. To this second question I would shrug, grin, and say, "Probably." The nurse would smile. A visibly gay friend of mine used to just answer "no" while batting his eyelashes as a dare, but no one ever rejected his "donations," likely because they test all the blood for disease anyway, and nurses don't seem to follow stupid rules that have no bearing on public health.

"Don't worry," the technician would always smile and joke, "we give you your blood back at the end."

Once, while sitting in the cot and staring blankly into my phone, I did the math: I made more per hour selling plasma than I did at any job I ever worked.

It is a strange thing to be lying on your back and watching your blood leave your body, and realize you are literally worth less than the sum of your parts, no matter how many books you read or how good you were at loading pallets into trucks or how good your band was. My plasma was worth more than bartending, nannying, in-home care for the intellectually and physically disabled, or even working the till at a garden center and loading mulch and fertilizer into the back of a truck with a forklift in the blazing heat.

At one point, my ex-husband got an infection at the needle site of his "donation." My head swam with ambitious litigious fantasies: "We could fucking sue them and never have to do this again!" I trembled breathlessly in the car. But we couldn't afford a lawyer, and BioLife paid for his doctor visit and antibiotics, so we kept farming ourselves out until eventually we decided to move New York, where we figured being starving artists would be more interesting and hoped we could at least find work more dignified—or at least less soul-crushing—than selling our bodies for scrap.

I knew I wanted to go somewhere big, somewhere we could maybe be worth more than the sum of our parts. I wanted to be where the action was.

Part II

NYC

4

YDS

I moved to New York in 2011, and it was the first year since joining DSA four years earlier that I hadn't attended "Socialist Summer Camp," the retreat for the Youth Section of Democratic Socialists of America, YDS. Back then we had so few members that it was held in an old Catskills "bungalow colony" in Sullivan County in upstate New York. This region, once known as the "Borscht Belt," still known as the "Jewish Alps," is littered with these little cabin resorts, once the favored vacation spot of Jewish urbanites escaping the unbearable heat of the city.

Many of the retreats were geared toward families but also had onsite bars and performance venues featuring cosmopolitan entertainment in the midst of country idyll. There was music and theater, but it's best known as the birthplace of stand-up comedy: Joan Rivers, Woody Allen, Milton Berle, Don Rickles, and Lenny Bruce were all Borscht Belt comics. Mel Brooks started his showbiz career first as a musician, playing drums in the Catskills clubs (he took lessons for six months at the age of fourteen from fellow Brooklynite Buddy Rich).

The Borscht Belt was also where red diaper babies received much of their socialist education, attending politically minded summer camps far more intensive and rigorous than the DSA retreat, often for months at a time. Not all Jewish summer camps were explicitly socialist, and the ones that were varied wildly in programming. Some were coordinated by parents living in New York tenement slums; others catered to comfortable suburbanites. Some integrated gentiles (including Black and Puerto Rican children), and some were no goys allowed. Some were religious, some secular, some Zionist, some antinationalist entirely. It sounded to me like an ideal arrangement for families looking to make summer plans outside the city; while the kids were off reading Marx, laboring collectively, remembering the Holocaust, and belting out "The Internationale," a Yiddish folk song, or a tune they learned from Pete Seeger, Mom and Dad could be a couple hundred yards or even a town away, drunk and guffawing at Lenny Bruce practicing the act that would later get him arrested for (and convicted of) "obscenity."

Despite my intense reverence for the history of both comedy and socialism, I wasn't too broken up about missing that year's summer camp since I'd have been expected to administer some of the programming and, as a "senior junior" socialist (still in the youth league but more experienced than most), babysit a bunch of middle-class college kids from the suburbs, many of whom were not accustomed to the thrills and subsequent dangers of underage drinking in the woods.

On my first summer retreat, a group of students from New Jersey went wild. They trashed the grounds, elicited noise complaints from an adjacent camp, broke something or other (I can't remember what) belonging to the resort— not expensive but not cheap either. Someone pissed in the swimming pool. I don't mean he was in the pool and pissed. I mean he stood at the edge of the pool, unzipped his cargo shorts, took out his dick, and aimed his stream into the same pool where his fellow barbarians were skinny-dipping. Someone cried. Someone fucked someone else's girlfriend, in *my* cabin, on *my* bed.

Maybe a third, or even half (if I'm being generous) of the other YDSers were fellow fuddy-duddies, annoyed and a little shocked by the idea of socialists who appeared not to consider the fact that they were at a camp surrounded by other people who were trying to enjoy their vacation, or that someone would eventually have to clean up after them, or even that we had education in the morning.

This is not to say I wasn't also wild at camp, but I didn't equate "youth" with acting like a child. During this time, I was finishing college, working nearly thirty hours a week, living not in dorms or at my parents' home but with the homeschooled, high-school educated man to whom I had recently become engaged, in a house where we paid the rent ourselves. By my second retreat, I was graduated, married, and working, but not in a professional job (either bartending or as a home healthcare aid, I can't remember). I think by this point my husband had become sick of being a short order cook and enrolled in college at the age of twenty-five, but he still worked nearly thirty hours a week as well. It's fair to say those of our class, income, education, and geography were not the norm among our fellow DSA youth.

A large part of our killjoy attitude was based on resentment: we had to take off work to come here, we had come a long way, by car, and though we had received some supplementary DSA funds set aside every year for low-income attendees, we were out of pocket. As silly as it may sound, we fancied ourselves militants, and we took it all very seriously. We were there to work and learn, and we were appalled and mortified that our socialist peers weren't taking an official event lasting only three days as seriously as we were. To be fair, we also tended to be better at handling our booze than the middle-class suburbanites, being seasoned professionals. An elder statesman of DSA called me "the Bolshevik" because, while I drank very heartily, I still woke up in time to attend, and later give, educational workshops. Maybe we took it a little too seriously.

The morning after pool-piss-gate, most of the revelers lost the first half of the day to hangover; when they finally woke up, the youth organizer spent about twenty minutes screaming at them. I liked him immediately; we are still very close today.

To their credit, the cul-de-sac hedonists were visibly ashamed and genuinely contrite. They apologized to the organizer and all comrades present, promising to pay any lost damage deposits, offering to speak to camp management and take full responsibility for any chaos or wreckage should they refuse to book us again, and taking extra care to clean up the remnants of their bacchanal. They were drunk kids and it hadn't occurred to them that their behavior might cost the organization money, the organizer trouble, and other YD-Sers time. It certainly hadn't occurred to them that pissing in a pool might not exactly be in keeping with the spirit of the event. So they filled up on humble pie, fixed what they fucked up as best they could, and . . . it was fine. We all let it go.

After the post-Bernie boom in DSA membership, this customary practice of restitution in exchange for forgiveness would undergo a drastic shift, favoring instead punitive measures, isolation, and excommunication. Witnessing the "callouts" and "cancellations," the smears and denunciations, I would think back on my first retreat. I can't imagine that someone whipping out his dick in front of a bunch of people who had not asked to see it, then pissing in a pool people were using, would be received quite the same way—"You fucked up, I am angry, apologize and fix it" seems like a pretty mature, constructive, and common-sense response to all but the gravest transgressions in an organization based on cooperation and contingent upon trust.

In order for this to work, restitution and forgiveness must both be paid in full, and all wiped clean. After that, it's just a funny story that we all laugh about. I even made friends with the pool-pisser. I know that a lot of people who joined DSA later on don't have any of these funny stories, or the kinds of friends you make by fucking up together, and it saddens me.

Of course, a little idiotic behavior is always to be expected of youth, but sometimes it was the elder socialists (often celebrity academics) who were the biggest pains in the ass, and they really didn't have as much of an excuse. During one winter conference, a famous Indian feminist literary theorist who taught at an Ivy League university gave the worst, most self-aggrandizing keynote speech in history. At times it was impenetrably worded in academic jargon, which I would later learn was the hallmark of her scholarship. She spoke something like five languages fluently, "Bullshit" chief among them, and name-dropped with the practiced fluidity of a linguist comfortable enough with the vernacular to improvise her own Komposita: "myverygoodfriendAngelaDavis," or "myverydearliberalfriendJosephStiglitz."

She very matter-of-factly informed us that she was there

to give us a "reality check," implying that we weren't real socialists, it was only that the US is such a "terrible fascist country that any kind of political work you do becomes left." Later I learned that this upbraiding of eagerly masochistic Western students was a key element of her schtick. In a 2022 interview, she clarified her sins-of-the-father approach to politics thusly:

"I tell my students, who live in the US, that they are children of a superpower. Look at your complicity—don't your parents pay income tax here? Therefore, remember, you are folded together with those in power."[27]

She does not seem concerned with the fact that income tax also pays for things like schools and roads, or that the very rich have enough tax loopholes to skip out on the bill for Amerikkka's store of B-52s, or even that those same rich parents pay the tuition at the Ivy League school where she collects a very comfortable paycheck. Nor does she insist upon any parallels of "complicity" between her own Brahmin caste and the subjugation of lower-caste Indians. It's not that she ever hid her background, but her gifts for euphemism and vague allusion certainly allowed her to gloss over the fact that she was, as she once told *The New York Times,* "unfortunately, a Brahmin," before quickly qualifying it with "but from an inferior sect of the Brahmin caste."[28] Ah yes, a humble peasant, then.

In a review of one of her books, literary critic Terry Eagleton summed up the appeal of a scolding, blameful lecturer to elite universities better than I ever could, saying, "for a 'Third World' theorist to break this news to her American colleagues is in one sense deeply unwelcome, and in another sense exactly what they want to hear. Nothing is more voguish in guilt-ridden US academia than to point to the inevitable bad faith of one's position. It is the nearest a post-modernist can come to authenticity."[29]

As myverygoodfriendMattChristman would say, you gotta respect the hustle, but I was baffled that we were being scolded by some Birkin Bag Brahmin for some bullshit idea of "complicity" in the oppression of the Third World. In fact, many of us weren't her usual target audience of wealthy, guilty, self-flagellating, liberal suckers.

Perhaps sensing some of the audience members' waning interest in her specious, sermonistic accusations, not to mention the increasingly tedious pseudointellectual blather (though I doubt it, she wasn't particularly self-aware), she switched tactics and started rambling about the immigration issues she "might" one day face if she wanted to become a full citizen (call me cynical but I don't think ███████ professors get deported that often) due to a DUI she had recently received, an incident she compared to Black drivers being profiled and pulled over for no reason. She admitted she had drunk "three or four" glasses of wine but that the charges were "fake" and "trumped up," since "nobody drove down that street without crossing the yellow line."

She also admitted that she had been drinking a lot in those days, and told another anecdote about falling asleep in her car in the garage after too much Eau de Vie de Mirabelle, which I later learned was plum brandy. I'll admit that I would have found that bit funny and endearing if she'd had any sense of humor about it. Or about anything at all.

"Is she . . . drunk right *now*?" I heard an incredulous senior citizen DSAer whisper-yell to another. She had been scheduled to speak that morning. I believe she arrived at 3:00 p.m., perhaps to conserve the energy she required for talking well over an hour.

I would later hear from a friend that the intellectual in question had her grad students clean her house, drop off and pick up her dry cleaning, and that she had hit one of them in the head with a book. Rumors are rumors, and the closest thing to a smoking gun was a leaked email, ostensibly from a university email list ("Prof. ███████████ is looking for a casual worker who knows the area, lives close to campus, and is willing to run professional errands at short notice. Please send resume and phone number to . . . and . . ."), but when you hear the same stories, over and over, from people who don't even know each other . . .

When considering rumors and speculation, I have a game I like to play. I pretend that I have been given $1,000 to place a bet on whether something is true or not. The odds are even, and I can bet for, against, or simply take the house money and walk. In this case, I'm pretty sure I would make two grand.

But at the time, socialism was démodé. Speakers that would publicly identify as "socialist" were few and far between, so we had to take who we could get.

Another time, I helped plan a YDS winter conference, and someone suggested booking self-identified "communist" Angela Davis, so we requested her speaking fee. When we read the number, we doubled over laughing. Who knew socialists could command that kind of cash? Lucky for me. . . .

For the record, many speakers have sliding fees depending on who has the money to pay them, and a lot of our speakers charged only the exact number we had in the budget. Some only requested travel expenses and/or accommodations, and some of them spoke for free. (Also for the record, I say get the bag from those who hold it. If it's a socialist youth organization, maybe figure out the absolute discount rate you can afford to work for. If it's TED, take 'em for all they're worth.)

Cornel West always donates his fee back to DSA. Once, when he was our keynote speaker, he took the National Political Committee out to a local diner, where I had a very brief but pleasant conversation with him about the NBA, and how McDonald's puts sugar on their fries, which shocked and distressed him, as he had been trying to eat healthier lately. He paid the bill for all of us—in cash—pulling a gold money clip of fifties from his pocket. When I asked if the birds on his gold cufflinks were nightingales, his eyes widened, delighted. He lowered his head, leaned in, and said, "Yes!" conspiratorial in the sartorial, and proceeded to almost whisper that his daughter had purchased them for him in China, I think as a birthday gift, but that may just be the memory of what I had assumed at the time. I'm generally suspicious of orators with a talent for theatrical sermons, but I trust Cornel West. And I like him. And I like his style.

And it was important to me to know that I didn't have to be an impenetrable academic, a pious scold, or (God forbid) a hippie to be a socialist. I could just talk to people about basketball and French fries, or I could be a grandiose eccentric. The privilege theory and intersectionality of the liberal college campus atmosphere, while fairly absorbed into DSA programming by that point, didn't really mean much to the daily life of anyone who hadn't made the campus (or the internet) their home, which was all well and good, because I wanted to make New York my home, and what I liked about New York was "very problematic."

5

COMING TO NYC

*The traffic on Canal Street's so noisy it's a shock
And someone's shooting fireworks or a gun on the next block*

—LOU REED, "HOOKYWOOKY"

In 2011, I crossed the Brooklyn Bridge at the crack of dawn with my two cats, Phyllis and Ernest, and the man who would one year later become my ex-husband. We drove a cargo van from Indiana, all in one go, the cats both howling in their carriers, deaf to my vain cooing to stop their howling. My husband was a good driver, but he had limited experience with urban traffic (I'd also had to teach him how to drive a stick a year earlier, bolstering my sense of confidence as the superior motorist). When we hit rush hour on Canal Street, he was suddenly too frustrated to merge. In standing traffic we did a quick Chinese fire drill in actual Chinatown, and I was behind the wheel. Never one to miss a corny cinematic opportunity, I put on Lou Reed's *New York* album, beaming with the possibilities of a new life all the way to the Property Management Company's office in Williamsburg. I got the distinct impression I was being judged for my tiny Soffes and children's wifebeater. It was hardly scanty attire for the neighborhood (that summer's Williamsburg Woman had been assigned a uniform of American Apparel dolphin shorts and a crop top), but the Orthodox man who handed us the papers and keys gave me an unmistakable "there's a whore in my house" once-over. I found this very funny; my husband found it annoying.

It was blisteringly hot, and I don't think we would have got all the furniture to the second floor of the once-grand 1930s Bed-Stuy apartment building had friendly new neighbors not held the door and helped carry some of the heavier pieces up the stairs. Despite the interior decay—missing hardware and fixtures, broken tile, cracked marble, crumbling plaster—it really was a beautiful old building. After more or less setting up the furniture and situating the cats, my husband spent the night. The next day he had to drive back to Indiana to finish up his remaining two weeks of work. Before we left, we had a big send-off with all our friends. One of them gave me a going-away present of a small chunk of hash. He was a veteran whose Humvee was blown up by an IED in Iraq. He had headaches now, and sometimes got furious for no reason; always embarrassed the next day, he was constantly apologizing. Fourth of July fireworks sent him into a silent panic. He said hash was the only thing that calmed him down. I just liked to get stoned.

We had to sign a lease on our apartment remotely after the place we viewed on our scouting trip got rented out from under us at the last minute. We had suspected the building we were moving into sight unseen would be in much worse shape than we had been led to believe, and we were right.

The gas was actually locked due to previous tenants' unpaid bills, which we dealt with by including a note with our rent indicating that we would be deducting what we felt was a fair discount on an apartment with no stove. The landlords never tried to collect, we assumed because they were just happy to be getting anything out of that slum. Many of the apartments were vacant, and for a few weeks some of the older Puerto Rican men from upstairs ran a card game in the uninhabited unit next to ours, blasting reggaeton hits until 3:00 a.m. on weeknights. I found this very funny; my husband found it annoying.

Once, the heavy porcelain bathroom sink fell off the wall and onto the floor, nearly crushing his feet while he was brushing his teeth. There was no weight on the sink. He hadn't even been leaning on it, just running the water. I found this very funny; my husband . . . well . . .

The only nice thing about the place was a massive antique clawfoot bathtub, big enough for me to lie all the way down in, and likely meant for a mess of children to be bathed all at once. On a pleasant day off work, I was watching Netflix on my laptop in bed and heard an eldritch gurgle from the bathroom. I ignored it in hopes that the issue would resolve itself, but then I heard it again, about twenty seconds later, and again about ten seconds after that, this time louder and more prolonged.

When I finally conceded and walked the length of the tiny apartment to investigate, I discovered at least two inches of brown water in my beautiful bathtub. I yanked the shower curtain out of the basin (figuring I'd have to burn it if it touched the filth) and ran back to my bedroom to grab the phone. I texted pictures to the super, then I watched, tense, perfectly still, staring at the spigot, waiting for another gurgle. When I finally heard it, I was surprised to see nothing come out of the faucet. Then the opaque brown water line suddenly went up about half an inch—the sewage wasn't coming from the faucet or showerhead, but from the drain. It was coming from . . . below. I updated the super.

The plumber arrived prompt and jovial, and he cheerfully reassured me in slightly accented but grammatically perfect English that he'd be done in a minute. His face fell when he saw the tub, and after dipping a paint stirrer in the "water"—which I would describe as slightly viscous, with a suspension of very fine particulates that I told myself was "just silt"—he crossed himself and began reciting the Lord's Prayer in Spanish while unpacking an elaborate-looking plumber's snake:

> *Ay dios mio. Jesus and Santa Maria. Padre nuestro,*
> *que estás en el cielo.*
> *Santificado sea tu nombre.*
> *Venga tu reino . . .*

I thanked him for his service and went back into the bedroom to sit on the floor with my head between my knees. For the next half hour I heard more gurgling, plus splashing, the clang of tools against porcelain, *"Ay dios mio,"* *"Santa Maria,"* *"Madre de Dios."* A lot of people had bad first New York apartments, but I had one that reduced a plumber to religious anguish, and in his mother tongue no less. I even found that incident funny . . . but not until a month or so later. I bought a gallon of bleach and didn't tell my husband.

A few weeks before the move, we had visited the city to scout apartments and interview with the Working Families Party for canvassing jobs. We were told at the time we'd mostly be doing electoral and campaign work (though we'd find out about a month in that it was primarily begging door-to-door for donations to WFP, a sell we both had trouble justifying to ourselves, let alone potential donors.

We were hardly WFP partisans to begin with, but we were at the time interested in the *idea* of WFP, though not so much for their electoral strategy of "fusion voting," where voters could cast their ballot for a Democratic candidate on a third-party line; it was only legal in a few states and still limited your picks to Democratic Machine politicians or whatever dark horse WFP might, on rare occasion, run as an alternative. No, we were interested in an organization that at least gave the appearance of working with the unions. Indiana would pass right-to-work legislation in 2012, but we knew it was coming well before, and we still believed in the labor movement.

Work didn't start for another two weeks, not until my husband got back, and everyone I knew in Brooklyn was upstate, learning about political economy, history, and a not insignificant number of liberal catechisms about "privilege" and "intersectionality," which I tolerated far more easily in those days. Alone in my new city, I spent that entire two weeks baked off hash and exploring. It was a heat wave, sticky and hot, and our neighborhood reeked of sweet, damp garbage, but the AC box we brought with us worked well, and the hash made the heat feel like a pleasant sauna. Plus, I only went out at dusk. The whole city was listening to *Watch the Throne*, which is a perfect summer album that you never listen to again. I went to museums and parks and rode the subway all over. I saw Ronnie Spector and Lesley Gore at Lincoln Center. I fucking love Ronnie Spector.

Once, in college, a guy I wasn't really interested in kept asking me out. I'd fake plans and put him off, knowing I'd see him again the next week in class, trying to come up with a new excuse to accompany every polite decline. One day though, he looked at me curiously and cocked his head. He paused a little before an expression of realization crossed his face and said, "I got it. You know who you look like? Ronnie Spector." We dated for nine months, eventually breaking up but becoming bandmates, then roommates. But I digress. . . .

It should be said that I didn't really have any long-term plan. I didn't think I'd rise through the ranks of WFP or even that I would try my hand at writing professionally. I just knew I wanted to be someplace big. And since there were no real career opportunities in Indiana, I figured, if we were going to be broke, let's be broke someplace where things happen. We sold some things on the way out (mainly the guns, firearms being one of the most reliable sources of liquid capital for quick and easy sale), but we came with the guitars and figured with all the venues, we could at least find a new drummer and play some shows.

We very quickly realized the Working Families Party was about one-third cult, one-third PR firm, and one-third barely paid internship program for recent graduates looking to pad their law school applications.

"John is making a speech," they would say breathlessly. The speech would be discussed later at not-exactly-voluntary bar nights—"mandatory fun," my mom calls it.

There were of course a lot of disgruntled employees, a few of whom I succeeded in drawing out by slowly testing the waters with increasingly candid conspiratorial bitching. It wasn't immediately obvious who was drinking the Kool-Aid; most of them knew well enough to keep their heads down, but it was easier for the men, whose lack of enthusiasm could be attributed to masculine stoicism. The girls were expected to be chipper cheerleaders. I must have looked like a stony bitch, which . . . fair.

I attended a Thanksgiving with coworkers at a boho-in-a-box decorated Bushwick apartment, where everyone went around the table and said not what they were thankful for but what they wanted to be "mindful" of. Later I referred to someone as a "garbage human being," and the host's girlfriend told me that "garbage human being" was offensive to the homeless. When I asked how, I learned that she was under the impression that homeless people live inside of actual dumpsters full of garbage, like Oscar the Grouch. Later her boyfriend—the one who suggested the "mindfulness" exercise—got way too drunk and started talking a bit too loudly (and explicitly) about how attractive he found me and, more specifically, what he would do to me given the chance; this was all relayed to me later by my first post-divorce roommate, a consummate gay frenemy who grew up Evangelical and poor in Bakersfield, California, only to get into NYU's drama program and graduate with a ton of debt, which most likely contributed to his passive aggressive hostilities. I was ambivalent about my mindful host's piggishness, because I found it inappropriate and disrespectful, mostly to his girlfriend. On the other hand, his girlfriend was a bitch, and he was hot. Such is the duality of woman.

The host went on to a career in campaign management.

I believe his then girlfriend (now ex, if you can believe it) went to law school.

Shitty job aside, I liked my new life. WFP was just another one of those shitty little towns my mother told me about, and I knew I would leave it behind soon enough.

6

WHOSE STREETS?

We arrived on [September 17] around 4 o'clock. We had been reticent to even attend because from the beginning it had been announced as an intentionally leaderless movement with no specific demands, but we went anyway, just in case they had something up their sleeve. Firstly, the entire event was organized in a public Facebook group, so very predictably, the cops had already blocked off Wall St. by the time we had arrived. Protesters gathered in a nearby park. They had no one directing people to this park. A very helpful cop actually told us where they were. We arrived at the park to a disorganized, confused looking bunch of kids arguing about assemblies and theory.

This being the absolute worst use of resources, we formed coalitions with some friends with WFP (particularly my coworker ▮▮▮▮▮▮▮▮) and ▮▮▮▮▮▮▮▮ from SPUSA [Socialist Party of the United States of America] and we started marching just around the park (at this point the Penn State Chapter of YDS and some Jersey

kids were also with us). After a few passes around the park,
we started to pick up some people and momentum, despite
the fact that one of the organizers of the demonstration tried
to pull us all aside to have a dialogue-based assembly, much
to the distaste of all the marchers. So we decided to march to
Wall St. anyway.

The majority of the people in the park ended up
following. We got loud, we got big, the cops started to
mobilize very quickly—lots of them. [We] tried to keep to
communication going from the front of the march to the
back, but there were just too many people.

—INTERNAL DSA EMAIL, LATER LEAKED TO BREITBART,
AMBER A'LEE FROST, SEPTEMBER 17, 2011

I was annoyed by Occupy Wall Street from the very first day. My husband and I showed up to what was advertised as a march on Wall Street and found . . . a meeting. Obviously, we already attended meetings pretty regularly both at work and through DSA, and by that point we were pretty sick of marching for this or that as well. But an actual show of populist contempt for the finance capital that got away with murder in 2008 seemed like one of those rare and maybe even promising occasions where getting out the poster board and magic markers might actually be the start of something. And again, I wanted to be where the action was.

We heard the hum before we even saw it, hundreds— maybe thousands—of people crowded into an ugly little office park in the Financial District, spilling out onto adjacent streets and sidewalks.

Aside from its size, the scene at Zuccotti Park was pretty much the standard protest tableau of the era, another ecumenical cattle call attracting a grab bag of advocates, crusaders, partisans, and "normies" (optimistic students, *Daily Show* Democrats, etc.). You had WikiLeaks vans here, drum circles there, lesser-known Trotskyite clubs hawking their papers along with the Bob Avakian cultists, Spartacist Leaguers, LaRouchites, and, ever dependable, the older white man with the thick New York accent who always slowly, almost hypnotically, barks out, "*China Daily! China Daily!*" advertising the English-language newspaper printed by the Chinese Communist Party at what I remember as every single major protest I ever attended in New York. Seriously. I saw that guy at Black Lives Matter.

All manner of pamphleteers for various causes vied for attention—fracking, fluoride, Free Mumia, Iraq, Iran, Palestine, Israel, legalize it, information wants to be free, Meat is Murder, corporations aren't people, jet fuel can't melt steel beams, forever and ever amen . . .

The crowd skewed, as nonlady, non-ethnicity-focused protests usually do, a bit more white and male than is representative of the general population of New York, but not exceptionally so for this type of thing, and not alarmingly so (I'm not sure if the women represent a sort of civilizing feature, but for whatever reason, the sausage-fest protests tend to degrade into confusion and/or intra-protest fights more quickly than the more coed events). There were more over-forties than I expected, which is always a good sign, as intergenerational sentiments usually indicate a broader, potentially "mass" appeal.

Mostly though, it was all the old faces, just on a much larger scale.

And for all the fringe regulars, the dominant vibe was still a broad resentment for "Wall Street," with a lot of references to Citizens United, the bank bailouts, "corporate power," and all those little asteroids orbiting capitalism, which I felt was a good sign. I even saw the "C" word on a few homemade signs not affiliated with any socialist organization, which I had never until then witnessed in person, except maybe at a Tea Party protest. It was an encouraging temperature check as far as these things go.

Someone handed us a flier with information on the "General Assembly" that was about to be held; it looked like a meeting to us. We also found instructions on the "consensus model" we were expected to learn and use during the General Assembly, which was explained thusly: "Consensus is a creative thinking process: When we vote, we decide between two alternatives. With consensus, we take an issue, hear the range of enthusiasm, ideas and concerns about it, and synthesize a proposal that best serves everybody's vision."[30]

"Well that's fucking stupid," my husband said.

I concurred and said something bitchy about the bait and switch between a political demonstration and a group therapy session with finger painting.

We learned that the General Assembly was being led by "facilitators" (appointed by whom we did not know, but we assumed it was *Adbusters*, the sanctimonious and humorless Canadian Gen-X anticonsumer magazine that appeared to assume the problem with America was overconsumption, and that the problem with *Americans*—i.e., "sheeple"—was their inability to understand that *advertisements* were trying to—gasp!—*sell them things, quelle horreur*!). In an uncharacteristic display of nationalism, I said something to the effect of, "I'm not taking orders from a goddamn Canadian," and scanned the crowd for familiar faces.

I saw a girl I knew from the Socialist Party USA and

asked her if she wanted to try to get a march going. We rounded up a few other DSA members and my coworkers from WFP, saying, "I didn't come here for a meeting, did you?" and they hadn't.

Someone said they weren't sure that anyone would follow us. I said that if you look like you know what you're doing, people will just join up. "Plus," I said, looking at the other woman from SPUSA, "we're girls. They'll follow us."

And they did, after maybe two circles around the park. At first only a few people joined in, somewhat tentatively, while a few facilitators with megaphones tried to insist that, actually, "we" were holding a General Assembly right now. Maybe they were, but *we* weren't.

We also weren't big fans of the suggested chants, "Whose streets? Our streets," etc., preferring instead, "What's disgusting? Union busting" and "No war but class war," both of which caught on. More and more people peeled away from the General Assembly and joined in, and then, very suddenly, we were very big, and we were moving. Eventually, someone shouted we were going to Wall Street. The crowd surged rapidly until we were no longer at the head of the march.

Dropping any attempt to exude confidence, I let loose an exhale of relief: I had no idea where Wall Street was.

At five-foot-three (and a half), I couldn't see what was going on ahead of me, but barricades must have been breached, because we got there. At first the only thing I could see was the shoulders of other protestors; then I looked up and saw the well-dressed people in a cafe terrace drinking literal champagne, laughing at us from maybe thirty feet above, hamming it up, flutes in hand, with smug mockery.[31] If not for the conspicuous presence of girl bosses in the kind of pricey professional woman's dress that always seems barely distinguishable from its knockoff at Marshall's, the scene would have felt anachronistic—like a heavy-handed cartoon out of a 1926 issue of the *Daily Worker*. "Eat the rich" became the new chant. By this point the crowd was incredibly congested, bordering on crushing, but suddenly people dispersed, and I found myself at the front of the pack again. Then I saw what had parted the teeming mass: paddy wagons.

Cops sprang from the rear doors, gracefully, I had to admit. One even spun his billy club in an elegant trick. "Big fuckin' man! What a tough guy!" we yelled. (Someone shouted that the taunt was "patriarchal and heteronormative.") The police advanced, and the crowd crushed tighter. I had no interest in being on the front lines of whatever was about to happen, and I had lost my husband in the mix.

People held up their phones, chanting, "The whole world is watching!" And they might have been, but I wasn't exactly sure how high ratings—even globally—were going to help us in that moment.

Someone screamed, "Who's ready to get arrested?!"

All power to them, but we sure as shit weren't. We had work on Monday, and we didn't have bail money (plus, my husband had a file). In one of those rare truly cinematic moments of my life (you can bet your ass I keep a tally), a male friend, not much bigger than me but definitely stronger, spotted me struggling to escape the chaos and very heteronormatively wrapped an arm around my waist, lowered his stance, and pulled me backward through the crowd, my heels dragging across the pavement. He cut a path shoulder first, like a peewee football player bearing down into a practice sled. I felt a bit like Fay Wray, in a romantic, glamorous, not-about-to-get-bludgeoned-with-a-billy-club kind of way.

I tried to observe the goings-on from further back in the crowd, but again, too short. (Being too short to see anything in a crowd is perhaps the defining aspect of protests for me, and I have yet to figure out a solution beyond perhaps assuming the outdoor concert position atop a man's shoulders, which is far too precarious and feels a little too "Free Bird" for a demonstration against capitalism.) Eventually, our dispersal assured escape routes for anyone trying to avoid contact with the police. The ones who decided to get arrested did, and other marchers split off into smaller parties to continue marching, go back to the park, or, like me, go home. I found my husband, we got on the train, and we wrote a report for DSA.

Funnily enough, this also appears to have been our first encounter with espionage, when the internal memo was immediately leaked to Breitbart, though nothing we said was particularly self-incriminating.[32]

I'm not gonna say it wasn't exciting. At times it was even fun—Fay Wray and all that. But that was the first and last day I thought that, maybe, Occupy Wall Street could actually change something.

7

WITH FRIENDS LIKE THESE . . .

While I didn't hold out hope for Occupy Wall Street, at least not as the "process" I was being instructed to "trust," I remained fairly active in it with friends from DSA who were searching for like minds and any possible germ of something more coherent that might be forming. My impulse, as I said, was to go where the action was, but the action appeared to be spreading by means of diffusion, like an ice cube melting into a wider and shallower puddle.

The initial strategy, which was coincidentally the only form it could possibly take, was the fracturing of the larger crowd into a million smaller crowds, which were expected to "self-organize" into self-directed, relatively autonomous "working groups," identity caucuses, and committees. Sometimes these groups did take shape, but in totally unpredictable and unstable ways, often according to identity, shared ideological affiliation, personal political hobbyhorses, and of course the labor that sustained the movement itself. The park had cleaners and librarians, direct actions had medics and legal aid volunteers, and the whole outfit had a social media army to inundate the internet with radical press releases.

The working groups themselves usually met very informally at or around the park, and though they were much smaller than the General Assemblies, they too were often confused and unwieldy, especially as they inevitably attracted a few newcomers who had yet to learn the language of Occupy.

In large crowds, activists circumvented city ordinances against sound amplification with "the human mic," also known as "the people's mic," where a speaker might enjoy the godlike feeling of hundreds, maybe even thousands, of fellow activists repeating their words back to them. This also meant that everything took at least three times as long to say. (One might initially assume, as many who objected to the human mic did, that it was only taking twice as long because everything had to be said twice, but there was also the matter of breaking up every sentence into a fragment short enough to be remembered and repeated by the crowd. Ergo, three times as long, at least.)

Then there were all the hand signals used to communicate in meetings—pressing both the thumbs and forefingers together in a triangle to indicate a "point of order," a raised fist to indicate you oppose, arms crossed over the chest to indicate you are blocking a motion, etc. You ended up feeling like a catcher signaling to a pitcher on the mound.

Then there were "twinkle fingers," basically jazz hands, the Occupy alternative to clapping intended to indicate support or agreement with a statement or idea. (In the cheerleading teen comedy classic *Bring It On,* they were called "spirit fingers" and were the signature move of a fascistic choreographer, the irony of which was lost on many occupiers, who were the exact age demographic for the film.) There seemed some sense to a silent mode of approval; applause of course draws out a meeting for ages, which is why clapping is for rallies, not for the work. But why must approval or disapproval be constantly announced throughout an entire meeting, even if it didn't slow it down with pauses for noise? Even when we weren't talking, we were expected to respond, to express our feelings constantly, relegating listening and actual communication to the back seat. Plus, it looked fucking stupid.

"I think it's cute," said one of the many middle-aged women writers who was always around, so eager to show her support for the young, lest they suspect her of being allied with "the Old and Evil."

Perturbed, I said, "I don't want to be cute. I want to terrify my enemies."

What's more, I wanted a populist politics, which was automatically precluded by a political subculture with its own native tongue and "cute" little sign language, both inscrutable to outsiders.

I attended quite a few working groups with people who wanted the same thing, but every group at Occupy was always unstable, always vulnerable to tyrannical personalities and disruption. One week a meeting might go very smoothly, with participants able to plan and coordinate while involving and guiding recent attendees. The next week you might have an antisocial personality, an obstructionist, an egomaniac, a zealot, a crackpot, or just an asshole. I watched efficient groups held hostage by pontification, and kind groups suddenly rife with not-so-subtle blind item admonitions of unnamed fellow activists, who sometimes sat there in the very same meeting, seething at the passive aggressive insult, usually in silence.

One such working group I attended was formed to establish a list of demands for the movement, although I later
learned there were many "Demands Groups" whose members did not always know about the *other* Demands Groups.
Mine was beset with obstructionists averse to demands, who
would demand we refrain from making demands, "because
if you ask for something," said one such antidemands advocate, "they can say no." By the end of such meetings we
demanded to go get a drink ("we" being the other people I
saw grinding their teeth into dust with frustration).

When someone did manage to get a lot of support for an
economic campaign, one *with* concrete demands and goals,
it tended to be very youth oriented and middle class. For a
while, there was some energy behind a "Student Debt Ju-
bilee," which would wipe the slate clean for current student
debtors but didn't do much for future students. I had no interest in any campaign that left the next generation hanging
out to dry, especially when I figured out that this "last one
out, turn off the lights" attitude was exactly why so many of
the kids at Zuccotti hated their parents. Besides, many of
us reasoned, healthcare affected more people, particularly
working-class people. Not just the ones who went to college.

Other student debt activists argued that we should ex-
ecute a "debt strike" and stop paying back our loans. The
results of such an action were merely speculated upon, so
there was a strategy, but no one was really sure that it would
do anything. Aside from the wild variations in risk to individual "strikers," I pointed out that a lot of people (like me)
had already "stopped" paying their loans out of necessity.
Apparently, my default status with Sallie Mae put me ahead
of the radical curve in my "activism." (Pro tip: debt collec-
tors can't call you if you just change your phone number.)

There was a lot of suspicion about money more generally, most likely due to mismanagement and lack of transparency, but I'd wager there was at least some corruption
and theft. Cash was donated and changed hands, and no one
really knew where it went. Rumors flew, and paranoia set
in. There was of course police infiltration, but even when a
cop was found out, the consensus model itself seemed to
be more effective at derailing any project—or even any
conversation—than the police could ever dream of.

The most famous interaction between Occupy and the
police was when a DSA member got wasted on St. Patrick's
Day and threw an elbow in a cop's face, later claiming she
was defending herself after he had grabbed her breast. She
became a poster child for police brutality and retained her
title well after a video was released showing her skipping by
the officer beforehand, pausing, rearing back, and throwing
her elbow backward into his unsuspecting eye before making
a break for it. After two years of waiting for her trial, she was
sentenced to three months in prison and five years' probation. She served fifty-eight days in the notoriously miserable
conditions of Rikers. DSA and many others campaigned for
her acquittal—my position being, "For chrissake, it was just
an elbow, and he's a cop, not a child with cancer"—but privately we resented all the time and energy we had to spend
managing an ongoing, sensational media spectacle surrounding a New School grad student being made an example of for
some frankly pretty harmless St. Paddy's Day antics.

It was a somewhat embarrassing way for DSA to make it
into the papers. On the other hand, it was fun watching the
anarchists clench their jaws to line up behind the new cause
célèbre, a socialist and therefore "statist." And she looked
good on TV.

Most of us avoided the spotlight, preferring to stay back-stage during the long run of political theater, though a few rising stars relished it, and some even managed to get paid. Every morning at the WFP offices, we were briefed on the day's agenda and assignments, meaning we were told who would be paid to "occupy" the park and who would resume normal duties. Sourpusses like myself, unmemorable white men, the less photogenic players, etc., never made the cut, so we would load up into the van like usual to go knock on doors in Ronkonkoma, begging for $60, ostensibly to supple-ment the "work" our fellow WFPers were doing at Zuccotti.

Sometimes that work just consisted of participation in OWS bureaucracy as conspicuous representatives of the Working Families Party, other times they were there to give 'em a show.

"███████████ is getting arrested today, everyone charge their phones. The photographer should be there, but he might not get a clear shot."

Or maybe:

"We have some new people coming in to bulk up our numbers at the park, just for this week's demonstration."

It seemed rude to ask what the day rate was for protest temp work, but I enjoyed learning which of them hadn't ever heard of the Working Families Party, which was infor-mation they tended to readily volunteer, just for small talk. I heard a rumor that WFP found its extras on Craigslist with-out mentioning the party by name, but I never found an ad that seemed to fit the bill, nor did I ever find an opportunity out of earshot of a superior to discreetly ask any of the temps how they got the gig.

I would later read a pseudonymously written article, "Ritual Protest and the Theater of Dissent":

I helped start a consulting firm to put on other people's protests. Organizations in North America would hire our team to organize "civil disobedience" involving anywhere from 10 to 10,000 people. They all have a standard set of goals, a never-changing list of menu items. A certain number of people will risk arrest. A specific group will be arrested. Something visually symbolic needs to happen with the appropriate backdrop. A US senator's home perhaps, or the post card [sic] zone in front of the White House.

We rent the stages and sound systems, walkie talkies and bullhorns. We contract out the production of hand painted banners and placards. We coordinate the building of massive props and facilitate "nonviolent direct action" trainings for our client's action participants. We can produce for our clients anything from dozens of people in koala bear suits to banners affixed to helium balloons to be released in designated convention center lobbies. We can fill an intersection with stuffed animals, if it will provide a moving visual for our client's narrative needs.[33]

I'm not sure that WFP ever used a boutique consulting firm, especially since a large part of their apparatus was in-house, but there were two sentences from the article that rang perfectly true:

We are hired to choreograph events intended to *appear* as manifestations of dynamic, broad based social movements, but any sense of spontaneity in our events is manufactured. Many of the protests that make headlines are less a coalescing of organized dissent than manufactured feel-good content for an activist's social media feed.[34]

Lights. Camera. Action.

Nonetheless, Occupy Wall Street really was more than the Potemkin protests, for better or worse. Much to my chagrin, the major opposition to the opportunism of Professional Managerial Anarchists were the Amateur Anarchists, for whom "spontaneity" and "organic" activity was the goal in and of itself. A sort of shitty Emerald City was formed from the energy roiling in and around the park; it's not that the outside world disappeared exactly, but it became less noticeable, and it was easier to forget the rest of Oz, much less Kansas. For a lot of people, this escape—a retreat, really—*was* the dream.

It wasn't totally clear to anyone how Occupy was going to build or even influence power by staging marches, arrests, and photo ops or, for that matter, by hanging out in an increasingly filthy park that had grown into a filthy combination conference room/kaffeeklatsch and just so happened to be constantly under siege by the NYPD. An aversion to productive discussions of nuts-and-bolts strategy was exacerbated by the growing hostilities between three more or less distinct camps. There were the anarchists who either believed that "the system" had to be destroyed, or that it was already on the verge of collapse, or that establishing an autonomous zone *outside* "the system" was going to eventually bring about its collapse; regardless of the scenario, after the collapse, we would then be primed to take over and institute a new model of society and politics. Then there were what old commies used to call "entryists," i.e., activists who sought to infiltrate, then influence, pressure, and (ideally) even lead existing structures and organizations. I'll clarify that entryism itself is just a strategy of "join them, be among them, and convert them." Every ideological camp at Occupy had entryists from every other camp; anarchists would attend Democratic Party Booster groups to evangelize about smashing the state; aspiring local politicians would join whatever Food Not Bombs knockoff crowd to get ballot signatures, promising that when elected, they would establish a "free store" or whatever. However, when I refer here to "the entryists," I am specifically identifying the activists who focused on making headways *outside* the park into traditional, professional positions of power and influence. Finally, there was the "Vote Blue No Matter Who" crowd, who maintained that the political problems of the country were primarily the result of Republican policies and could be reversed and corrected if we simply got out the vote for the Dems.

I never associated much with the most devout of the latter, at least not on purpose (there were plants at the park on the Democratic National Committee (DNC) payroll so they were impossible to avoid completely), but their perspective didn't take much rigor to understand or complicate; the white cowboy hats (Democrat) must defeat the black cowboy hats (Republican), without much distinction between politicians and voters, much less rich or poor. But most of us understood the old way wasn't working, and we had to try new things here, so I did hear the theories from the anarchists and the entryists frequently expounded upon, though their proponents always stopped pretty short of explaining how A might lead to Z.

The entryists seemed to have reverse-engineered their politics according to what they (hastily, I thought) assumed was the most pragmatic strategy; they wanted to accomplish as much as they could, which they assumed was very little, so that's what they shot for. This usually meant finding new left-wing candidates to run in state and local elections. I sympathized with them a bit, and not only because they were routinely denounced by the be-the-change-you-want-to-see-in-the-world lifestyle anarchists as "reformists," "electorialists," and (just like us socialists) "statists." I liked that they had concrete goals and definitions of "win" and "lose" that would be recognizable to the average person on the street: did you win the election? Yes, or no? But I had major objections to both the limits of their aspirations and their analysis of the playing field. For one, I always thought we would need a lot more than a few social democrats on the city council to get anything done. A stronger labor movement, to start. Of course, little races are easy to win because they're for positions that don't have much power, thus big money doesn't care who gets a state senate seat, especially if it's in Bumblefuck; a few impotent progressives in office might even offer plausible deniability to the elites insisting the game wasn't rigged in their favor. If we tried for something ambitious on the electoral level, even with a labor and social base behind it, capital would obviously intervene. Forget the Republicans; the establishment Democrats would be certain to nip any growing electoral wave in the bud. To me, the entryists seemed to subscribe to a wide-eyed optimism bordering on obliviousness: "Let's use this moment to get our foot in the door the old-fashioned way! They can't stop the people's vote! There's still some juice left in American democracy!"

Initially I assumed this was all pure naiveté, but I was underestimating them. Of course, there were a few Pollyannas who really believed that Occupy could move the Democrats to the left with a combo of popular pressure from the park and an electoral strategy, but the majority of entryists

would, when pressed or when feeling boozily honest, ac-
knowledge that progressives would never manage a hostile
takeover of the Democratic Party, and that even if we did,
politicians run the country only as much as capitalists allow
them to. What the entryists could do, however, was secure
positions as brokers on behalf of the people. They worked
their way into academia, got bylines in legacy media, established think tanks, got jobs at nonprofits, started their own
consulting firms, embedded themselves in NGOs, etc. This
isn't to say those jobs always make the world worse, but as a
political "tactic," you can't help but notice that the profes-
sionalization of activism does more to shore up power for
a growing class of "movement managers," and that, rather
than relying on democracy (much less democratizing anything new), they were joining the very institutions used to
circumvent democracy. Granted, they would ostensibly be
taking these posts to capture the king's ear and thus wield a
little "soft power" in the name of justice. It made sense, on
some level. You had a glut of angry, educated, progressive
millennials who recently found themselves on the professional and economic downslide. They knew they were a
bit screwed, but they also knew they were way less screwed
than everyone else; and they needed jobs. So of course they
wanted to pursue positions where they might exercise a little
Professional Managerial noblesse oblige that might benefit
"everyone else." I admire the people who go pro for the
cause, but I can't take seriously anyone who thinks they can
change the world by getting a job. And some of those jobs
did make the world worse.

Prospective nonprofits that came out of Occupy (or,
like most, were born there but died in the crib) were usually named something either dynamic or important-

sounding; they favored words like "movement," "project," or "initiative." "Collective" was popular, though it tended to bely an internal dynamic that was more Ivy League literary salon than democratic organization. "People's" had a moment, as in "People's Mic," though you had to be careful with that one, since it might elicit an accusatory "Which people are you talking about, because I see a lot of straight white cis men in this working group right now!" So "people's" sort of fell off; it was ultimately too divisive. "Group" was completely démodé, though I'm not sure why; maybe because it stank a bit of dusty old Ralph Nader's Public Interest Research Group—the college Boy Scout program for aspiring young professional–managerial class (PMC) Democrats—or maybe because it didn't seem to celebrate the individual, whereas even "collective" sort of implies a "which Spice Girl are you?" BuzzFeed quiz-style performance of identity, a space where you will be acknowledged for the snowflake you are. At any rate, the million NGO flowers blooming betrayed the entryists' not-so-secret skepticism toward electoral politics: if they really had faith in democracy, they wouldn't need to form a 501(c)(3) with an inspiring name as a backup plan to circumvent it. Compared to the other two Occupy camps, they were pragmatic; cynicism is, after all, one way to be pragmatic.

If the Blue Dogs believed a beautiful future was easily in our grasp if we could just beat the bad guys (i.e., anyone who disagrees with us) fair and square, and the entryists believed that a tolerable future was possible—at least with a progressive professional managerial elite in place—if we just got in the room with the bad guys, the anarchists believed that a horrible future was a pit stop on the way to utopia.

The only problem was, they couldn't agree on anything about this horrible future, which split them into three *more* camps. The first is the storied anarchist of yellow journalism, a conscious accelerationist who believed we had to "burn it all down" with direct confrontation, violence, riots, "by any means necessary," etc., to destroy whatever metaphorical machine had corrupted whatever perfect Rousseauian harmony mankind would naturally adopt were it not for that darn snake in the garden, the state, because on a long-enough time line, anarchists tend to be pretty consistently antimodern. Contrary to right-wing propaganda, ultra-accelerationists were a fun-sized sect. Even the middle-ground accelerationists, who believed they had a role as midwives to the coming apocalypse, weren't picking up a lot of bricks. And still many other anarchists believed acceleration required no help from "us," adopting a millenarian eschatology, insisting that any day now, the state would crumble on its own, so their "praxis" was mostly about preparing the park for capital's downfall.

"Praxis" was a word you heard roughly ten thousand times a day, and it meant everything and nothing. "Praxis" could refer to the quotidian "activisty" things you do in daily life to bring about change, which sounded a lot like "lifestyle" to me. So praxis could be like . . . making soup. But radically. Praxis could also be the way you navigate the social world within and without "activist spaces." So, for example, calling your mom. Or apologizing to a fellow Occupier for "doing harm." Praxis could be self-reflection about that harm. So, looking inward and feeling bad about yourself. "Prefigurative politics," meaning the belief that if you change yourself you can change the world, was a big part of "praxis." I found prefiguration not only antisocial (people don't need to be told how to be good, people are already good), but also an ego-driven cart-horse misunderstanding of power; no one cares if you're good.

There was some pushback on prefigurative politics; "Goldman Sachs doesn't care if you raise chickens" was a tidy slogan of a rebuttal I liked, but looking inward for the political and moral purification of ourselves and the movement at large was still heavily prioritized. And of course it was. We couldn't think of anything else to do.

I hated praxis. I still hate praxis.

Ironically, while Occupy was somehow highly individualistic, it championed crowds as its strength, energized by the size, growth, and rapid duplication of occupations across the country, even to other countries.

Some assumed we would reach a critical mass of occupiers, and then . . . something *had* to happen, right? There was a vague idea that if enough people joined the movement—and why wouldn't they?—if they just refused to play, just took their ball and went home, then "the system" couldn't possibly persist and would collapse merely from the lack of us. Some went further, insisting that a large-enough bloc of Occupiers would idiopathically develop some sort of organic group coordination, like fish that seem almost telepathically connected to every other fish in their school, then act en masse as a nonhierarchical, horizontally organized blob that would eventually seize power. The blob here is very important; the prescribed form of Occupy was that of an undifferentiated mass, spreading ever outward. Don't get me wrong, I would never call us a cancer. Cancer is a threat. We were more of a benign tumor, one that capital was able to mostly ignore.

At Occupy, leadership was "hierarchy," and hierarchy was "violence," and "horizontalism" was the alternative to violence. Opposition to this theory was generally tiptoed around, but it certainly came up at any number of sparsely attended YDS events I coordinated or joined. Of course, DSA was "hierarchical," which I never had a problem with, nor considered the possibility that anyone else would, until Occupy brought me face-to-face with a generation of middle-class kids for whom "Fuck you, Dad" was a political slogan. As toothless as we were, what I liked about organizations like DSA is that we *did* have demands and we decided how to prioritize those demands—i.e., designating our limited energy and resources to one or two campaigns—by voting on what campaigns the organization should pursue. Everyone in DSA lost a vote at some point, including the leadership.

I rarely took a major role in anything OWS that wasn't a "statist" DSA project. I went with my friends to strike solidarity actions and antieviction demonstrations, and I tabled and organized YDS events intended for political education, usually in hopes of scouting new members. Alas, it seemed everyone was an anarchist that season; *statists* were démodé and hierarchy was hopelessly out of fashion. That's obviously not the only reason DSA youth membership didn't surge with Occupy, but it was part of it. And of course for many, especially the "star" activists, the quotidian work of a structured organization will never be as sexy or romantic as endless direct-action demonstrations in front of TV cameras. Any real movement requires a lot of spreadsheets; nobody wanted to make the spreadsheets.

Once in a while someone at Zuccotti would suggest that accountable leadership could be a healthy, if not necessarily innate, impulse, and that it was something to be cultivated socially by the group through the work of organizing together. A lot of people might agree with this person privately, but more than once I heard some version of the reply, "That's not what we're doing here." They weren't wrong. For all the alleged experimentation and creativity, coordinating a formal structure—or even admitting an informal one had already cohered in the power vacuum—seemed to be the only thing explicitly against the rules. Later a friend quoted a line to me from French Marxist and philosopher Michel Clouscard, a critic of the Paris '68 commune and the New Left more broadly: "Everything is permitted and nothing is possible." I hate giving credit to the French, but when they nail it, they nail it.

For example, meetings and assemblies were facilitated with "progressive stack," which was intended to prioritize speakers "of marginalized identities," meaning women and minorities got to cut in line to talk. The thinking was that this would correct the outsized influence of "dominant groups." In practice, it only served to highlight the fact that "marginal people" are just like un-marginal people; some of them are leaders, some of them are soldiers, some of them are quiet, some of them are vocal, some of them are team players, and some of them are giant assholes. One of the guidelines for progressive stack is usually, "Ask yourself, 'Why Am I Talking?'" a question that people who dominate conversations or meetings tend to avoid by their very nature.

Rather than "leveling the playing field," progressive stack not only frustrated those lower/higher on the totem pole, but also gave tyrannical personalities outsized influence over the proceedings and saddled women and minorities with social pressure and extra obligations to speak, whether they wanted to or not. And as you can imagine, ranking the right to speak according to identity demographics produced some pretty fraught math. Does gay beat Black? Should we ask somebody if they're gay? Do lesbians beat gay men? Often, these theoretical calculations lead to increasingly hostile conversations about things like "butch privilege," something that came up once during some committee meeting I attended. I watched a woman in Dickies and an oxford shirt run a nervous hand over her flattop, shifting on her seat in an attempt to recede inconspicuously back into the group of friends she came there with.

As for "the consensus model," the "creative thinking process" intended to "synthesize a proposal that best serves everybody's vision," it appeared to underestimate both the size and ideological diversity contained in the category of "everybody."

A few of us tried (and failed) to promote and discuss "The Tyranny of Structurelessness," second-wave feminist Jo Freeman's 1972 essay about her experience with "leaderless" organizing models in the women's movement:

> The source of this idea was a natural reaction against the over-structured society in which most of us found ourselves, and the inevitable control this gave others over our lives, and the continual elitism of the Left and similar groups among those who were supposedly fighting this overstructuredness.
>
> The idea of "structurelessness," however, has moved from a healthy counter to those tendencies to becoming a goddess in its own right.

There were a lot of "goddesses" at Occupy Wall Street. There were also a lot of macho pissing contests over what you were "willing to do"—violence, arrests, riots, etc.—for "the cause" that precluded any conversation that might define what "the cause" even was. When this was questioned, it was couched in conversations of who was "privileged" enough to engage with police violence without fear of imprisonment, injury, or even death. To me these debates missed the point, or at least skipped a step: "Maybe I'd be willing to go to jail," we mused among ourselves privately, "but . . . for what?"

There was in particular a fixation on "diversity of tactics," the euphemism for rioting and violence, that suggested if someone found either of those approaches less than appropriate for a particular action, they were not only a coward but also antidiversity.

There were a few little riots, which I never opposed on moral grounds, though I noticed they didn't really seem to be doing anything either. But, riots don't require a leader, so they appealed to the horizontalists of OWS. Plus, they're fun.

This is not to say that OWS was a "leaderless movement" as so many declared, or even boasted. I don't think that even a majority of the most faithful ever truly believed that. None of the techniques intended to "horizontalize" participation did much to change the fact that some people like being in charge of some things, other people like being in charge of other things, some people just want to put in a day's work, and others thirst for power.

Of course there *were* leaders, if only informally—leaders both wise and foolish, noble and opportunistic—otherwise there would have been nothing but utter gridlock, which was already rampant. If one not-actually-a-leader went up against another, consensus mediation became a prolonged battle that was usually won by attrition (or thinly veiled personal attacks or rumor-mongering with the intent of character assassination). Eventually, a decision was made to shift from consensus to 90 percent majority, but some Occupiers still clung to consensus, the ideal organizing principle for ideal people. Any suggestion that there might be one or two intractable differences of opinion in any group of two or more was resisted heavily by the evangelists of consensus, who insisted that there was always an option that would please everyone: no one should ever have to feel like they lost a vote, sort of like how a movement without demands can never really "fail" to achieve them.

There really is a nugget of truth to the right-wing trope of "entitled millennials" who all want a participation trophy.

The one thing I cannot stress enough is how so many Occupiers absolutely could not bear the thought of losing, re-fusing to ever entertain the idea, and looking with suspicion at anyone who even appeared to exhibit a hint of skepticism. So many of them suddenly couldn't even consider—couldn't *stomach,* really—the possibility of failure, so much so that suggestions for improvement were often met with flippancy or irritation. Often there was outright hostility to contin-gency planning, which some believed betrayed a lack of faith in our inevitable victory.

Tinkerbell is dying and only you can save her, so if you believe in fairies, let's see those twinkle fingers.

★　★　★

I'm still not sure why some of us felt that rah-rah pressure of obligatory triumphalism, while others, like myself, didn't see any point in either optimism or pessimism, but I think it had something to do with how they wanted people to see them—as in how badly they wanted eyes upon them and how they wanted those eyes to regard them.

When OWS chanted over and over again, "The whole world is watching," I would concede that we were getting some press, but I'd inevitably return to my mother's reassuring words: "No one even notices you." I remember reading a tweet around that time from a friend in the art world, who observed the recent obsessive fixation on themes of surveillance and drones in the then very hot "net.art" scene; she suspected much of it was wishful thinking, a bunch of aspiring celebrity artists just hoping that someone was paying attention.

Occupy was always bubbling with an intense ambivalence about "the whole world watching." When there was mainstream press coverage, some would rejoice, insisting that it was evidence of our momentum and therefore progress, while others would fret over the bourgeois press's disingenuous, disdainful, or even condemnational coverage of the protests. Conversely, when coverage was scant, some would bitterly obsess over being "ignored," while others saw it as a vain attempt by capital to close their eyes to the inevitability of our rise, which was of course evidence of their fear of us/our power. After all, they'd point out, the revolution will not be televised.

Still, some of the more ambitious, PR-minded, millennial strivers at Zuccotti were willing to say anything to raise "the movement's" profile, and if they got some press of their own in the process, they certainly weren't opposed to it. Around late September, one such enterprising little turd "pranked" a few media outlets by spreading a rumor that Radiohead was set to play the newly christened "Liberty Park," including to Gawker, which you may be shocked to learn was extremely relevant at the time, and one of the rare outlets that gave us unreservedly sympathetic coverage.[35]

Having covered him previously in a *New York Times* Style Section takedown titled "The Literary Cubs"[36] (a profile of the sort of vanity magazines Ivy League kids start in order to get noticed by the publications they actually want to write for),

Gawker gave the farceur—oh how droll, what a card, a mischievous and incorrigible little Loki/imp/Puck/rascal, like the Coyote Trickster of old, he's simply *too* much, etc.—an article of his very own to make his statement, titled "I'm the Jerk Who Pranked Occupy Wall Street." Usually, the editor picks the title of any post, even a statement, but while Gawker's admirably humble "we were suckered" mea culpa introduction still betrayed a bit of contempt for him, I find it just as easy to believe he wrote the headline himself to cultivate some sort of righteous enfant-terrible celebrity-activist persona.

Most of the "article" was a dynamically narrated play-by-play of the stunt, apparently inspired by an April Fool's Day prank he played on his family as a middle schooler; it was sort of like if the *Ocean's Eleven* heist was about twenty minutes of tweets and emails.

> It started like this: an autonomous group of Occupy Wall Street activists were sitting around brainstorming ways to get more people out to Zuccotti Park over beer and pizza. This was a little over a week into the occupation, before the mass arrests on the Brooklyn Bridge, and it still wasn't clear whether the whole thing would catch on. Someone suggested we should get Radiohead to play a free concert—they were in town for a couple small shows and fans were ready to sell pounds of flesh for tickets. The band wouldn't even have to play the thing, people just had to think they were going to.[37]

By the time I caught wind of the Radiohead rumors, I was familiar with the nature of crowdsourced games of telephone in so-called "activist circles," as were most of my friends and fellow DSAers at Occupy; my ex-husband's comment was something to the effect of, "These kids will believe anything, because they believe that *if* they believe, they can make whatever they want happen." I agreed, suspecting the hearsay was being spread with the hope of "manifesting" the band, à la *The Secret*. We also considered the possibility that it was an intentional lie, prank, or some kind of hustle; we just didn't suspect a fellow Occupier to be behind it.

Still, we figured there would be a surge in crowds at the park, with at least a few people showing up on the off chance they would get a free concert rather than political activity. So we attended some out-of-park meeting that day, I believe in the cramped DSA office, which had one window facing a dark airshaft but offered a quiet respite from Zuccotti despite being conveniently located very nearby. Worse than a crowd of angry, disappointed music fans mixing with territorial Occupiers (the photo Gawker supplied was the crop of a sign being held by one such hostile protester, hand-painted with the words "IF U R HERE ONLY FOR THE BAND, GO HOME") would be if Radiohead *did* show up. I hate outdoor music festivals, and counter to the "Jerk Who Pranked Occupy Wall Street," I don't think most Occupiers—not even my skeptical self—would have agreed with his premise: I would have said it was pretty clear by that point that Occupy Wall Street *was* "catching on." Perhaps the autonomous group in question were a bit bleary from their oh-so-relatable proletarian sup of beer and pizza, or maybe I'm just bad at crowd estimates. Who's to say.

Toward the end of the statement, the Merry Prankster insisted that "it was never the goal to troll the OWS bureaucracy . . . but that didn't stop me from laughing my ass off when I heard [my coconspirator's] incredulous voice on the phone: 'They just confirmed it. Officially. "It is confirmed."'"

As he saw it, the credulity of whoever happened to believe the rumor actually made some sort of point: "It was a pompous exercise in the exact sort of discourse the occupations are about undermining. I don't know how much of that conference was a genius exercise in publicity through Zizekian over-identification on their part, and how much was just rogue organization kids getting bamboozled."[38]

I don't know about all of that—really, I have no idea what the fuck he's even trying to say—but I felt then, and still feel now, that it's a strangely brief explanation of the reasoning behind a bait-and-switch strategy of lying to a huge number of people and implicating your fellow activists in that lie without their knowledge or permission, and without much mention of any consideration you might have given to the possibility of it backfiring. Of course, as Gawker put it, "He made us look like chumps and ensured nobody would take Occupy Wall Street's press team seriously ever again." If you'll forgive my mystified tone—I'm still baffled to this day—it's just such a fucking *weird* thing to do, and so seemingly at odds with OWS's stated values: it was strikingly individualistic to the point of being antisocial, confusingly petty, politically ill-considered, and deceitful to the people you were supposed to be working alongside, nearly all of whom appear to be a mere afterthought, written as minor characters in your epic saga of "it was just a prank, bro." Also, it was just mean.

And for a writer, he could have used an edit. But he got his byline, and if it seems like there's not much introspection, much less contrition, in his account of the "prank," the Jerk is just one of many activists who subscribe to the old Hollywood bromides: "all press is good press." In my experience, stitching together activism and celebrity is a tricky thing, and it's rarely a chocolate-and-peanut-butter situation. It usually ends up more like chocolate and dish soap: too performative and exhibitionistic to be focused and serious-minded, but too pure and sanctimonious to be cool and fun.

The Jerk was arrested a few days after the Radiohead debacle, I suspected at the time to his delight, during the Brooklyn Bridge March he mentions, when on October 1, 2011, more than seven hundred protesters were taken downtown for blocking the roadway. Many of them may not have heard warnings from the police that they would be arrested if they left the pedestrian walkway and spilled into the road, others certainly did and chose to proceed into all-but-certain zip-tie handcuffs. The tactic of "kettling"—i.e., lining the perimeter of a march with a phalanx of police officers, bottlenecking or corralling them into a manageable space—is used by both the authorities (for crowd control) and protestors themselves for intentional arrests, whether as an act of civil disobedience or just a good photo op.

That said, there is a long history of activists getting purposefully arrested for noble and strategic reasons, notably during the civil rights movement; I just didn't see much to compare, for two big reasons. First, the coordinated acts of civil disobedience against segregation were planned centrally, through established organizations that had been developing strategy for years; the newness and spontaneity of Occupy meant that no such track could have been laid yet. Second, there was just the question of capacity; when Martin Luther King, Jr., advocated intentional arrest in his speech "A Creative Protest," it became better known as "The 'Fill Up the

Jails' Speech." But when hundreds of people from near and far targeted the Woolworth's lunch counter in Greensboro, North Carolina, for a six-month-long campaign of boycott and sit-in, the city itself had around 120,000 people, and with careful planning and organizing, it was possible for the protestors to exceed the workload capacity of local law enforcement and the capacity of local jails (and again, this was over the course of six months of tactical planning that emerged from decades of organizing). Conversely, 2011 NYC, with a population then of about 8.2 million and 34,000 police officers—left us with about 4.18 police officers per 1,000 citizens.[39] On top of that, with ten prisons—Rikers alone can hold up to 17,000 inmates—and definitely at least a few black sites we don't know about, a jail cell might be the only real estate with reliable vacancy in NYC (aside from Airbnb of course). A little bar napkin math convinced me that what worked in Greensboro in 1960 wasn't going to work in the Big Apple in 2011.

On top of that, I just never found the idea of getting put in cuffs exciting or romantic. To this day, I have managed to never be arrested, and I maintain the hope that if I ever am, it will be either for a righteous, politically strategic reason or for something fun and trashy like, say, drunk and disorderly behavior at a water park where I brought my own margarita in a Nalgene and started fights with strangers for "judging me": I am as God made me.

What is certain is that the Jerk Who Pranked Occupy Wall Street did know that he was being kettled, and he did hear the police, meaning he was not able to claim, as so many arrested that day did, that he was unaware of the police warnings/threats.

We know that he knew because he live-tweeted it before

quickly deleting the posts after realizing he had incriminated himself. During the year-long legal battle leading up to the trial, the prosecution attempted to subpoena the tweets, while the National Lawyers Guild defense argued it was a violation of privacy to subpoena public tweets. The argument failed to sway the judge, and two tweets were brought before the court:[40]

They tried to stop us, absolutely did not want us on the motorway.

They tried to block and threaten arrest. We were too many and too loud. They backed up until they could put up barricades.

Court transcripts weren't particularly flattering: "I had no idea what was in those tweets until about a month ago," confessed the defense. "If you really want to get into it—"

The judge interrupted the scrambling attorney: "Not really, nor are you doing any service to your client."[41]

The Jerk pled guilty to disorderly conduct.

To the average person, live-tweeting illegal activity in full admission that it is illegal may have looked like a bone-headed move—one tends not to announce they are breaking the law unless they hope to be arrested and possibly prosecuted for it. I'm no mind reader, but the Jerk managed a PR pivot from Occupy prankster to civil rights poster child, and eventually to spokesman for his generation—literally. His first book was a sort of political economy of millennials, which comes to this conclusion (according to the marketing copy):

We are the most educated and hardworking generation in American history. We poured historic and
insane amounts of time and money into preparing
ourselves for the twenty-first-century labor market.
We have been taught to consider working for free
(homework, internships) a privilege for our own
benefit. We are poorer, more medicated, and more
precariously employed than our parents, grandparents,
even our great grandparents, with less of a social
safety net to boot.[42]

(What's all this "we" shit?)

The same copy describes him as an "early Wall Street
occupier" and lists his birth year (1988) after his name on
the cover.

For the *New York Times* piece concluding his trial, his
picture was taken by East Village photographer John Marshall
Mantel, known for his dynamic photojournalism and beautiful portraits of everyday New Yorkers and their lives in the
city. The Jerk looked sharp, because he was sharp. He chose
six days community service of his choice over the option of
three days for a service assigned by the judge.

And he was, I have to admit, a man of his time: a gifted
director of spectacle and adept at sowing misinformation and
suspicion at the park (while still somehow retaining most of
his credibility). But he wasn't particularly cynical or even
ambitious compared to his peers. I think he stands out because his trial felt like the acme of our cognitive dissonance;
an adamant demand for privacy and a desperate desire for
publicity, the two mutually exclusive positions that Occupy Wall Street tried to square. Live-tweeting your illegal

activity then trying to get it thrown out of court somehow didn't seem so ridiculous at the time.

At Zuccotti there were constant heated arguments about transparency, secrecy, what information should be public and what might be better kept under wraps, whether or not covert organizing was even possible, and, if it was, did it undermine the horizontalist, "all-are-welcome" movement of the 99 percent?

Fears of surveillance, infiltration, and espionage by the authorities were rampant, and not without merit. If we hadn't been surveilled, we'd have been the first "movement" anywhere near its size in America not to be. I still never found out who leaked the DSA internal memo I wrote.

At least a few cops were always around, including plainclothes detective Rick Lee, the so-called "hipster cop" who made waves with his 1950s-style browline glasses (Ray-Ban for J.Crew, we later learned), shaggy-chic haircut, slim-fit oxfords and khakis, and skinny ties.

Although his clothes were denounced roundly by many Occupiers as a "disguise," it's not clear if he was ever technically "embedded," as the plainclothes he wore were literally his own everyday clothes, as an article in Gothamist leaked from an anonymous source in his precinct:

> He's actually been called "hipster cop" for years—the nickname originated with someone at the mayor's office who was directing someone to Lee by saying, "Oh you'll recognize him, he's the hipster cop."[43]

He was even interviewed in GQ, saying, "This is pretty average for me. For work anyway. The jacket and cardigan are Ralph Lauren. The tie is Burberry. The shirt is Ralph Lauren, too. These are J.Crew pants. And Ralph Lauren shoes. Lot of Ralph Lauren."[44]

It turns out the "spy" was just a community affairs detective like any other, in any other precinct, doing what he had always done, just as he had always done it, "acting as liaison between the precinct and the community we serve." The nefarious "disguise" was just the eccentricity of another clotheshorse New Yorker. He wore his badge on his belt, and sometimes an official NYPD-issue raid jacket with POLICE printed in letters four inches high, on both the front and back.

There were, however, actual instances of espionage to spy on and undermine OWS, though even to the untrained eye at least a few of them weren't much less conspicuous than Detective Rick Lee with his clearly displayed badge.

In 2013, undercover NYPD detective Wojciech Braszczok was arrested when police placed him and his fellow bikers at the scene of a felony gang assault. One of the bikers cut off an SUV then rapidly braked to create a longer stretch of uninterrupted highway, a common technique for bikers using city streets to try out stunts—not too dissimilar from kettling, really. The man in the SUV, obviously unable to slow as quickly as a motorcycle, tapped the biker ahead.

The mounted crew then surrounded the now-parked car and began pounding on windows, knocking off a rearview mirror. The SUV gunned it, knocking down a few bikers and paralyzing one. The driver was stopped by a phalanx of the bikers that were driving ahead, and they began bashing in windows, eventually dragging the driver out of the car and attempting and failing to drag out his wife. She said in court her seatbelt stopped them (remember kids, always buckle up). Eventually, a bystander intervened, and the pummeled driver was able to return to his car and his terrified wife. Their two-year-old daughter was unharmed but covered in shattered glass.

The bikers filmed the entire gang assault and uploaded it to LiveLeak. But what works for the Jerk Who Pranked Occupy Wall Street very much does not work for a crowd of violent bikers, and the assailants, who included many NYPD members, along with Braszczok, were immediately identified. Some of them had their names on their jackets.

Braszczok was charged with riot and criminal mischief and eventually sentenced to two years. He initially hid his face in court on the advice of his lawyer, who insisted that in light of his undercover work and his five years of "infiltrating various organizations" (though how hard could it really have been to infiltrate a cattle call like Occupy Wall Street?), "to disclose his identity would jeopardize his life, his family's."[45]

I can't help but think that he didn't face much threat from Occupiers, especially as they had already sniffed out something pretty fishy early on, a few even accusing him outright of being a cop. In addition to the fact that the ostentatious biker dude with the thick Polish accent didn't exactly "fit in," his online footprint was suspicious.

He had started his Twitter account in April of 2010; nearly every one of his seventy-four tweets was activism-related, and his posts promoted a number of seemingly unrelated actions, particularly demonstrations that were likely to lead to police confrontations. (Never trust the guy encouraging you to throw the brick.)

★   ★   ★

In Richard Wright's two-part essay, "I Tried to Be a Communist," published in the August and September 1944 issues of *The Atlantic,* he recounts his disillusionment with communism; from his mother's "disgust and moral loathing" for the belligerent cover art of *New Masses,* the party periodical, to the internecine hostilities and domineering personalities within the group, his initial feelings of inspiration and enthusiasm slowly tempering off before collapsing completely.[46]

The final straw for Wright landed him with a life-altering despair for communism. He was recruited into the party through the Chicago John Reed Club, an organization for the support and advancement of left-wing artists founded by some editors of *New Masses.* The club was broadly socialist, but officially unaffiliated with the party, favoring an editorial approach unbeholden to any party line in order to reach a wider audience. Wright, who was Black (I'll reiterate that I find capitalizing the word biologically essentialist and grammatically silly, as if all Black people hail from Blackistan or something), had suspected he was being tokenized by members courting his involvement in the JRC, but he eventually decided these were well-meaning people with a noble vision of an egalitarian world—and after all, they published a few of his poems. (Writers are such whores.) He also decided that he had something to contribute to the club as a Black man and that communism had something to offer Black Americans.

Almost immediately there was a coup; the painters, who had unofficially run the group up until then, were upended by the writers, who favored resources for the club's magazine, *Left Front.* Nominations were made to elect a new executive secretary, and Wright was among them. He declined, citing his inexperience and ignorance of the project, but after debate ran from night until morning, he was elected. It wasn't until much later that he learned that the writers had used Wright, as the sole Black man in the club, to insist upon the primacy of literary endeavors, their only Black member being a writer.

The power struggles intensified when a faction of Communist Party members (many of whom had kept their membership a secret) fought to absorb the club into the party proper. Writers resisted, and the party threatened to dissolve *Left Front*. Wright was told he had to become a member to maintain his position; hamstrung, he signed the card under duress.

Suddenly an unprepared leader in a political party he barely knew, Wright was stumped when a newcomer, a Party Member from Detroit, showed up at his own Chicago chapter of the JRC. Comrade Young was a painter, and while Wright found him nice, he found his paintings and personality inscrutable, though the latter were certainly embraced by his comrades. Young had difficulty answering basic questions about his background beyond having come from Detroit. Wright wrote off the behavior as the eccentricities of a nice but nervous "queer artist" type, invited him into the JRC, and granted his request to sleep in the party offices until he got his grounding in Chicago. Just in case, though, he requested references from the party offices.

Whereas Wright was reluctantly dragged into the party, Young dove in immediately, before the national offices could even confirm he was a member. One night, Young submitted for a spot on the meeting's agenda.

[H]e rose and launched into one of the most violent and bitter political attacks in the club's history upon Swann, one of the best young artists. We were aghast. Young accused Swann of being a traitor to the worker, an opportunist, a collaborator with the police, and an adherent of Trotsky.

As a card-carrying member of the Communist Party, Young's accusations were met with deference, even though most of the club never believed Swann was a traitor. Wright moved that the charges be sent up the ladder and handled by the executive committee, but Swann insisted on defending himself publicly. The executive committee, however, consisted largely of party members, and the JRC feared unjust retaliation against Swann. Members loyal to Swann but afraid of the party demanded Wright dismiss the charges and keep the executive committee/party out of the loop entirely, then accused Wright of being complicit in Young's attack on Swann. He was "hurt and humiliated" by the suspicions of his comrades.

Wright confronted Swann; who was he taking orders from?

"I've been asked to rid the club of traitors."

"But Swann isn't a traitor," I said.

"We must have a purge," he said, his eyes bulging, his face quivering with passion.[47]

Members threatened to resign if Wright didn't dismiss the charges. He wrote to the party: Why had they ambushed Swann? Why had they sent this agent to charge him and with what crimes? The party wrote back: they hadn't.

Wright finally convinced the club members to send the matter to party leadership. Members reported to an office, while the accuser and defendant stood ready to state their cases to an official.

Young had his charges ready. Young had them printed off. Young gave a copy to the official; he could keep it. Young had made ten carbon copies. Young "didn't want anyone to steal them."

Swann threatened to resign and scream to high heaven if his persecution was humored. Young insisted this was evidence of his police collaboration. The party leader dismissed all present but promised to read all of the charges and make a decision regarding Swann's guilt or innocence.

A few days later, Wright decided to confront Young a second time, but he wasn't at the club. For a week, no one heard anything from him, and members harangued a clueless Wright to reveal his whereabouts, still suspecting him of collaboration.

Young had disappeared so quickly that he hadn't even taken his luggage from the club office where he had been sleeping. Wright and a friend, "Comrade Grimm," snuck in one night to learn what Young had left behind and discovered a madman's manifesto.

> [A] scroll of paper twenty yards long—one page pasted to another—which had drawings depicting the history of the human race from a Marxist point of view. The first page read: *A Pictorial Record of Man's Economic Progress*. . . . There were lengthy dissertations written in longhand; some were political and others dealt with the history of art.

Finally, they found a Detroit address and wrote to it in hopes of finding some clue as to who or where Young was.

Their correspondent, unlike the Communist Party officials, was swift to reply:

> *Dear Sir:*
> *In reply to your letter, we beg to inform you that Mr. Young, who was a patient in our institution and who escaped from our custody a few months ago, had been apprehended and returned to this institution for mental treatment.*

Wright made a motion and the charges against Swann were dropped. He apologized to Swann personally, but he makes no mention of an apology from the party or any internal evaluation of procedure regarding sabotage, disruption, verification of party membership, internal mediation, or management of "affiliated" organizations like the JRC. He never really recovered, leaving readers with this:

"What kind of club did we run that a lunatic could step into it and help run it? Were we all so mad that we could not detect a madman when we saw one?"

And so it was. And so it is. And so it ever shall be.

There were rumors and accusations against Officer Braszczok throughout Occupy but no real mechanism for investigating or evicting him, much less making everyone aware there was a fox in the henhouse.

The Communist Party of Wright's memory had a traumatizingly disorganized bureaucracy and an absolutely Kafkaesque judicial procedure. Occupy sought to avoid such mistakes by forgoing bureaucracy and procedure altogether. It was just as easy to lob false accusations, but now it was impossible to verify and act upon actual traitors.

Were we all such psycho cops that we could not recognize a psycho cop among us?

None of this is to say that OWS was a threat to power.

The now declassified 1944 CIA (then OSS) document titled "Simple Sabotage Field Manual" remains the gold standard for anyone who wants a primer on the history of American espionage.[48]

- Insist on doing everything through "channels." Never permit short-cuts [sic] to be taken in order to expedite decisions.

- Make "speeches." Talk as frequently as possible and at great length. Illustrate your "points" by long anecdotes and accounts of personal experiences.

- When possible, refer all matters to committees, for "further study and consideration." Attempt to make the committee as large as possible—never less than five.

- Bring up irrelevant issues as frequently as possible.

- Haggle over precise wordings of communications, minutes, resolutions.

- Refer back to matters decided upon at the last meeting and attempt to re-open the question of the advisability of that decision.

- Advocate "caution." Be "reasonable" and urge your fellow-conferees to be "reasonable" and avoid haste which might result in embarrassments or difficulties later on.

"Irrelevant issues" abounded at Occupy. While initially a movement primarily focused on economic justice, it quickly attempted to absorb every other cause. If they wanted to be "legitimate," they believed they had to be everything to everyone: every injustice, every crusade. There were fractures, splinters, and backbiting as competing activists attempted to shove their pet issue or strategy to the fore. "We can't talk about [X] if we don't talk about [Y]." Everything was "problematic." There was a campaign to change the name, because the word "Occupy" was "erasing indigenous people" of "Turtle Island," the winking little name they gave for America in the increasingly prevalent land acknowledgments that preceded meetings and events. "This Land is Your Land" was problematic. Endless articles were churned out announcing only the most conditional and qualified support for Occupy Wall Street, whose own activists agreed was too white, too male, too privileged. My skepticism of identity politics had been far milder before watching hundreds of people reduced to anxious terror or even crippling self-flagellation over a few losers on Tumblr. Those losers, however, often had bright futures ahead of them.

Years later I would write, in a book review of *#Hashtag Activism*:

For the life of me, I cannot remember a single insight from any book written about Occupy Wall Street during its brief window of apparent promise, though I do remember that the website occupywallstreet .org (taken down only a few weeks after this review was written) now advertises one—*The End of Protest: A New Playbook for Revolution,* from the "cocreator of Occupy Wall Street." As one of the more high-profile, media-savvy activists to make a name for himself in Zuccotti Park, the author, Micah White, also plugs his business ventures, including "Boutique Activist Consultancy," which bills itself as "an activist think tank specializing in impossible campaigns." In 2019, White was named "Activist-in-Residence" at UCLA's Institute on Inequality and Democracy, but if you missed that and were unable to attend any of his speaking engagements at Harvard or Yale, you can still enroll in his Activist Graduate School, an online streaming service of "exclusive content" where students receive no grades or credentials but can "learn from leading social movement creators." It's $19.99 a month, but you can sign up for a free two-week trial, which might be worth it just for the class taught by Rachel Dolezal.[49]

A lot of people got careers out of "the movement," which never bothered me. It's the ones who see their career *as* the movement that you gotta watch out for. For the ambitious politicos and NGO aspirants, Occupy Wall Street bestowed credibility as an "activist."

For the ambitious academic and media types, Occupy Wall Street established credibility as an "intellectual." There was always something to *discuss,* and discussion was a chance to insist upon your expertise.

I watched one such discussion on a panel featuring two (millennial) anarchists and two (baby boomer) socialists, the latter of whom weren't quite ready to give up on the state just yet. One of the anarchists, another writer who'd been recently arrested at the first Brooklyn Bridge kettling, breathlessly declared in a prim British accent that Occupy was here "to teach us new ways of fucking."

I remember later saying to a friend, "I think I pretty much figured out all the ways of fucking worth knowing," before adding, "and I don't think the revolution is here to teach her to not use teeth."

But I whispered it, very quietly, careful that only my friend could hear, because there were "leftists" around, and it had at some point been decided that people who made these kinds of jokes weren't committed to justice. I was a part of a movement where I couldn't make jokes about sucking dick. Never again.

Once in the van for a canvassing shift for WFP, I made the mistake of being honest about my lack of faith, expressing my concern that the diffuse nature of Occupy's spectacle-based strategy, combined with a lack of organizational structure capable of coordinating a division of labor and prioritizing demands, was about to go tits up. I believe my exact words were, "This is fucking dumb, and it isn't doing anything."

I like to think I'm better on the page.

A coworker who I had actually been quite friendly with suddenly hissed at me, "You sound like CNN right now! Maybe give it some time, OK?!?"

But I had given it some time, specifically my rare free time away from work, leisure, my social life, and DSA, a shit show of an organization that drove me insane, but a shit show with an organizational structure. A shit show with demands. My first loyalty was to a shit show that also required work and participation and debate and seemingly endless meetings, but with one crucial difference: the express purpose of an organization like DSA was to create a world where, one day, maybe there could be *fewer* meetings.

Toward the end of my participation in Occupy Wall Street, "fewer meetings" was my *only* political issue.

And there's the real rub: back in the 1940s and 1960s you *needed* the police or the CIA to interrupt meetings; now we did a much better job of just sabotaging ourselves, without even knowing it, and for free (a certain class of millennials were always quick to take unpaid internships, so why would being an inadvertent stooge for capital be any different?).

Maybe some of these people were cops, but would it really matter if they were? When a group's strategies and tactics are indistinguishable from an "op," aren't cops and activists a distinction without a difference?

"With comrades like these, who needs capitalists?"

8

HURRICANES

[S] annoyed the shit out of everyone, though I think this was mainly because whenever we saw her she was nearly always drunk, very loud, and off-puttingly oblivious to boundaries. And this was back in Indiana, where ridiculous drunken behavior is usually tolerated with patience and generosity, if only for fear of our own hypocrisy ("well, that was me three weeks ago"). At bars, parties, and shows, she would corner you in an inescapable conversation that consisted mainly of her yelling, often incoherently. This was always in an attempt to be friendly, but she was the ultimate example of what musicians, strippers, and now even some podcasters refer to as a "punisher." I would only later come to realize the endearing egalitarian nature of her intrusions; she would treat anyone like that, not just the ones in cool bands, or the funny ones, or the beloved party animals. Everyone got the star treatment from [S].

Like me, she married in her early twenties. Her husband was tall and handsome, and an equally aggressively friendly drunk. He had a massive Mohawk, and they never seemed to be spotted more than five feet away from each other, much less one without the other. Like my husband, she was a townie—a local rather than a transplant who had moved to attend Indiana University, the campus of which they both drove by every day on their way to work.

My husband told me she once interviewed him for her high school newspaper. This was when he was a skinhead in a punk band (not exactly Oi! but close enough to Cock Sparrer to count), which I found cute when I met him but later mocked him mercilessly for, until he grew his hair out. There was something self-loathing about a Pentecostal preacher's son moving out of the trailer he grew up in to emerge an Anglophile, and I thought it ridiculous to be obsessed with a place that hadn't done much I cared about since Shakespeare. (The joke was on me years later, when I started traveling to and writing about the United Kingdom, then the most promising beacon of renewed socialism in the world.)

[S] loved Oi! and skinhead fashion, and though I found her bleached white Chelsea haircut a touch costumey (Chelseas are sexy, but the peroxide really gilded the lily), I secretly envied the balls it took to shave most of your head into something so bold and louche. I was always too scared of scaring boys to get a "statement" haircut. So I was surprised when she admitted to me that she was "scared" to go to Planned Parenthood, scared someone might see her go in (honestly not an uncommon fear in Indiana) but also just scared of the examination itself. Unless it was moshing at a punk show, being touched by strangers made her incredibly nervous. Even hugs made her uncomfortable. I remember thinking to myself, *This girl has "sedition" tattooed across her knuckles, but she's squeamish about a Pap smear.*

I figured out later that while I was worried about looking unfeminine, she was worried about looking awkward, inappropriate, or stupid. She had debilitating social anxiety; the booze lubricated it, and the fashion was an icebreaker. Of course, after half a bottle of Stoli, she was breaking more than the ice, sometimes in someone else's house.

If you were in the right mood, though, she was fun, and before her light buzz of Dutch courage reached critical mass, she was still pretty wild, but no more so than the rest of us. Plus, she was always warm, and she laughed a lot. It was a real, unselfconscious laugh.

I used to have girls over for movie nights back then, and one time I invited [S]. When I told the regulars, one girl just said, "Oh no." Another said, "Hide your glassware," but the latter was joking, and everyone else agreed the more the merrier. "We really should hang out with [S] more," we'd say, "she just gets out of hand at parties because she feels like she has to."

She arrived last, but not late, glancing and smiling at the other guests quickly. I told her there would be "some girls," but I didn't think to tell her there would be six or seven of us, a few of whom she had never spoken to, except for maybe an inebriated rant at some party or show. Dead sober when she arrived, she was soft-spoken and visibly shy. Girls' Movie Night wasn't exactly a "dry" event, but my ample selection wasn't enough to get my regulars, plus [S], shitfaced. Perhaps anticipating this, she brought her own bottle, but slowed her pace to something approaching commensurate with the rest of us, no slouches ourselves.

We watched Pam Grier's blaxploitation classic *Coffy* with subtitles on, chattering throughout, except for [S], who just watched and listened to us, her eyes intermittently darting

between the screen and our faces. She seemed to be concentrating on sipping her drink to keep from chugging it.

After a little vodka loosened her up, she finally spoke,
leaning over to me on the couch and whispering with gen-
uine concern, "Are we racist for watching this?" To be fair,
when you have a skinhead haircut, you might be a little
more anxious about people thinking you're racist than most.
And she was already anxious.

Plus, she was out of her element. This was a rare solo
appearance; before they split up, you almost never saw her
without her husband. But I wouldn't say they were bad for
each other. They dried out for a while together, and they
both only resumed drinking in moderation. Instead of arriv-
ing already wasted, [S] started smoking a bit of weed before
going out, which I think calmed her down.

Even before they broke up, she started going out alone
more, just to hang, no longer either silent or bellowing and
no longer attached to her husband at the hip. I never got the
impression he was a bad guy, she just seemed to lean on him
a lot, both figuratively and literally. Friends speculated that
she had developed a new confidence, as if only then realizing
she could socialize just fine without him, and without even
blacking out. She got a new job at a liquor store (we joked that
she picked a helluva career change for someone with a recent
interest in the health of her liver), where she worked with
my ex-husband's roommate, a good-hearted former meth
head whose only residual effect was an inability to regulate
his body temperature; he always wore a hoodie, even in the
reliable heat waves of southern Indiana.

"I love that girl," he said. Everyone did, he said. She's
the easiest person in the world to work with, he said. Sweet
and easygoing and great at her job, he said. All the employees

agreed she was funny, and she makes you laugh off the busy days and laugh at the shitty customers. She makes you laugh and laugh and laugh.

Everyone in "the scene" noticed the change and was pleasantly surprised to finally meet this new person, whom they had already met before, multiple times, even though she usually didn't remember it. Me and [S] weren't Sisterhood of the Traveling Bondage Pants or anything, but we got friendlier in a way that suggested hangs to come. That is to say, when I left Indiana, she was A New Friend. We hugged now when we saw each other, though we both admitted that neither of us were totally comfortable with it. We seemed to have shared an unspoken agreement that sometimes it was good for you, and maybe even important, to be uncomfortably close to someone.

Once, we ran into each other at a bar that had been converted from an old small farmhouse. We started bitching about "the students," and we noticed a girl so fucked up she had regressed to a preverbal state, mumbling wordlessly while nodding off into her glass. We also noticed a guy noticing her, and we noticed him "introducing himself" to a now totally silent, nearly unconscious woman before offering to drive her home, even though her eyes were closed. When she did not stir for a moment, he took her hand and the eyes fluttered as he slowly pulled her up out of her chair and led her weaving to his car.

I called campus police ([S] didn't have a cell phone), and we watched the guy leading the stumbling heap of a girl through the crowded bar toward the parking lot. We agreed to intervene if they made it to the car before the cops got there. But they showed up in time. I didn't want to build my new friendship with [S] by blocking a business student's Audi to prevent a date rape, but in retrospect, the prospect of vigilantism offered a closeness far more comfortable than hugging for both of us. College Town Seditionists sheepishly calling cops didn't quite feel hypocritical, since university police pretty much exist to babysit the students, but it did feel lame. Then again, feeling lame together offers another kind of bonding.

I deactivated my Facebook not long after moving to New York, and then I started a new one, for my new life. Unlike [S] in her early years, I've never overstayed my welcome; I've been Irish goodbye–ing my way out of different lives without looking back since I was able. I eventually deactivated my "New York Facebook" well before I cut and ran to Los Angeles.

Sometimes though, I reactivate my old Indiana account, just to go back and read our exchanges during that period of her life. My new friend:

Still down for brunch . . . going to sleep now, though.

The next day:

We're waking. Brunch? Or . . . Lupper? Whatever time it is . . .

I canceled that one, but we made it up a few weeks later, at a place that did mimosas by the pitcher.

There's one message from a few months before I moved to New York where she sounds just as nervous as she could be:

*Hey, I was thinking about checking out a movie (**Idiots and Angels**) playing at [redacted bar/restaurant where I slung craft beers to meek and polite grad students who were under the impression they were drinking at a real live dive bar and not the rustic-chic basement of a trendy small plates eatery] next Thursday, but haven't been able to find out* *how much it costs, so I thought you might know? Also, I've never been there and don't know what to expect, really. Is it in the restaurant part, or the bar (if they're separate)? I've heard the menu is a bit pricey, so I've been looking for more details. Sorry if I was mistaken about you working there!*

I replied:

Hey, I do work at ▮▮▮▮▮▮▮▮▮▮ *, usually in [the bar], where they hold the film series! It's downstairs, and it's a separate bar area from the upstairs, but you can order food down there, too. The movie nights have changed prices the past few times I've worked there, and since I don't always work movie nights, I'd just call and ask what the price is this week. . . .*

The food is kind of pricey, but sometimes they do specials where they give you a free bowl of fries or something for coming in on a movie night. The pizzas are your best bet—thin crust gourmet things, medium size, for about 13 bucks. 2$PBRs and 2$well-drinks. I'm not sure if I'll work that night, but if not, I might come in for the movie!

She replied:
Hey, thanks! Hopefully I'll see you there one way or another!
I don't think she saw *Idiots and Angels*, but she saw a few others. I got her free fries once, I think when I was tending bar during a screening of *Fantastic Planet*. Or maybe we just talked about *Fantastic Planet,* and I got her the fries during some Béla Tarr movie. Or maybe John Waters. Or maybe Wim Wenders. I can't remember.

Sometimes I go back to my Indiana Facebook and read her final status updates:

> **August 26, 2011:**
> Don't feel well. Left work early.
>   I have chills and my skin hurts. Think a headache is coming on.
>   Stopped in on my way home from [restaurant]. Didn't drink anything. This is the first day I haven't in forever. I don't like it.

> **September 6, 2011:**
> Anyone want to sleep on my couch and listen to me cough all night and make sure I don't choke and die?

This was a joke. Kind of.

> **September 7, 2011:**
> So who's hiring? My liquor store sold out.

The owner, who had promised to sell his business to my hoodie'd friend, had decided instead to sell to a chain liquor store, which quickly fired every employee, I believe for their preexisting, though long since passed, familiarity with the wrong side of the law.

> **September 9, 2011:**
> Someone come give me a back massage. I really think it would help.

This is where I remember thinking how uncomfortable she could be with being touched.

> Seriously dying here. Don't care if you're a pro, need a massage. No comfortable position.

Sometimes, I even read her mother's posts from years later.

> 3 months ago today I found out you were sick . . . had no idea that in less than 15 hours you would be gone . . . why you didn't tell me you were sick sooner . . . ask for help sooner . . . I will never understand. would have done absolutely anything to help you . . . miss you. love you.

Later, she would lash out in blame:

> a year ago he knew you were sick . . . in a couple days, you would respond to a text from him telling him that it hurts so bad you could hardly move or breath and that you had no meds. he did nothing. did not even bother to text me that you might need help . . . that week that he knew and did nothing cost you your life. . . . it cost those of us that love you one of the most precious gifts we had . . . I don't understand how someone who knew [. . .] any sort of conscience or character could do that . . . especially to supposed 'family'. weighs heavy on my heart all the time . . . even more so as September begins. . . .

I have always assumed this was directed at [S]'s husband, but I don't know if they had reconciled in the end. If his wife's mother was talking about him, I hope he never read it. He was always sweet to me, and we all got the impression he adored [S].

When I think of why someone might post something that cruel, I try to imagine what it would be like to have a baby and watch her grow up, watch her struggle and thrive, fail and succeed. Then one day, you get a call from the hospital: your baby (who grew up) is very sick. Your baby (who grew up) has been very sick for a very long time. I try to imagine what it must have felt like to have had fifteen hours left to be with her daughter, and then to know that she would be alive today if she had just not waited so long to go to the hospital.

I try to imagine it, but my brain just goes snowy, not like postcard-of-a-polar-bear snowy, and not like blizzard-on-bare-cornfields snowy. This snow is like television static, jittering and hissing with electrical white noise. Sometimes I can actually hear it in my head.

She was twenty-six, and I remember thinking as I walked to Zuccotti on that very first day how strange it felt to have known someone younger than me who died of a treatable disease. It was only five days earlier that I had learned of her death from Facebook. The announcement was from a mutual friend, and I almost missed it, buried in all the posts advertising the forthcoming protest movement of the 99 percent.

I know I sound contemptuous of Occupy Wall Street. I am. I resented the idea of hanging out in a corporate office park on a doomed mission to found some new utopian society while the real world went on with business as usual. I wanted everyone in the real world to have healthcare, housing, decent work, and time off to go to the doctor (or just to fucking relax). I believed then, and still believe now, that these things require not a community, or a process, but the democratization of the economy, something that's historically been advanced by organized labor, not a bunch of downwardly mobile middle-class kids playing revolutionary commune.

[S] had a community. She had friends and family who loved her. She had a husband. She had a bunch of great guys working with her at the liquor store who would have done anything for her. She had great hair and a sense of humor, and she had punk rock. But nearly everyone in her "community" was as terrified as she was of going to the doctor and racking up a ruinous medical bill. None of us went to the doctor if we could possibly avoid it.

Some of us had parents who could help. Many of us didn't. A few of our friends had parents who took the bootstraps approach not uncommon to Midwestern Protestants and our pathological work ethic:

"Don't worry, it will clear up; you're young and healthy!"

"Walk it off . . ."

"You got yourself into this mess, you can pay for it."

Etc.

A lot of our parents were in massive debt themselves, and even if they'd have rushed to find a way to pay for anything their kids needed, their adult children often felt too guilty to ask for help.

In a parody of Hoosier idiocy, my husband broke at least one rib at his bachelor party—he was drunk and wrecked a Jet Ski. (Irresponsible or a life well lived? Judge not lest ye be judged.) He hid his injury from his friends, who only noticed the severity of it the next day. When he confessed to me how much pain he was in, I became terrified that he was bleeding internally. He said if that was the case, he'd probably be dead by now, or at least a lot paler. A few days later, he limped down the aisle with nothing but whiskey for painkillers. I'm not kidding; *none* of us went to the fucking doctor.

We had all at some point been nearly as sick as [S], and

just like her we all decided to "wait it out." We all gambled with our lives, all the time, without even thinking about it. She just got a bad hand.

★ ★ ★

Lest your takeaway be "Woe is me, the Cassandra of Occupy Wall Street, and no one even appreciated my charm and wit!" I would never say the experience was traumatizing, or even tragic; I already knew what real tragedy was, and she wasn't at Zuccotti Park.

It's true I have no glorious memories of Occupy; it was frustrating, exhausting, and eventually a little demoralizing. But the disappointment faded long before the "movement." Just as many women secretly admit to never really mourning the miscarriage of an unviable pregnancy, I didn't feel the need to grieve. Not for Occupy. But it wasn't, as I thought at the time, a complete waste. Occupy had to happen so that the next, more important thing could happen, and I met good people and I figured out a lot of stuff about organizing, though most of it in hindsight.

It took a while for the smoke to clear enough so that I could make sense of things; the indignation of being ignored and the smug satisfaction in having been correct had to wear off first. Only then could I be honest about my own "contribution" to the movement.

Maybe you find my account of Occupy Wall Street self-aggrandizing and selectively flattering, which is fine by me (I mean, what do you expect, it's *my* book). But do know that I was just as clueless about what to do as everyone else.

It's easy enough to remember everyone and everything that annoyed me about Occupy, but I'm sure I was just as insufferable as the average fool I imagined myself to be suffering. If nothing else, I know I wasn't great for morale, my own being weighed down with scorn for the optimists, loathing for the chancers, and pity for myself. (If you think I lack humility *now* . . .)

I got a little too proud of being a Cassandra, as if "I told you so" was a declaration of victory, rather than the petty, defensive retort of an egoist who wants an excuse to give up and slide into comfortable bitterness. I took consolation in my prescience, ineffectual as it was, because feeling smug is a cozy little blankie for when you don't know what to do, but you know everyone else is doing it wrong. I portended doom pretty accurately, but what good did that do me? I thought constantly about what couldn't work and why, and I was really good at it, probably due to some combination of exposure to experienced elder DSA members, my own reading of socialist memoirs, and a little bit of prior experience. But I never had the patience to sit and think of what could work, or even what was already working. I never took an honest accounting of our strengths, and I never tried to organize something better. I had no alternative program, no positive advice, because I was just as lost as everyone else and too frustrated to notice. I didn't notice a lot of things.

I didn't, for example, notice that the emotional rewards and sense of belonging people got from activism were extremely important to them, and that those values aren't a weakness or a lack of vigilance or true commitment. I saw so many Occupiers searching for "their people," and I would scoff at them because "they're just searching for meaning," perhaps the most fundamental thing a human being can do. My values are pretty thoroughly compartmentalized, with my moral, spiritual, social, cultural, and political principles operating more or less distinctly. It's much tidier that way, though certainly more rigid. But for a lot, maybe most, of the people at the park, those principles were fuzzier, more adaptable and intertwined. I knew that a desire for community or comradery or God or art or whatever-the-fuck is never a good foundation for an anticapitalist movement, but I didn't appreciate that that desire is also a very human impulse, so I didn't understand why everyone wasn't just punching in every day and getting down to the task at hand, rather than participating in what often amounted to salons, pep rallies, and group therapy sessions. I didn't understand—and more importantly, I didn't try to understand—what mattered to them, and why.

I didn't know how lost and lonely so many of them were, and I didn't see that they were scared of the inarticulable things that financial security and professional opportunity wouldn't fix. I wasn't scared of those things because I had never really thought about them, save maybe for a few times when I got too stoned. (I remember the day I finally got a paycheck big enough to come with a dividend of existential dread; who knew that rising to a higher tax bracket would dig up ennui?)

These weren't the sort of discoveries I could have made in the moment. Even if everyone knew and understood and could explain what was important to them (no one can, there's not enough therapy in the world), I wouldn't have been able to hear them. I was conflict-averse, but in my own, counterintuitive way, meaning I was fine with making enemies and starting fights; what I didn't like was arguing. If I surmised, rightly or wrongly, that a political opponent was hostile, I also assumed they were a lost cause, so I was quick to say something shitty and walk away. My thinking was that I was standing firm and not wasting my time. In reality, I was just giving up, because I was a bad listener, too impatient, and too easily exasperated. I will say I've become much better at listening, though six years on a podcast where everyone is trying to get a word in edgewise has eroded some of my progress. I certainly enjoy listening more, and I'm generally pretty interested in what people have to say, though I still get excited enough to interrupt them when I know a relevant fact or anecdote, or if I have a joke or story that might charm them, perhaps even endearing me enough to them that they'd hide me one day if the Cossacks ever ransacked Silver Lake. Making people laugh isn't so much a defense mechanism as a survival plan.

Even during OWS, I knew that I was bad at listening, but I was good at being heard, so I tried treating the park like a DSA recruitment outpost. A good rule of thumb: if you don't like someone doing it to you, you're probably not going to be good at doing it to anyone else. For all my annoyance with the entryists, I was more annoyed at being an unsuccessful one. I didn't respect entryism as a tactic, and I didn't think it really worked for anything long-term, but I thought it would work for me, because I was right. My approach was condescending; I went out looking for the unaffiliated, ignoring the most engaged activists because they had already picked anarchism; after all, the former were searching for answers. It's not that I thought I knew everything, it's that I knew I didn't have to.

After Occupy, I learned my organizing talents lay more in the propaganda wing—the millennial equivalent of radical theater, writing for party papers, radio evangelism, whistle-stop tours, etc. Even before I was on a podcast, I understood that I moderated a good panel and threw fundraisers people actually enjoyed. Despite WFP's many attempts to beat it out of me, I'm also actually good at canvassing, so long as I believe in whatever's on the pamphlet I'm pushing. But at the time, I fucking sucked at getting people on my side; I was just too angry, and I resented even having to justify my position. You can't be smug and bitter and convince people to join you. At least, not for very long.

I don't actually believe I could have strengthened Occupy if I had known all this stuff at the time, but I would've been less frustrated, and maybe I could've recognized more opportunities. Live and learn.

By the summer following OWS, I had left the Working Families Party for a nearly full-time job in the DSA office as an "administrative assistant," which was the formal title and feminist-approved euphemism, but I still said "secretary" because I thought it sounded sexier. Whatever you want to call it, I usually made coffee, coordinated mailings, processed donations, updated the spreadsheets and databases, called and emailed donors, and answered the phones. I was one of four employees. That got me health insurance. I was also writing the odd music review and drove a forklift part-time in a cocoa warehouse alongside my husband, where we sold kosher baking chocolate to Orthodox Jews who refused to interact with me when he wasn't in the room, but always left me a gift of babka or rugelach. I had a nice little life, and I was meeting new people with leftist politics outside of DSA, and (thankfully) outside the surreal social order of Zuccotti Park.

A DSA friend had just begun dating a high-strung labor journalist who made a lot of misandrist jokes where nobody could tell if she was kidding. The aforementioned friend spoke on a panel one day, and afterward the three of us, plus his best friend (a stoic Palestinian activist and graduate student), went out for lunch. It was a sunny day, and we were all having a good time laughing over burgers and beers. Someone mentioned in passing an article that had just come out:

everyone was calling it "the Occupy postmortem." None of us were particularly convinced by the author's analysis, albeit, I was soon to learn, for very different reasons.

The Palestinian activist insisted that it was the cops who crushed the occupation, which to me seemed a sort of tautological excuse, as if to say, "Well, we only lost because they beat us." (Great note, I knew we forgot something—next time we'll remember to not let them do that.)

I said that I thought the article was reductive, but understandably so since it was almost impossible to observe and analyze all the chaotic moving parts of Occupy Wall Street.

I continued, saying that there were probably too many reasons to count "why Occupy Wall Street failed."

The journalist suddenly stiffened, irate, and to my surprise, began tersely upbraiding me for using the "f-word," and in the past tense, no less. She became more and more agitated as she expounded on all the ways OWS was still alive, how it was developing and growing, until hot, angry tears streamed down her face. In a finale befitting a maudlin opera, she screamed through sobs, "Occupy! Didn't! Fail!"

This was in the early afternoon. Surrounded by friends on a warm—but not too warm—day, right by a window with the sun shining (but not in our eyes). This was during our second round of good beer, and with good burgers. Not the foodie kind of good, which uses too little fat and where the patty is overly thick, compromising flavor for "presentation." I mean just very good burgers.

Obviously, she was still sore. I don't know why I wasn't. I was just tired, and I was relieved that Occupy had run its course so we could move on to something more productive. I didn't want to even think about the park, but here she was, still in it, whatever "it" was now. It was like she was scared to leave a condemned building, and was lashing out at anyone who noticed the extent of its decay. It was harrowing—not in a "strange drunk girl crying and screaming at you" kind of way, but in a "there but for the grace of God, please don't let me succumb to delusional denial" kind of way. I realized that if I didn't confront failure, I'd end up squatting in the rubble, out of commission, incapable of navigating real politics and totally cut off from the real world, including the good parts.

Yes, Occupy failed. But I realized then that there are worse things than failing; I had just witnessed a far more tragic defeat.

It was such a good burger. And such a perfect day.

Part III

BERNIE

9

MAYBE . . .

Before Bernie announced his first run, all I wanted was a party. A Labor Party, to be precise. We don't have real political parties in the Land of the Free and the Home of the Brave because parties have members. No one is a "member" of the Democratic (or Republican) Party. You can certainly *register* as a Republican or a Democrat, but unlike, say, the Labour Party of the United Kingdom, there is no way to become a *member*, i.e., someone who pays dues and chooses both the party leadership and the machinations of its politics.

I specify a Labor Party rather than a Socialist Party because the distinction is more than academic. As the political wing of the working class, a Labor Party not only consists of members but also incorporates the trade union movement into its architecture; labor doesn't just steer the party, it powers it, with the coordinated strength of an organized and militant trade unionism. The thinking is that labor makes the world, so labor should run it, and the unions are the muscle. That sounds about right to me.

A Socialist Party, on the other hand, is a collection of

like-minded progressives with a critique of capitalism. Even with a radicalized rank-and-file membership, a Socialist Party would differ very little from any other third party in function, and since I didn't lose my virginity in a Prius, I find nothing promising about reproducing the impotence of the Green Party. Without the muscle of the unions, a party doesn't have the threat of industrial action to flex on the capitalists. A Labor Party, however, doesn't rely on liberal lifestylism, coalitions, or social movements; it's motivated by the material needs of the working class. The working class makes the world go round, so the working class, more or less, gets to drive.

American unions seriously made a go of a Labor Party as recently as the mid-1990s, and to be honest it wasn't a bad effort, given the recent so-called "End of History," Francis Fukuyama's term for the new certainty that liberal capitalism in every nation was all but a fait accompli. In the first weekend of June 1996, nearly 1,500 trade unionists from the United Mine Workers, International Longshore and Warehouse Union, American Federation of Government Employees, California Nurses Association, and a number of other locals gathered in Cleveland, Ohio, to found a Labor Party. Their leader was Tony Mazzocchi—"The Man Who Never Sold Out"—of the Oil, Chemical and Atomic Workers International Union. His motto was simple and perfect: "The bosses have two parties. We need one of our own."

Before Bernie announced his 2016 run, progressive "It-girl" Elizabeth Warren was favored by both the left-liberal intelligentsia and the electoralists of the erstwhile Occupy movement, which had gone more or less fallow after Hurricane Sandy provided the sort of immediately rewarding disaster relief work that endless meetings never could. Just before Bernie threw his hat in the ring, I managed an invite to a

"Draft Warren" event, featuring such professional progressives as Lawrence Lessig, Van Jones, and Zephyr Teachout. I was Bernie or Bust from the beginning, and the day he announced, my article "Screwing with the Democratic Party: Fear and Loathing on Champagne Trail as a Bernie Sanders Admirer Travels to Elizabeth Warren Utopia" went live on Salon. To this day, I believe that if the editors had even *imagined* Bernie getting as far as he did, the article never would have been published in a mainstream online mag.

My endorsement-turned-prediction-turned-manifestation—if you're a vision board kind of girl—was exciting, but neither I nor any of the Berniecrats I knew thought he could win the primary. We knew Hillary was the favorite of middle-class liberals and of the Democratic Party, and we knew Liz Warren was their chosen dummy candidate, plausible deniability that "no, we swear, the fix isn't in!" We also knew that even if the game wasn't rigged, Bernie didn't have the name recognition to reach the critical mass of voters he'd need to get the nomination. And we knew the 2016 Bernie run was predicated on this knowledge; it was a "realignment campaign" that would show Americans they could demand more than what the Democrats offered, and maybe even nudge the party a little bit to the left.

Over the course of 2016, though, there were two big surprises.

First of all, Bernie caught on. Not just with young left-wingers, but—and this part was far more important—with a fair number of the sort of people who usually ignored politics, and for good reason. It had been a long time since a politician had offered Americans anything concrete, anything that improved their lives in any way, so why would they pay attention to politics? There were only two parties, neither of which possessed an ounce of integrity, and neither of which were at all accountable to voters.

Bernie first made waves because he was an outsider. He was detested by the Democratic Party and the liberal elite, something that only increased his credibility in the eyes of many. He was an honest man in the public eye, and he was exposing the venality and corruption of the DNC.

The second thing, of course, was that Hillary Clinton lost.

I should have seen it coming. We all should have. I should have seen it coming with NAFTA, with right to work, with how much the country suffered during eight years of Obama. And we knew absolutely everyone hated the Clinton dynasty, and how much they resented her sense of entitlement, her smug confidence that she was destined for the highest throne in the land.

For a moment, everyone sort of lost their minds. Trump was going to be the end of the world, or at least the end of America, they wailed. Disheartened, I feared the momentum and ambition we had built around Bernie would recede into a cloud of panic and lower their expectations, that they would retreat to the dubious safety of "Blue, No Matter Who."

But then, at the risk of going full Adam Curtis, something funny happened. A curious and encouraging rush of outrage erupted toward the Democratic Party; not only were they uninterested in fighting for the little guy, it was now obvious they would be completely incapable, even if they tried. But, wait a minute, if Trump could get elected president, who's to say Bernie couldn't? A few weeks after the Chicken Little–ing surrounding Trump's inauguration, there was a soaring optimism in the air. DSA was surging in membership, and little cultural projects—my friends' left-wing podcasts for example—were developing small but politically engaged audiences who were suddenly excited about the new possibilities that Bernie's campaign/Hillary's loss/ Trump's win had illuminated.

Later that year, I was invited to speak at a DSA fundraiser, a Christmas party at the dreaded Verso Loft. I was as sick as a dog, wearing a floor-length muskrat fur coat over what I insisted was a dress but was far closer to lingerie; I looked like a consumptive whore. I gave a speech that I can't quite recall, though I do remember getting a few laughs. The room was packed, and not a single face was dour; even the grad students were smiling and laughing. (I didn't even know they could do that.) Sanders had raised the bar, not only for the politicians who failed to deliver what Americans already knew they deserved, but for socialists, who for the first time in decades were being called up from the reserves of Marxist reading groups and sparsely attended discussion panels. No one was really allowed to admit outright that Trump's election had a silver lining, but now we knew, without question, that people were ready for an outsider. That election proved that the future wasn't written, that anything could happen, that the plans made in the halls of power could still be sabotaged by popular will, or even upended by a little bit of chaos. We were ready to go as far as we could; we even allowed ourselves to believe—not just say— that we might be able to take power back from the billionaires and their sclerotic toadies, the "elected officials."

Just as I was about to pour myself into a cab, I got a call: everyone on the Chapo Trap House podcast had discussed it, and they wanted to add me as a cohost, as well as Virgil Texas. We would be joining Will Menaker, Matt Christman, and my roommate Felix Biederman. Our producer at the time was Brendan James, who retired after our first tour to work on his own successful projects. After that, we brought in Chris Wade to produce.

I knew two things that night for sure.

One, I was about to get paid for screaming about politics with my friends on a show with a growing audience of tens of thousands of politically motivated people who were all sick of the Democrats.

And two, Bernie would run again.

I wasn't *quite* optimistic, but I definitely wasn't pessimistic, though I'm almost never either one. Optimism is for suckers, but pessimism is for pussies.

★ ★ ★

The Baffler, January 11, 2019:

IT'S BERNIE, BITCH[50]

The substance of Elizabeth Warren's political rhetoric is dominated by banks and corporations—obvious and odious targets, to be sure. She speaks positively, but vaguely, about labor unions. In 2013, she advocated for a minimum wage increase to $10 an hour over the course of two years—tragically modest in the time of Fight for $15. She's helped make some mild reforms to student debt, but nothing so great as to be noticeable for a young person debilitated by loans. She's made no great stink about socialized health care or higher education. Aside from financial regulation, it's actually quite unclear

> what a Warren presidential program would
> be . . .

This dandy little bit of self-plagiarism is from three years ago, when I attended a painfully nerdy and shamefully self-congratulatory event to "Draft Warren" into the presidential primaries. It was a farcical gathering of type A Tracy Flicks, barely worth the free booze, and even the assembled nerds quickly realized this Lisa Simpson of a dark-horse candidate wasn't as inspiring to the masses as she was to them, and we all moved on.

And what we moved on to was Bernie—our indefatigable, unwavering, incorruptible Bernie! And we very nearly won, despite despicable sabotage from the DNC. Bernie was the leader of a movement that fundamentally ended the Cold War of the American mind; he changed the face of American politics, acted as midwife to a nascent insurgent left, and achieved more in a few months of mass political action than Elizabeth Warren did in her whole political life.

It was true then and it's true now: Bernie Sanders is the best candidate—the *only* candidate who could be considered anything even close to socialist, and the one to beat Trump. A President Sanders isn't some idealist fantasy, he is our best bet by a mile. He has *consistently* polled as the most popular politician in America since the primaries, and while everyone else has been tweeting (or following up with 23andMe), Bernie pressured Amazon into raising wages, followed up by going after Walmart, condemned Saudi Arabia and sponsored the resolution to end support for the war in Yemen, introduced the No Money Bail Act, committed to a federal job guarantee, campaigned so powerfully for Medicare for All that he shifted the entire Democratic Party, and *saved a woman from being hit by a car.* Not only is he the best candidate politically (as in, *the only social democrat*), he has the best chance of giving the "pragmatists" what they *say* they want: a presidential win.

Unfortunately, a few of my media colleagues appear to have caught the Warren bug yet again, but this time around she lacks the good sense to refuse to run.

Elizabeth Warren's politics aren't impressive, and they never have been; all she has ever leaned on is a rigid obsession with the sort of basic financial regulation that *barely* mitigates capitalism's greatest crimes. She's not charismatic and appears to have absolutely zero understanding of what voters want in a candidate, as indicated by her precampaign soft launch on a bit of specious family lore about Native American heritage. Literally, *no one cares,* and yet she *keeps doubling down on it.* She chokes, she flinches, she reacts *every time* Trump insults her, and thus the public is far more familiar with her defensive "Orange Man Is Mean to Me" ethnic delusion than they are her "Accountable Capitalism Act" (really inspiring name there, Liz).

Warren, who didn't stop voting Republican until 1995, said in 2011, "I was a Republican because I thought that those were the people who best supported markets. I think that is not true anymore." Again displaying her tone-deaf penchant for doubling down when the situation desperately calls for changing the subject, she explained further that "I was a Republican at a time when I felt like there was a problem that the markets were under a lot more strain. It worried me whether or not the government played too activist a role," and then she declined to say if she voted for Ronald Reagan. (Incidentally, these quotes came from a *Daily Beast* interview titled "I Created Occupy Wall Street," an ungenerous fudge on Warren's original statement that she "created much of the intellectual foundation of what they do," and her professed support for the Occupy insurgency. One might still accuse her of taking too much credit for the "movement," but given the futility and ultimate failure of Occupy, I'd argue it's actually pretty fair to call her its Fairy Godmother.)

There's no reason to believe that a goody-goody technocrat would fare better in 2020 than fellow neoliberal loser Hillary Clinton did in the prior presidential cycle. And yet here's Hamilton Nolan in *Splinter,* who titles his anyone-but-Trump political polemic "Bernie Don't Run"[51]:

> I don't really give a damn who it is. Warren, or Kamala Harris, or Sherrod Brown, or whoever. Pick one and get behind them from the very beginning. Any solid top-tier true left-wing candidate should, barring a serious fuck-up, be able to win the Democratic nomination if Bernie Sanders hands them all of his supporters on a platter.

I hate to break it to you, HamNo, but the voters actually *do* give a damn who it is, as evidenced by the fact that Bernie was previously unable to hand Hillary "all of his supporters on a platter." They didn't want Hillary, or really any neoliberal. And why should they?

Barack Obama was the very last "horoscope candidate"—a politician who manages to speak so vaguely that his platform could mean anything to anyone. It's not going to work this time around; the Democratic Party is not going to be able to trick people into believing that Liz Warren is a social democrat. Ditto for Kamala "Cop" Harris, a woman whose duplicitous record as a prosecutor includes the defense of the death penalty, three strikes laws, and the imprisonment of single mothers for the truancy of their children. You really think you can convince anyone that Kamala Harris is a woman of the people? Sherrod Brown has gone all in with Russiagate hysteria (also he signs his tweets). And before you even think of it, don't even bother with Beto, who is to the right of all of the aforementioned, *and* votes to the right of the median Democrat. His district is majority Democratic, so he *could* plausibly vote to storm the Winter Palace and still keep his seat, but he joined the New Democrat Caucus in order to advance business interests. You can't just astroturf any shitty neoliberal hack into the hearts and minds of the Bernie voter; if you could, we'd have President Hillary right now.

The coming election cycle will be an extremely difficult and fraught one. The Democrats might not be able to win with *any* candidate; even the worst presidents seem all to serve for two terms now, and frankly, a lot of people have very little faith in electoral change. And despite all the #resistance hysteria, for the time being, the majority of the electorate haven't seen the sort of plummet in quality of life that inspires droves of voters to cast a ballot for Anyone But Trump. The Donald hasn't *actually* deviated that much from the neoliberal trajectory of his predecessors (remember, Obama shot tear gas at the border, too), and you can't expect people who don't spend all day on Twitter to feel that motivated to combat what is essentially the gradual continuation of previous administrations. (Hell, he's already more antiwar than Obama.)

And even if we *could* get a President Gillibrand in 2020, another lukewarm Democratic presidency will not only further impoverish and destabilize the working class and its suffering institutions; it will also all but *guarantee* that 2024 brings us POTUS Hamburglar in an SS uniform. No, HamNo, it's Bernie or bust. I don't care if we have to roll him out on a hand truck and sprinkle cocaine into his coleslaw before every speech. If he dies midrun, we'll stuff him full of sawdust, shove a hand up his ass, and operate him like a goddamn Muppet.

At first glance, it might seem strange to abandon the winning candidate for "pragmatic" reasons, but I have my suspicions as to why a lot of people who should know better are doing it right now. I suspect it has something to do with caution, or at least the professional credibility a writer gains by appearing to heed such caution. Call it "pressimism" if you want, but journalists are generally treated as more judicious when they aim low during times of crisis (it was one thing to support Bernie when we all thought Hillary would win, but now we have to get "serious" and stump for a shitty candidate, lest *The New York Times* think you too idealistic). Pressimism is regarded by the industry not as cynicism, diffidence, cowardice, or even just plain poor judgment, but as prudence. I call it hedging your bets. But since we have a real shot here, it's time to keep the faith and go all in. Otherwise, (1) no one will *ever* let you forget it; and (2) you'll have to spend years eating crow.

And for the love of God, *learn to exercise your scoffing muscles.* Don't get drawn into show-trial debates when someone is *obviously* merely attempting to defame, discredit, or otherwise malign the Sanders campaign. Yes, there *are* guileless and gentle souls who might voice concern about Sanders's prospects, policies, or appeal to women and minorities, and with those people we have conversations. Kindly, confidently, and thoroughly we explain, over and over, again how Bernie Sanders is *the best candidate for the working class*—and we then spell out, with the same saintly patience, that this means *all* of the working class. But as for the liberal media, and for those who would disingenuously invoke identity politics to attack the socialist, just remember the magic words: "I know what you're doing right now and it doesn't work on me." Remember, they're trying to trip you up, wear you down, and waste your precious time. (Luckily, they're utter clowns; elite whiners who pout that everyone is being too mean to them and to their favored milquetoast candidate.) The hit pieces against Bernie have already started to pour in, and we cannot concede a *single inch* to bad-faith liberals. Steel yourselves against the pseudoprogressive manipulation tactics and moral blackmail that put you on the back foot.

Fellow soft-handed scribblers, if indeed you are

a socialist first, then indeed you must be a contrarian pundit second, and this is your *one* opportunity to drop the professional artifice of "constructive criticism from the left" and choose socialism over media strategy. There are no "impartial" spectators on this one; only partisans and compradors. This is not some college debate where you get extra points for novelty and precocious dissidence, and it's not some office pool where heated but distant speculations on the tournament are an amusing pastime with colleagues around the water cooler. This involves nothing less than the real, live fate of every single person in America (and most people outside of it).

If you have strayed, all is forgiven, but you better come to Jesus *right now,* because memories are long and history judges the cowardly squish far more harshly than the honest enemy. And you can't say that no one was there at the time to tell you that *this* was it, that *this* was the pivotal moment where you had to make the right choice.

Partisan isn't a dirty word, it's nice out here (on the right side of history), and if you keep sitting on that fence you're gonna get splinters in your ass. So hop aboard the Bernie train (choo-chooooo)! We got ourselves a winner. It's Bernie, bitch, and it's the only game in town.

January 21, 2019, The Baffler:

Editor's Note: We have removed the January 11, 2019, column by Amber Frost from our website after determining that

*it does not meet The Baffler's guidelines for coverage and com-
mentary concerning political candidates. The essay is an expression of Ms. Frost's personal views. While The Baffler supports
a robust discussion about political issues and candidates, as a
nonprofit organization it does not support or oppose any individual candidate or potential candidate for political office. We
are sorry for any inconvenience to our readers. We appreciate
Ms. Frost's other contributions to The Baffler, which you can
find here.*

**January 22, 2019, republished as "It's Still Bernie" in
Jacobin.**

★   ★   ★

We knew the odds were stacked against us. And we certainly
knew the energy behind Bernie's first run had surprised and
scared the Democrats, who were now activating to nip his
second campaign in the bud. It's a cliché for a reason: first
they ignore you, then they laugh at you, then they fight
you . . . and I forget the last part.

I was never given a straight answer as to why my article,
"It's Bernie, Bitch" was removed from The Baffler—their
own explanation didn't hold water. My fiercely loyal editor
had gone to the mat for me more than once, and I knew this
came from the top—I suspected the porcine little second-
generation publisher who was always cowering before the
shrieking hydra of online liberal feminists (who were not my
biggest fans, to say the least).

Jacobin, by then fully Bernie Bro'd, reprinted the article
the next day—albeit with my nasty little jab at Owen Jones
removed—as "It's Still Bernie." Editor in chief Bhaskar Sunkara was himself too genteel to keep the word "bitch." It was

a fair compromise. Moreover, the retraction backfired, as outlets like Common Dreams and Spectator US decried the censorship. But the real outrage came from the Twittersphere.

It's difficult to trace the trajectory of Twitter as a landscape, but before it became LinkedIn for New York media—a formation that solidified around the 2016 election—it had gone through a series of evolutions.

I was a late adopter, as I always am with new technology, mostly because I know the majority of it ends up going the way of Google Glass. Why would I start *another* social media account when every Next Big Thing on the internet never seems to last more than six months, even when it manages to attract a seemingly promising user-base? And 140 characters? It'll never last!

The idea of "microblogging," as the company described it, felt insipid, and I was already bristling at the rapidity and vapidity of the online news cycle, the emerging hot-take economy, and the increasingly lurid and artless voyeurism in the new rash of misery porn confessional essays.

I liked writing. I liked writing essays and fiction and poetry and polemic. Privately, I liked writing love letters, which were as much a self-indulgent creative exercise as they were an outpouring of emotion with a motive. Like a polemic, love letters always have an agenda.

A few months after I moved to New York, I got a job as an arts and culture writer for a niche online outlet called Dangerous Minds, where my bio was "Freelance writer, Musician, I'm the Girl Friday of Socialism," having recently been hired for the administrative assistant (secretary) job at DSA.

By day it was spreadsheets and fundraising for the glorious cause of the workers' movement; by night, I was posting, "Hey look, it's your new favorite band you've never heard of." I was proud of both gigs but unsure of how to promote either my writing or DSA. Turned out 140 characters was just perfect, and at that time the weirdos of early Twitter were a perfect target audience for both.

I also discovered that among those weirdos were some of the funniest, most creative people I'd ever read. The platform lent itself to a certain kind of humor, later dubbed "Weird Twitter," that was completely born of the form, but not without precedent. Back in 1990, David Foster Wallace wrote beautifully and sincerely about the postmodern turn of both television and literary fiction, which left both suffused with a slavish devotion to cynicism and irony; if he'd been resurrected to scroll through a Weird Twitter time line, he'd hang himself all over again. The brevity, the disconnect between individual tweets (remember, you couldn't even thread at that point) meant there was a complete lack of continuity that induced a sort of manic ADHD high. And it was all very disposable, as small things usually are. A "bad" tweet couldn't be salvaged, only deleted. At the same time, a "bad" tweet was almost always quickly forgotten after another few rounds of compulsive scrolling. No one was quote-tweeting or screenshotting or really even scrutinizing other tweets at that point. It wasn't that the environment was warm and welcoming; it was actually mean as shit. But the stakes were so low it didn't matter. If someone didn't like your tweet, or didn't like you, you might get roasted a little, but you were never crucified. It wasn't punitive; no one was "canceled" or "called out" or fired, because nobody took it seriously. I loved it, but again, I've always had a bully's heart.

I recently discussed the shift in the social dynamics of Twitter with fellow veteran Felix Biederman, who noted, "It was way meaner, but it was way less cruel." I compare it to rugby versus football. Rugby is played without padding or protective gear; it's violent and you get knocked around, but serious injuries are rare. In football, you're padded from head to toe until you look like the Michelin man, but there's a good chance you'll destroy the part of your brain that prevents you from murdering your wife. Twitter used to be way more brutal, but it didn't destroy people.

I can't pinpoint the date I reluctantly joined to tweet my writing and promote DSA events, but I insisted on using my real name from the very beginning, an extreme novelty for a platform largely populated by message board migrants who nearly always posted anonymously. I used my name *and* my actual picture, because I wanted credit. It wasn't long before I became a "poster," i.e., not only tweeting things like "Look at this article I wrote" or "Join DSA" but "If I had a dick I would wade into the ocean and scream 'I am fucking the sea.'" I was never great at it, but I was decent enough at rebounding the more talented posters and even better at dragging the bad ones. As shameful as it is, I smile when I remember my reply to a distinctly bland and stupid writer defending her recent appointment to a legacy publication. Amid the mockery, she tweeted, "I'm not here to please everyone," to which I replied, "No, you're here because of low standards." Not exactly Dorothy Parker, but it got me blocked (not muted), which meant that I won. Kick flip.

I still maintain the meanest thing you can do is repeat someone's own words back at them without comment. When the Hillary diehards began demanding Bernie Bros "take a seat" and start listening to and "signal-boosting" women of color, I complied, retweeting Roxane Gay @ing the Hillary Clinton campaign to request "I'm With Her" shirts in XXXL. She blocked me in record time. I was just impressed she could move so fast. Demands to "signal-boost" women of color never quite turn out the way they want.

I realize how painfully cringeworthy it is to read someone reminiscing about tweets long past. Believe me, I'm more ashamed than you are disgusted, but shitty little interactions like this are a decent representation of my fair to middlin' presence among the denizens of a significant social media phenomenon. Imagine if the Algonquin Round Table was a bunch of NEETs with social anxiety and benzo addictions who grew up watching beheading videos instead of reading books; that was Weird Twitter. It was fun as hell.

Around this time, "abuse on the internet" became a hot-button issue . . . for adults. I had a few truly disturbing comments on my articles in Dangerous Minds—"I'm going to find you and fuck you with a knife" being the most memorable—but "abuse" on Twitter was generally more along the lines of replying to someone with a picture of a hog's testicles weighed down by its own shit. There were some nasty little creeps, to be sure, but the platform just didn't attract the sort of men virile enough to really scare you. Gross you out, sure, but they weren't a menacing bunch. There was also an unspoken rule that the one sin of Twitter was getting mad; anger was an intrusion on the "safe space" of being stupid in a zero-stakes environment. It was convivial, because it drew out the miscreants and the maladapted. Thus, the atmosphere was shaped by the cultivation, or at least acceptance, of innocuous taboo. It wasn't for the thin-skinned, but it was also a little sanctuary for eccentric, unoffendable losers. You know, fun people.

The truly punitive viciousness of Twitter emerged much later, from a combination of increased posting from Occupy and Occupy-adjacent activists and a migration from "Social Justice Tumblr." From there emerged a particular "scene" that we—meaning, Old and Stupid Twitter—referred to as "The Discourse." Around that same time, "social justice warrior" was coined. Soon, any reference to "SJW" was declared a dog whistle; if you used the phrase, you risked accusations of right-wing sympathies. At the very least, you were a suspected reactionary. Some said it was a smear against the left, or even against anyone with a sense of compassion. But those who said it derisively were generally just using "SJW" as short-hand for scolding, sanctimonious liberals. Funnily enough, "social justice warrior" originated unironically, and in self-identification, by online figures whose activism usually consisted of little more than posting on Twitter. That's what they called themselves, before deciding it was an insult. Such is the moving target that we call "discourse." "SJW" went from badge of honor to insult because too many people began rolling their eyes when they said it. Ditto "virtue signaling," once used by Social Justice Twitter to refer to disingenuous posting by manipulative opportunists and "pseudoleftists" who were usually just trying to get laid. More recently, the woke position has been denial of the existence of "cancel culture," when once again, the etymology of that term traces back to their own torch and pitchfork declarations that "[X] is canceled."

Social Justice Twitter had lit up and expanded around a series of campaigns and social causes—Occupy, the Arab Spring, opposition to the execution of Troy Davis, outrage around the murder of Trayvon Martin, and others—when activists and supporters had used the platform to raise awareness (although, as I would later write in an article titled "The Poisoned Chalice of Hashtag Activism," none of that "awareness" won a single one of those fights). But the biggest flashpoint—or at least the biggest spectacle—by far was Gamergate.

There's not much to explain about Gamergate. In 2014, a

woman game developer named Zoë Quinn cocreated a game called *Depression Quest,* a text-based sort-of choose-your-own-adventure where players navigate the world as a character suffering from depression; gaming blog IGN called it "an adventure in empathy." Inspired by Quinn's own experience with depression, the game tasks players with trying to stay employed, maintaining a relationship, taking their meds, going to therapy, etc.—you know, "adventure." Full disclosure, I've never played the game; I just suspected that if I didn't want to kill myself before playing, I certainly would after.

The personal nature of the release, the game itself being a "we need to have a serious talk about mental illness" confessional, plus Quinn's aesthetic hallmarks of an SJW techie—brightly dyed hair, piercings, tattoos, etc.—hit a nerve with a bunch of nerds when a positive review came from a "journalist" she had dated. Then *another* nerd she used to date wrote a blog post excoriating her for the conflict of interest. Soon a mass of nerds began mobbing Quinn online under the banner of "ethics in gaming journalism," a charmingly naive ideal in an industry that runs on payola between developers and the venerable periodicals that review their products.

There have been moments in my life when I have failed to properly articulate my lack of interest in a conflict beyond "I don't care," but I'll try now.

Once, sitting on a subway platform and waiting for a train, I saw a visibly homeless and mentally ill man approach another visibly homeless and mentally ill man and begin yelling. When someone is having an episode of delusion, hysteria, or psychosis—online or IRL—I believe the kind thing to do is to avert one's eyes or, at the very least, eavesdrop with discretion. Since this was an unignorable conflict, I chose the politely nosey approach. It seems the approaching Homeless Mentally

Ill Man—we'll call him "Bob" for the sake of clarity—was upset with the other Homeless Mentally Ill Man—we'll call him "Jim"—because Jim was behaving in such a way as to inadvertently attract a massive cloud of bats on the unused platform on the other side of the track. I would be doing the reader a disservice here if I did not make it perfectly clear that this cloud of bats did not exist, nor did a single bat, nor was anything that might resemble a cloud of bats on the platform. Nothing was on the platform; it was completely empty.

Social contagions being far more rapidly transmitted among the deeply mentally ill, particularly in cramped cities like New York, Jim responded with hostility, but with a complete and total acceptance of the bats as a reality. Jim then accused Bob of calling the bats, not obliviously or even unintentionally, as Bob had accused Jim, but in fact to *frame* Jim for the ensuing plague of bats.

This is the incident I use to explain my response to Gamergate. I have no dog in this race, and therefore feel no compulsion to take position on it, not in a "both sides" kind of way but in a "this has nothing to do with me or really anything of import" kind of way. In a "who gives a fuck?" kind of way.

As far as I was concerned, the "lesson" of Gamergate was twofold:

1. People were starting to seriously resent the degradation—if not outright elimination—of fun in the name of social justice and "empathy." I don't "game" in the sense that I don't think that word should be used as a verb, and I feel the adoption of "gamer" as an identity is more embarrassing than "virgin," but emerging titles like *Depression Quest*; *Papers, Please*; and the heart-wrenching *That Dragon, Cancer* seem to really stretch the definitions

of words like "game," "adventure," "play," and especially "fun."

2. The class composition of Twitter meant that an entire, seemingly endless news cycle was manufactured to revolve around a video game, the conflicts within a niche culture war within a niche subculture, and—most importantly—tweets. Twitter exists to insist upon the importance of Twitter and the political, social, and cultural importance of people who tweet.

I am not interested in arguing about the bats. There are no bats. I am however concerned that two people are homeless and require medication and care that they are evidently not receiving. I am concerned that the ambient hostility of a decaying city with mind-blowing levels of wealth disparity is absolutely exacerbating absurd and delusional animosities between crazy people. Likewise, I am not concerned with "the gamer and tech community." There is no "gamer and tech community." And I'm not concerned with "ethics in gaming journalism"; no combination of any of those words means anything at all. The thing that actually concerned me about Gamergate was that it passed for politics. I wanted to talk about anything but nerds and bats.

I got my wish, and during the 2016 primaries and general election, the broad liberal media pivoted to rah-rah the Hillary campaign with the zeal of suicide bombers, while Bernie fans suddenly dove into serious discussions of policy and boiled with fury, not at bats or nerds, but at the people who were actually in charge. Niche campaigns and culture wars didn't dominate the online conversation for once, as "the discourse" focused on the actual status quo, the big

picture. We were finally talking about the change we really wanted and refusing to consume whatever the bourgeois
press prescribed. Monkey's Paw.

Although a late adopter, I have a sixth sense for when a
party is about to go sour, so just after Trump's inauguration,
I quit Twitter. It seemed to me the bread and circuses, the
nasty careerism, the libidinal animosity and paranoia hadn't
done much to tip off the media that Hillary was not, in fact,
a shoe-in. And people on the broad left and liberal end of
politics were starting to froth and fantasize about some im-
pending apocalypse that I believe on some level they craved.
Unable to process new information, they glitched out over
Russian interference, the prospect of World War III, and
Nazi takeovers. *Slán leat,* my little bluebird.

The first message on the internet was sent in 1969—"LO."
The biblical gravity of the word—a command to look, and
perhaps even "behold"—was a fluke: the scientist had been
meaning to type "LOGIN," but the system crashed.

A portentous synchronicity.

The most famous program—one still used today by
anyone who learns to code—is the display of two words,
"Hello world," popularized and likely created by scientist
Brian Kernighan in 1972.

A beautiful, Promethean greeting to all.

March 21, 2006, Twitter founder Jack Dorsey made the
first ever tweet, "Just setting up my twttr." If the Silicon
Valley–mandated amputation of vowels wasn't bad enough,
he originally wanted to call the site Stat.us.

Professional ambition masquerading as communication.

I never thought that "owning" liberal shills online ever
accomplished anything, but before Trump, it had at least been
fun. And if I'm honest with myself, it's given me a career. But

something had gone irreparably sour in the online microculture, and since I didn't need to tweet to promote anything anymore (thanks, Chapo), why stay at a shitty party?

By the time Trump was finally inaugurated, I was relieved to delete my account.

I could go back to writing love letters. They might not have been great, but they were better than my tweets.

10

I ENJOY BEING A GIRL

Note: The following chapter was written over a year before the overturn of Roe v. Wade, making it (in my eyes, at least), a far more interesting artifact, both personally and politically. I was in San Francisco for the first time since campaigning for Bernie when I heard the news, visiting a friend whose two-year research stint at Stanford had come to an end. He was flying to the UK to take a tenure-track job in Leeds at the end of the week. Unbeknownst to me, our goodbye-for-now hurrah coincided with Pride Week, and the streets now teemed with leather daddies and go-go boys, all trying not to trip over the homeless people and junkies, with a few muddled tech bros in the mix trying to swim upstream. Maybe it was the surrealism of the scene, but we had a gay old time, shopping for hand fans, attending a tea-tasting, and drinking strawberry nigori in a park before catching a movie (he's not really a "march in the parade" kind of gay). This may all read like the sort of disconnected, irrelevant prose that's meant to give an affect of depth or disillusionment, but I do have a point: my reaction to the news was delayed. I tucked it away until I got back to Los Angeles. Abortion was the first activism I ever got involved in, and so much had happened in the world (and to me) since I was making signs and protesting on the Indiana State House lawn. I needed the drive "to process." I had been on hiatus from podcasting duties for a while at that point, but I made a point to come back on the show for that episode because I "felt a responsibility." I don't really remember what I said, but I'd be shocked if I had the grace or humility not to screech a self-righteous I-Told-You-So to any liberal feminists who might be listening; that just doesn't sound like me.

October 3, 2016

My wanderlust inflamed by romantic failure, I have decided I absolutely must spend money I don't have on plane tickets I don't need. I want to buy them soon (before I either come to my senses or succumb to some Victorian lady sadness disease), and I want to go in early January.

Berlin was my original first choice, but my German is nonexistent and every Berliner I know is actually Irish and will have returned to Dublin for the holidays. It would be a difficult city to navigate alone, and I dislike the idea of having to rely on Teutonic hospitality, although I suspect that at any given moment 90 percent of German citizens are actually trudging through the streets of NYC in those awful fucking square-toed loafers, so who knows.

I do love Dublin and have many hard-drinking feminist comrades there, but you can cover the whole city in a

*day and I'd prefer to see some place new before clinging to
the Samuel Beckett Bridge like a maudlin rhesus monkey
while vomiting into the Liffey (again).*

*Everyone who has suggested I go to Moscow alone is
an unbelievable idiot, especially* ███████████, *who
should certainly know better, since the Russian government framed him as a neo-Nazi despite his being so visibly and obviously Jewish and Chinese.*

*Paris is out, as my ex is a translator of French economics
texts, and I fear a trip would send me straight into the arms
of the Caliphate. I assume heartbreak is not an insignificant factor in the radicalization of young men, and at the
moment cannot help but see the appeal of suicide-bombing
Thomas Piketty, with his stupid fucking haircut and his
terrible tiny teeth.*

*Which brings me to London, or maybe some combi-
nation of London and Edinburgh (where the only person
I know will be visiting her parents in the US, but it looks
adorable and the Scots almost speak English). You will
probably be in London, though, and it would be nice to
see you again.*

*So, if I came to London in early January, would you
have a little time for little me?*

Amber A'Lee

Monday, December 12, 2016, 1:50 p.m.
Subject Line: I'm sorry I jumped out of the cab

*I would like to open by saying that you caught my eye
immediately. I remember looking at your sexy shoes,
straining under the red light to discern if they were mustard*

or chartreuse. I liked your jeans, which were somehow casual and chic at the same time (something I can never seem to pull off). And I liked your eyelashes and your elegant Josephine Baker hair. And I liked kissing you.

This is all just to say: I'm sorry I jumped out of a still-slightly-moving cab to get away from you; I was wasted and suddenly so unsure of myself that I had to go that very instant. I just have an extremely primitive fight-or-flight response. And a primitive everything else, I suppose.

Also, I long ago vowed never to be the other woman, a policy I have never failed to uphold, and which I publicly justified with vague feminism, even though it's far more likely the result of my own ego. "I am no man's getaway car," I like to say. I like to say that because it sounds very Bette Davis.

The fact that you are a woman obviously renders the gendered angle null, but as I said before, the actual feminist politics of my "never a side chick" ethos are pretty thin—mostly I'm just greedy, and I don't like to share anything I really like. (Also your boyfriend seems nice, and I didn't want to cuck him, nor did I want an audience or a third participant.)

When ▮▮▮▮▮▮▮▮▮ *and I dashed out of the cab, we didn't have anywhere to go, so we just sat on the steps outside of some Chinatown park with the bag of cat food he picked up earlier. We had some drunken but reassuring conversation while I panicked over your text messages before we eventually both just vomited, in tandem, no less. Still too wasted to really move, we used our shoes to brush some dry leaves over the piles of spew and pretended they weren't there. Then he asked if he could kiss me—very politely,*

to his credit, but I immediately responded "No, because of
███████████████*," who is my dear friend and his ex. But*
even if it weren't for her, I had no interest in kissing anyone
else that night, much less in front of barely concealed piles of
our own vomit, the bile still clinging to our tongues.

I woke up deathly hungover—a skull full of glass
and a belly full of bears—and a friend had sent me this
song, "The Heavens" by The Raveonettes. The track
has fakey record static on it, and I hate all those phony
pops and crackles—gimmicky, corny as a retro Instagram
filter. Also, it features a Danish man's ludicrous attempt at
a hillbilly accent, but while I suppose I should be offended
on grounds of cultural appropriation or whatever, in a sort
of ethnic polymorphous perversion I am always flattered
when Europeans like redneck music. (As you know, I like
people who like me.) . . .

I love that you write in cursive. I'd love to see your
handwriting.

We should get soup dumplings, or maybe soup noo-
dles. Definitely something soupy; I'd love to watch you
suck the broth from some xiao long bao, or slurp up a
noodle. I like the chaos of noodles, when you eat them too
quickly, so they go awry and slap wetly on the face. I will
sit across from you, at a ladylike distance.

December 13, 2016
Wow. This was interesting to open up while I was show-
ing a film to my second class. I mean it was extremely hot
but I'm really conflicted. I don't want to lead you on. You
know I'm trying to make it work with ███████████████*.*
I get how shitty/tenuous my relationship looks from the

outside, but I do intend to see it through. If he doesn't live near me soon, I obviously can't keep doing this, but I'm not scouting the room for better offers before May (when he said he'd move back to NYC).

    If this is uncomfortable for you, I think you should cut me off. I would hate to see things go sour between us. I'm really enjoying our time together, and I'd be lying if I said there's not something very appealing about you romantically, but I could see this going very badly.

After Bernie was out of the 2016 race, I wasn't really sure what to do with myself. I mostly let *other people* do things *to* me.

I had been married at twenty-three and divorced at twenty-seven, then immediately fell into a long-term relationship, but in the autumn of 2016 we split up—not for the first or last time—when he moved upstate to complete his dissertation. It wasn't too long before we got back together, but in the interim I had a fling with a visiting Brit who I initially found obnoxious (but eventually found sexy) under the assumption that I would benefit from a wholesome palate cleanser with someone I assumed I would never want or have to see again (wrong). After that began the affair with an (unbeknownst to me) extremely mentally ill colleague, who *I* thought was cool with it when I said I didn't think we were a good match, and that it looked like I was getting back together with my ex, who had been creeping back into my life as a long-distance boyfriend. I *could,* however, see myself leaving my long-distance boyfriend for the girl who leaned over the table at the bar after some panel I spoke on and kissed me, despite the fact that her boyfriend was right outside. (Victory favors the bold.) Unfortunately, the boyfriend somehow figured it out, and in an absolutely horrifying attempt to appear "fine with it," he suggested that, since we were all going the same way home, my male friend and I should just share the cab with them. You're just going to have to believe me when I say this man did not want a threesome, nor did he want to watch; what he wanted was a thousand times more perverse—to abolish the primitive sexual jealousy innate to all erotic human beings. He overestimated his level of enlightenment, I realized, as I sat in the middle seat of a cab between my friend and the girl's boyfriend; she for some reason sat in the front seat, and they proceeded to "whisper-fight," hissing indiscernible but unmistakable animosities at one another between the plexiglass barrier, but very quietly, as if they thought this would allow my friend and I to plausibly deny the obvious tension.

Before we reached the bridge to Brooklyn, we stopped at a red light, and my friend broke his stiff posture, turned to me pleadingly and said, "Do you want to get out?"

"*Yes*," I said, relieved. We both leaped from the car just as it began to move, surprising the couple but leaving them to quarrel at a volume more befitting the situation. We ran to a park where we sat on some steps and laughed for a moment, giddy with the relief of our escape.

I'm not sure who started vomiting first, but I remember noting that it looked and smelled as if we had both been drinking the same red wine that night. Emptied and panting over bile and autumn leaves, we caught our breaths. Then he turned to me again and, very politely, asked, "Can I kiss you?" I, equally politely, I hope, declined. He took it in good stead, and we are still very chummy to this day, but the moment called for a measure of self-reflection I was in no state to confront.

It wasn't until I flew back from the UK after very nearly becoming a man's getaway car (second base doesn't count when you're drinking like the British, or so I told myself), that I could admit to myself that my experiment in licentious adventurism was a bust: too tumultuous, labor-intensive, and time-consuming, and while the company of others can always offer a little comfort, it certainly wasn't worth the heartache or headache.

At Heathrow Airport, security opened and checked my bag for whatever contraband I might have been smuggling across international waters. I'm still not sure if the abortion medication the uniformed woman removed from my toiletries bag was technically illegal, but I held my breath until she packed everything back up, handed me my luggage, and said, smiling, "Have a good flight!"

"I have *got* to get my shit together," I thought. I flew home, ghosted one, gently broke it off with a second, and cut ties with the third.

I write about this time in my life not as some repentant woman with a cautionary tale, "woe betide the girl who falls prey to the transient thrills of earthly romance!"; it was just one of those chapters of misadventure that becomes a running joke among the friends who knew me back when. We can laugh about the time I tried to sneak out of a formerly promising suitor's window while he slept because he called me a "chinky little bitch" during sex (we'd been dating two months, came out of nowhere). Mine was not the kind of experience that leaves any girl with a sense of humor haunted or scarred. The truth is, I was bored and a little lonely; I needed a hobby, so I took up juggling so to speak. I wasn't cut out for it, but you never know until you try and all the pins (or paramours) land on your head.

What I do hope to convey is what a goddamn hassle going wild can really be. I defend and enjoy a little fun, harmless drug use from time to time, and I don't believe every romantic encounter need be long-term, meaningful, or even rewarding, and there are some nights where you really should stay out long enough to curse the morning's songbirds. "There'll be time enough for rocking when we're old" goes the song. But I must openly refute the nefarious misconception that hedonistic abandon has some sort of radical or liberating political content. There are no radical drugs or "radical ways of fucking," even if you don't get in over your head (catting around and hangovers really eat up a lot of your evenings and weekends). Whenever I hear someone extolling promiscuity or nonmonogamy as some sort of political principle, all I can think is, "Jesus, who has the time?" There are only so many hours in the day, only so many days in a life, and "excess ain't rebellion,"[52] but it can be easy to confuse the two when you're having fun.

A few weeks after getting back to New York, I had to threaten one of the former paramours with a restraining order, renewing my resolve.

Thus concluded my brief career as a heartbreaker.

My first visit to the United Kingdom was primarily motivated by curiosity about what appeared to be promising political developments around a Labour MP named Jeremy Corbyn, but if I'm perfectly honest, I was also entertaining the idea of meeting up with the aforementioned Brit a second time should the opportunity present itself. (To this day, I've never technically pulled off a one-night stand; they always seem to stick around.)

Plus, between adjuncting at NYU, freelance writing, and my podcasting gig on Chapo Trap House, for which I had just begun receiving supplementary income, I now made enough money to actually travel. At that point I had about $30,000 worth of student debt, and all loans were in default, so it was arguably not very advisable, but I had just then solved the problem of incessant hounding from Sallie Mae by changing my phone number, and I was determined to leave New York, preferably for some place I had never been, and preferably out of the country.

After much deliberation, I decided to bounce around Britain as a whole, but I fished for the Brit's interest (knowing full well I wanted to go somewhere in the UK to feel out this Corbyn thing for an article) by sending him a mendaciously indecisive love letter with the subject line, "I want better for every bastard (myself included)." It was something I had said to him when he was last visiting New York, a belligerent reply to his flippant declarations that "Brits and Americans don't deserve socialism." I've never believed in "deserve." Blessings and curses are distributed arbitrarily across the world, with no regard for the virtues, work ethic, or moral fiber of the gifted and/or afflicted. Best to just establish a universal baseline standard of living from which the "undeserving" will no doubt benefit. No skin off my ass.

I initially balked at the banality of visiting the original Anglophone city. I wanted to go to Manchester, the cradle of industrialization, and therefore capitalism, and therefore socialism. Manchester is Jerusalem for socialists. But I didn't know anyone in Manchester, and London did meet my criteria for a good vacation: cold, urban, and not entirely devoid of people who speak a language I also speak.

The Brit was amenable to being my tour guide (eager, even), and I bought the tickets cheap, figuring I could take a few trains to different parts of the country. Despite still reeling from the 2016 election, I was optimistic. I was sure Bernie would run in 2020, and I was pretty sure I was living my best life: I had a ridiculous career as a New York City mercurial artistic type, finally a little bit of spending money for dumb pretty girl shit like a signature perfume (Le Labo's Tubereuse, a girlish floral homage to the old-enough-to-know-better Norma Desmond), and I could afford airfare for adventures in foreign lands. On top of that, I had re-acquired the bad penny of a boyfriend, but he didn't much care if I dated while he was upstate (something I should have recognized as a red flag by how much the bloodless absence of jealousy always disgusted me in other men, but live and learn). Of course, I had drafted an understudy until such time as we were reunited, plus an entirely new prospect that might have even unseated the bad penny. So that was three, plus the possibility of the overseas paramour.

The juggling caught up with me. Just after purchasing my nonrefundable tickets, I found myself pregnant (again), and I preferred not to be. The soonest I could get into a Planned Parenthood was in the middle of my trip, and I didn't have the money to burn for new tickets. On top of that, with the long wait for the appointment (apparently, there had been a lot of ho ho ho'ing in NYC that winter), I would be further along and would therefore have to get a dilation and curettage rather than a simple medication abortion I could do at home. Having already experienced both (look, I'm a real fun girl), I was an informed consumer, and I knew that I very much preferred the medication to the procedure, as a slightly heavy period curled up in my own bed is far more convenient and comfortable than hours in the clinic and a crampy ride back to Brooklyn.

I was, however, going to be in Ireland for a short spell and remembered Women on Waves, a Dutch NGO that delivered abortifacient medication to women in antiabortion countries from the international waters of a floating barge. I messaged them and explained my situation, and they said I qualified and they could send the pills to a British address (I made a hefty donation). The problem was, I had no address for them to send it to, because the friends of friends I was staying with resided in a disused warehouse that had been repurposed into an anarchist squat. I can't remember if their mail was all delivered outside the gate in a pile or if they really just didn't have a postal address, but my host informed me that they all used PO boxes. I thought of another friend of friends, a lefty Northern Irish writer who now lived in London; he had once been "canceled" (before that was a thing) for saying of a right-wing public figure who had been severely burned to the point of unrecognizability in the Falklands War, "If he knew anything, he'd still have his face."[53]

I thought, *This is the sort of writer who would help out a goodtime girl like me,* and shot him a message.

> "█████████████, *I need the discreet help of a London-based comrade. The mission is 100% legal and requires zero effort on your part, but nonetheless will put you in such standing with feminists that you will be among the protected if ever there is a violent uprising of knife wielding, Monique Wittig–inspired misandrists.*
>
> "*Do you know what Misoprostol is?*"
>
> "*I have no idea.*"

[A minute or two passes]
"Ok, Wikipedia has informed me."

I explained my conundrum as briefly as I could, given the differences in our healthcare systems.

"Well, due to bureaucracy, outsized demand for free services, onerous legislation, and cost, it's very difficult to get it in the US. In the UK, you can get it through the mail through a women's health nonprofit. The trouble is, where I'm staying is basically a squat, and doesn't have a proper address. I need someone with an address to accept the package."

He was of course amenable (eager, even) to come to my rescue, so I made the arrangements for the mailing, and we agreed to do the handoff over drinks (I was delighted to learn he lived somewhere called "Cockfosters," a synchronicitous destination if ever there was one).

★   ★   ★

"Being born a woman is my awful tragedy. From the moment I was conceived I was doomed to sprout breasts and ovaries rather than a penis and scrotum; to have my whole circle of action, thought, and feeling rigidly circumscribed by my inescapable femininity. Yes, my consuming desire to mingle with road crews, sailors and soldiers, bar room regulars—to be a part of a scene, anonymous, listening, recording—all is spoiled by the fact that I am a girl, a female always in danger of assault and battery. My consuming interest in men and their lives is often misconstrued as a desire to seduce them, or as an invitation to intimacy. Yet, God, I want to talk to everybody I can as deeply as I can. I want to be able to sleep in an open field, to travel west, to walk freely at night. . . ."

—SYLVIA PLATH, *THE UNABRIDGED JOURNALS OF SYLVIA PLATH*[54]

Since puberty I have been cursed by a rampant fertility. And I'm pretty open about the fact that abortion has thus far been the correction to my always-around-the-corner "condition." Once, when I still shared an apartment with Felix, he walked outside to find me cleaning a box window AC unit with the garden hose, spraying out a disgusting, pulpy mass of formerly airborne, rust-colored Brooklyn filth that had collected in the grating of the box, which had faced a mechanic's garage for the last two years.

"Jesus Christ, Amber," he said, "another abortion?" This kind of joke is more than friendship—it's brotherly.

Women on Waves was providing abortion number three. I topped out at four (knock on wood). Early on I figured out that I was allergic to latex. Shortly after, I learned that non-latex condoms break more easily (though the materials and design have since improved). There was, of course, lambskin, but even after my lapse in vegetarianism, the very idea of a sheep's guts in my own guts would have killed the mood. So that was Abortion Number One. I began to suspect the pregnancy when I went with my then ex-boyfriend/guitarist to one of the three Creole restaurants that had recently been opened in Indiana by post-Katrina transplants. The frog's legs came out, and the smell made me retch.

After that, I switched to pills, but despite my religious use of hormonal birth control, which I always bought months in advance and never missed, I was confounded by the intrusion of a second pregnancy a few years after the first—Abortion Number Two. Many months after this encore procedure, I returned to Planned Parenthood for my regular exam and to renew my prescription. I mentioned the name of the pill I had been on when I got knocked up the second time, which I assumed had failed due to user error.

"Oh," the doctor said, a bit surprised, "we don't prescribe that one anymore."

"Why not?" I said, somewhat annoyed, as I had gone through a few different hormonal birth controls before finally finding one without depressive side effects.

"Well," she sighed, "people kept getting pregnant on it."

Sick of the Planned Parenthood lines and bureaucracy, I had been patronizing a black-market pharmacy based out of the volcanic island nation of Vanuatu. They were fairly reliable, save for one delay in international mail due to eruption, which was understandable. Unfortunately, they also carried more than a few discontinued, recalled, and expired products.

Abortion Number Three followed the failure of the then newly over-the-counter "morning-after pill," which I learned was not as effective as originally thought and was revealed—the very week of my condition, in fact—to be even less effective for women with a BMI over twenty-five. At that point I was pissed to have to get another abortion, but I was even more pissed to learn that I had ballooned to 137 pounds, which, for my five-foot-three (-and-a-half) frame, was "Brooklyn fat" but, luckily for me, still "London skinny."

Taking an exploratory research trip with an unwanted pregnancy in tow may seem overwhelming, but you have to remember, this wasn't my first rodeo. Being slightly pregnant wasn't even an obstacle to my flirtations (kick flip), nor to the man they were directed toward, who upon being told over Szechuan dumplings (why is Chinese food so sexy?), replied, "Wow . . . that's impressive," in a tone betraying a hint of erotic thrill. Nonetheless, a third abortion would be the final punchline of the long-running joke my body was clearly playing on me, I thought.

Did you know that many supplements and medications, including common anticonvulsants, antiemitics, and even some antibiotics reduce the efficacy of hormonal birth control? Me neither! That's the working theory for Pregnancy Number Four. A few weeks after a bad flu, I was feeling sick again, but found that I had no temperature. "Huh," I thought, and went for a walk.

"Huuuuhhhhh . . . ," I thought again, but more carefully this time.

It couldn't be. But just to reassure myself, I bought a pregnancy test at the dollar store on a whim. "I'm not pregnant again," I thought. "That would be ridiculous." I told myself this was just to confirm that I should make myself some soup and go to bed, but my anxiety increased on the walk back to the apartment and I had to know right then. I stopped into a bougie new Cuban restaurant, ordered a prosecco at the bar, and pissed on a stick in the "rustic-chic" bathroom under one of those ridiculously dim Edison bulbs that were plaguing every new "a-bit-much" bistro in Brooklyn around that time. Staring at the plus sign once more, I decided that being a woman is a comedy, and if you're going to judge me for anything, judge me for having sex despite being sick with the flu. Frankly, I even disgust myself with that one.

Well before any of this, the first "activism" I cut my

teeth on was in defense of Planned Parenthood, an organization always under siege in Indiana, usually through circuitous legislation designed to make it impossible for them to operate, rather than outright banning abortion. Going to the statehouse with my best girlfriend and a few DSA members to protest its defunding could not have been more different from any of the demonstrations I would go to later on in New York. For one, you had to interact with the opposition, who screamed about murder and hell and held up giant signs of inscrutable gore. My sign had read, "Don't take away the only doctor I can afford," and I wore a red bandana that read, "Democratic Socialists of America" above a rose-and-fist logo. I had printed it myself with a homemade stencil and supplies from Hobby Lobby, a craft store owned by virulently antiabortion Republicans.[55] At that point DSA didn't have the money for merch beyond the one-inch buttons I would later press by hand working at the offices. Even if they had sold T-shirts, I wouldn't have been able to rationalize the expense. Plus, an entire T-shirt would have been a little ostentatious at the time. At this point the Tea Partiers of Indiana were still calling Barack Obama a "socialist," but I always suspected that even they knew they were being hyperbolic, and the introduction of the word in earnest self-identification would have diffused the focus of the event. A real, live, self-proclaimed socialist would have been as disorienting to Hoosiers of all political stripes as an actual unicorn trotting by.

When I started making money, I donated monthly to Planned Parenthood. After all, they did me a solid (three solids, but who's counting)—but I never will again. I still support women's health nonprofits and abortion funds, including Women on Waves, but never, ever, ever Planned

Parenthood. When asked why I, as a serial abortion-haver, no longer support the organization that's done so much for me, I answer simply and truthfully: they don't care about women.

★   ★   ★

Planned Parenthood turned one hundred years old in 2016, the same year, incidentally, they made their first ever primary endorsement for (you guessed it) Hillary Clinton,[56] on January 7, despite Bernie Sanders's superior record of support for abortion rights.[57] While Sanders opposes any restriction on abortion, favoring the well-worn but always chic "a choice between a woman and her doctor," Clinton supports bans on so-called "late-term" or "partial-birth" abortions—the termination of a pregnancy twenty-four weeks or older—with the standard "exceptions for rape, incest, the life of the mother" catechism, natch. Always worth mentioning that that diplomatic and reasonable-sounding fine print at the end is redundant; abortions performed after twenty-four weeks are incredibly rare, but they're always medically necessary. Were such a law in place, any "humane" exceptions would just be another inhumane barrier to access, as the onus would then rest on the pregnant woman and/or her doctor to justify the necessity of the abortion to . . . whom? Their congressman? The supreme court? The FDA?*

And what would be the burden of proof? Would you have to prove you were raped by your father? Would you have to

---

* As of writing this, the answers to these questions are in flux, so any legislative updates I can provide will likely be moot by the time you read it; resources like the Guttmacher Institute's interactive map keep their information up to date and easy to search.

convince someone that yes, you will hemorrhage to death from this ectopic pregnancy? Well, that one's a little clearer cut, even if being forced to provide evidence would be humiliating and painful. But what if you only *might* die giving birth? Say you've got something like pulmonary hypertension, and a fifty-fifty shot at getting out of this pregnancy alive, would you have to stick it out? What if you would live, but your baby was going to be born without a brain? Would you have to carry it, knowing full well that even if the anencephalic fetus growing inside of you makes it to term, it would only live for a few days, weeks at most? Even if you believe the abortion of a healthy fetus after twenty-four weeks is wrong, you can see the slippery slope of banning it, even with "exceptions."

Many assumed Clinton and Sanders had the same position on abortion. If her history of equivocation came up, and if her legions weren't able to wave it away ("they basically agree") or pivot ("as mother of a daughter," or "Hillary is her mother's daughter," "our feminist foremothers," or some such permutation of or variation on "mommymommymommymommy"), they would say that the quote was from a long time ago, a different time entirely, in fact. That defense did her a disservice, I thought; it made her seem wishy-washy when, in fact, Clinton had no problem boldly doubling down on her position that abortion should be (sort of) legal. During a Fox News Town Hall in March of 2016, she stood firm: "I have been on record in favor of a late-pregnancy regulation that would have exceptions for the life and health of the mother."[58] So give the girl some credit: she may have updated the euphemisms (though "late-pregnancy regulation" sounds like it would involve some sort of obstetric meter maid), but when it comes to hedging her bets, Hillary is consistent and reliable. Planned Parenthood did not rescind their endorsement.

Nor did they when in July of 2016, the Clinton campaign picked Senator Tim Kaine as her running mate. His positions on abortion have also been pretty consistent since at least back when he was Governor of Virginia in 2005:

TIM KAINE ON REDUCING ABORTIONS IN VIRGINIA[59]

I have a faith-based opposition to abortion. As governor, I will work in good faith to reduce abortions by:

1. Enforcing the current Virginia restrictions on abortion and passing an enforceable ban on partial birth abortion that protects the life and health of the mother;

2. Fighting teen pregnancy through abstinence-focused education;

3. Ensuring women's access to health care (including legal contraception) and economic opportunity; and

4. Promoting adoption as an alternative for women facing unwanted pregnancies.

This was the campaign that Planned Parenthood stumped for in the primaries, when there is zero benefit in endorsing anyone unless you're currying favor or returning one—not that I'm making any accusations. I suppose they could just be morons, but unlike Clinton fans, I tend to give credit to strong women: I think they knew what they were doing.

Planned Parenthood does have a concrete political agenda; it's just that women's health isn't at the top of the list. As a nonprofit, they require funding, and they have to justify their own existence to receive that funding. Bernie

Sanders's Medicare for All program would secure abortion, "on demand, without apology," and most radically, for free. Think about it from PP's perspective: sure, Medicare for All would do so much for women, but (and this is the important part) what would Medicare for All do for Planned Parenthood? I don't mean the patients, or the doctors or nurses, or even the support staff—they'd be gravy. I mean, what would happen to the CEO, to the Board of Directors? What would happen to all those poor women in business casual, sitting around massive tables in neutral conference rooms, meeting with politicians, writing press releases, and organizing their fundraisers? What about those fresh-faced young women getting in their internships so that one day, they, too, can wear business casual?

Those are the women Planned Parenthood fights for; it's nepotistic at best, dynastic at worst. I'll avoid trying to convey a byzantine conspiracy corkboard in print, but just as an example: Planned Parenthood's Clinton endorsement was under then-president Cecile Richards, whose mother was Texas Governor Ann Richards. Cecile's oldest daughter, Lily Adams, worked on the Clinton 2016 campaign before working on the Kamala Harris 2020 campaign, and is now something called "Principal Deputy Assistant Secretary for the Office of Public Affairs" at the US Treasury. Before that, though, she was press secretary to freshman Senator Tim Kaine.[60]

I didn't know that before the Clinton endorsement, but I wasn't surprised at the incongruity between Planned Parenthood's stated feminist principles and their political agenda, mostly because I had already been in New York for a while. Once, the drunken frog-faced editor of a publishing house ran his hand just under the hem of my miniskirt at a bar while his girlfriend—whom I didn't know well but had invited me out—was in the bathroom. I slid off the stool. When she got back, the frog said he had work in the morning, it was nice to meet me, and he'd call the girlfriend tomorrow. When I told her what happened—not in an "I feel violated" kind of way, but in a "heads up, your dog don't wanna stay on the porch" kind of way—she explained that "he was just so drunk" in a tone that one generally saves to reassure someone who has just received bad news. She later became an important editor at a legacy publication, and I'd smile a little bit every time I saw something she wrote or commissioned extolling the #MeToo revolution.

Like Planned Parenthood, she's only contradictory at first glance. When defending gross men was beneficial to her career, she did. When it was good for her career to denounce gross men, she did that too. And maybe she loved him—I'm not that cynical—but I'm not sure there's a difference where pens in the company ink are concerned. If Planned Parenthood's primary goal was securing healthcare for women, they'd support Medicare for All, which would secure doctors, nurses, administration, and other staff into a universal healthcare system, but that would leave the Girl Bosses out of a job. Not that they'd be on the breadlines, but their power, influence, and the informal jobs program for their type A sisters and daughters would be gone. Planned Parenthood isn't going to push for their own obsolescence; careers are at stake.

It's the nature of the beast, and has nothing to do with whether or not the higher-ups at Planned Parenthood are sincere. If any of them realizes they're a morbid symptom, they can't actually do anything about it; they'd be swimming against the tide, and unless blessed with a rare clarity of judgment, they would still most likely pave the road to

hell with their best intentions. I'm sure many Girl Bosses
care deeply about securing and expanding women's access to
healthcare; they just want to have the monopoly on it. And
that's the problem.

★   ★   ★

An addendum on "choice": I don't think I'm reckless, but I'll
admit I'm not overly risk-averse, so I wouldn't take it personally at this point if a reader said aloud, "Jesus Christ, Amber,
four abortions?!?"

There is an intractable conflict between freedom and
safety—or, if you like, danger and restriction—that govern-
ments, political parties, and individual human beings have
always had to negotiate. I try to keep this in mind when I
am making decisions, and like most people, I try to be at
least somewhat methodical. I "do the projections," consult
experts and colleagues, do cost-benefit analyses, throw in
a little guesswork, that sort of thing. Sometimes, though,
when I know a choice is likely to backfire, I throw caution
to the wind anyway, because I know the remorse of "wish I
had" is a thousand times heavier than the remorse of "I wish
I hadn't." Obviously, I'm not just talking about sex anymore.

I won't tell anyone how cautious or adventurous they
should be, I'm just saying that I've never regretted a disaster
I knowingly ran toward. I make informed decisions, I didn't
say they were good ones.

I sleep in open fields. Because I can.

11

TRUMP HYSTERIA

This is a mournful discovery.
1) Those who agree with you are insane.
2) Those who do not agree with you are in power.

—PHILIP K. DICK, *VALIS* [61]

February 11, 2016

I'm currently writing something on the pathological hostility toward any dissent from the "fascism is coming" narrative, hopefully for Damage. At this point I think it's pretty clear liberals and leftists don't need rational arguments, they need psychoanalysis.

I dislike having to put down the Marx and pick up the Freud, but I think in dealing with a delusion this deeply held, evidence and even expertise are generally a waste of breath. I think I'm better off zooming out from the debate itself and asking, "In a post-QAnon world, where far more divergent interpretations of reality than my own are surging,

*why does it make them so angry that I don't believe exactly
what they believe?"*

People got really mad at you for not being scared of
Trump, even after his administration had failed to pursue
most of the policies he had run on.

I'm not antidiagnosis, I'm merely procontext.

I would describe bipolar II as a propensity toward states
of mind during which thoughts and/or feelings reach the
point of diminishing returns.

The majority of my life does not meet this definition, but
I can't deny that there have been moments. I will say that the
mood stabilizer I was prescribed and took regularly on a few
occasions did an excellent job of tethering me, preventing
both the depths and heights of my moods without flattening
a reasonable range of emotion. The side effects were temporary but physically visible: an irritating (but not unbearable) rash along with some notable facial swelling, primarily
under my eyes and in my lips and cheeks. Already being
somewhat squinty, lippy, and cheeky, the reaction intensified
my features cartoonishly, but for me it was worth looking
like I was enduring a shellfish allergy for a few weeks if that
meant evading the constant feelings of inevitable doom and
the sort of hypomania that does not result in psychosis but
does interfere with one's ability to function in the world.

Perhaps the best endorsement of medication I can give
for people like myself is that you can stop taking it if it doesn't
work or you don't like it. I am highly averse to "dependence"
on any person, place, or thing, but I am not opposed to
medication, just avoidant; I prefer to manage without it. But
there are only so many times you can decide "I SHOULD
GET A FUCKING GOLDFISH" before staying awake for

forty-eight hours straight, researching aquariums with the intensity of an immunologist racing to find the cure for his beloved wife's unknown tropical disease, before you start to consider better living through chemistry.

OCD is also an issue, which is exacerbated by the "racing thoughts" associated with the bipolar family. It certainly ate up my time, which I always felt I should be using more productively; that made me even more anxious. Trying to write the perfect sentence, organize the perfectly scheduled day, I'd review things over and over and over in my head until I was paralyzed by the frustration and indecision that accompanies a fixation on optimization. And there were the classic neurotic perseverations: "Is there something I forgot to do that will result in disaster?" I checked locks, sometimes getting to the end of the block before telling myself that yes, I had already checked it three times, but if I went back and jiggled the handle just once more, it would relax me, and I could stop thinking about it (it did not, and I did not). I never checked the stove though, which is apparently the most common one. I never perseverated about my home going up in flames, but I was terrified by the idea of anyone getting inside, and I can never tell if that's worth reading into.

However, I would always insist, my "rapid cycling"— meaning both my hypomania and depression—while extreme, were also extremely conditional. When I had no money or no prospects, medication stabilized me to think clearly and prudently, a state that is impossible while experiencing either despair or paroxysm. When my life got less chaotic and desperate, I would wean myself off with no withdrawals.

Before the right-wing Orthodox Jew, I briefly saw a therapist (Lebanese feminist this time) through a low-income service. The number of therapists in New York who help with "fear of success" or "fear of missing out" is staggering; that's not what I was looking for. I read up on her areas of expertise—her dissertation was on domestic abuse in the Levant—and decided if she could handle that, I would be a walk in the park. Like my later therapist, she specialized in cognitive behavioral therapy, i.e., mental health for Protestants, because unlike Freudian psychoanalysis, CBT helps you get back to work.

Eventually, she "broke up with me" for being too emotionally withholding, which was fair enough. When she asked me how I felt about her terminating our services, I shrugged.

After Trump was elected, I experienced a brief, mild depression, followed by a brief, mild hypomania, during which I was creatively invigorated and extremely productive. Then I reread an epistolary stream of consciousness poetry . . . experiment that I had written during my "mild" hypomania and sent it to a friend for notes:

December 17, 2016
    My darling ▮▮▮▮▮▮▮▮,
    So this motherfucker says to me, "You're not getting any younger," like I should marry him to capitalize off my fading beauty. (Joke's on him because my beauty has always been negligible at best!) And who the fuck is he? I do very well for myself, admittedly it's a small but loyal following, but I'm more of a cult classic than a blockbuster. I do not love him.
    I am in love with someone else, it is revolting. I am so lovesick I am literally sick. This is something that has always happened to me, I suspect because my heart is so filled with bile that any stirring throws me into a

vertiginous nausea. I have contracted the sort of undignified dramatics that only women hotter than myself can get away with. As a girl that generally inspires neither lust nor tenderness in men, I usually adhere to a sort of dignified code of secrecy when it comes to my own romantic yearnings, maybe a slight limp from holding it all in. I love him with all the bile in my heart and all the blood in my mouth.

It's a full-body affliction. My amorousness has metastasized and migrated to my gut. I love him with my intestines, which feel like they're peristalsing razor blades and powdered glass. I must have eaten some on a dare.

My eyes burn from staring at other men, trying to distract myself with lustful deviations. When I finally remember to blink, my eyelids drag over my dry corneas like rasps over a pine box. I worry about going blind.

I grind my teeth and clench my fists until my short nails leave little slivered impressions in my palm like young moons.

I have become overly prone to metaphor and sensory language. I retch and twitch and up they come, on my lips, the page, the screen.

My back is bending at obscene angles from the weight of the sprezzatura, but when I remember to stand up straight, I am better on pointe than I have ever been in my life. Maybe all great dancers are lovesick.

I wish his name was an object I could put in my mouth and chew until it dripped down my chin and onto my tits.

He is an intrusive thought, and I am never able to remove him from my mind entirely, only push him to the periphery. I want to lobotomize the part of me that thinks of him. I want to make him coffee and purr in his lap.

I want to wear things that he likes me in. I really want to Lean In to the Male Gaze.

I want to parade all the others in front of him. I want to jettison them all at his behest. One time he said, "Fuck you," and I was relieved.

I hate these austere white walls, austerity posing as style, Helvetica hair shirts. I need a new perfume. I like this one I got from my mother for my birthday, but it won't do anymore. I need to smell like victory, and revenge. I need to smell like Lady Macbeth. I don't mean like "all the perfumes of Arabia," I mean like her: cold, metallic ambition. Bitch, let's go shopping.

I want to buy new sunglasses, I want to eat oysters, I want to eat my heart out, I want to eat every page of Anna Karenina, *one by one. I want to wake up and go the whole day without thinking of him, only to be reminded of him again by someone interjecting. Then I want to laugh at how trivial I now find him. "Remember when I had that massive stupid crush on ▮▮▮▮▮▮▮▮▮▮▮?" I'll text you. And then we'll laugh and laugh.*

The other day, though, I was walking around Clinton Hill, and I saw a sign outside of a little secondhand shop, "Tarot Readings on Sunday." It was actually Thursday, but I figured maybe if the person was there I could cajole a reading out of her anyway on the grounds that I was in dire need of divination. When I went in, though, I saw expensive boutique clothing next to the carefully curated vintage and used clothing. On a shelf there were high-end candles and beauty products, right next to the crystals, charms, and bundles of sage that looked straight out of a suburban witch's Pinterest. In the back there were two salon chairs and sinks, and two

women who looked like what Alexis calls "California
clean" were chatting away about how they just had to go
dancing that night. A third girl smiled knowingly and
nodded along from the chair while one woman styled her
white-blond hair, which coated the round brush like sweet-
ened condensed milk.

I picked up a brochure—it was Rose Quartz, of
course: $250 for highlights.

I turned right back around and went home. I mean
all tarot is totally fake, but Etsyfied boutique Clinton Hill
tarot is somehow even more fake.

I have no justification for even wanting a tarot reading,
except that I desperately need a vacation from common
sense—a spa day of bullshit mysticism for my world-weary
psyche. It's counterintuitive, of course, not only because I'm
a positivist that believes in nothing supernatural whatso-
ever, but also because all I want in life is to be surprised. It
would stand to reason that if prophecy was real, it would
ruin the surprise.

I thought again about ███████████, who was
very funny, but who I had anticipated being unimpressed
by. But after he came over, I got us both beers and he cor-
nered me against the wall to kiss me. Forever the barmaid, I
was immobilized trying not to spill the beer in each hand—
bondage by High Lifes (High Lives?), if you will. It was
opportunistic, and he snapped into a natural skill, and his
sleepy eyes were suddenly focused, and his long, rangy body
was suddenly elegant and deft. He was profusely sweaty,
too, but it somehow only made him lovelier, like a slick
Modigliani. That was a nice surprise.

I finally managed to get my tarot read yesterday! I
went to Namaste Bookshop at 14th and Fifth Ave, and

it was exactly the environment I wanted. High, wall-to-wall shelving filled overflowing with books on numerology, witchcraft, astral projection, and all that. Nearly every other square foot of the space was a display of some mystical paraphernalia for sale—idols, candles, incense, charms, crystals, stones—the works. There were scented oils for sampling, I dabbed on an Amber and Violet blend "for protection." I didn't feel like I needed protection, but it smelled nice.

I purchased a ticket at the register up front (I'm embarrassed by how much I paid), and went in the back where a woman waited at a table behind a semidiaphanous curtain. She was perfect, with a gentle but serious voice, and ageless skin that belied her gray hairs. She put me so at ease that when she asked what area of my life I wanted a reading on, I completely abandoned my plan of asking for career advice and instead blurted out "romance."

I explained that after a brief breakup and a few paramours in the interim, I was back with someone I had dated before, and that while I was cautiously optimistic, I remained generally unsure and nervous. She nodded, and she understood perfectly.

She laid out a bunch of cards, which I don't remember but I sent you a text of. "This draw is unusually unpredictive," she said, sounding curious. "I can't see much about your future. It's mostly about thoughts and feelings." (Goddammit.)

Nonetheless, she managed to orient some of my recent experiences in a useful way.

She gestured to a man lying dead, impaled by a spear, and said, "It looks like you're fucked, but don't worry."

They were all there: my mother, my man, even my middle-class Modigliani.

It ended with the Queen of Pentacles, who looked very beatific and maternal, which I liked. Anyway, you ever see that Raphael Soyer painting, Consolation*? I figure that could be me—right down to her fat ass. I don't see you as social realism, though—all that brown and those smears. You're like Klimt, and not in some bullshit dorm-room-poster way. I mean you're shimmering with gold leaf. You're a goddamn Snapchat filter. I don't have Snapchat. I've never even sent a nude.*

Now I'm just looking for a cheap, tight, sparkly dress for holiday parties; I want to be tits and ass in tinsel. And I want an even cheaper, tighter, sparklier dress for New Year's; I want to look like glitter in cum.

Let's go to the ballet, let's wear furs.

Yours,

Amber A'Lee

I went back on meds.

I also vowed to stay away from experimental fiction, at least for a while. These things can get out of hand if you're not vigilant.

So a few of us have asked around a bit and no one really seems to know what her situation is anymore. She has no political or social circle in ▮▮▮▮▮▮▮▮▮▮▮ *that we can find, and the very few people I know who live and work there don't have any contact with her and say they've never seen her at any lefty functions or events. A few conceded that this is understandable, because*

██████████████ politics aren't exactly the most dynamic thing at the moment, and they don't exactly have a vibrant left, but at least two mentioned that they found her obsession with American politics odd, and that if she was motivated to do so she could have easily gotten involved in ██████████████ politics as a respected writer. If only she could log off.

It sounds conspiratorial, but I truly believe we have yet to grapple with the socially and mentally corrosive results of the internet. There's a reason none of those Silicon Valley guys let their children look at screens for their entire childhood, and I'm sure like the big tobacco executives who never let their kids smoke, they're suppressing their own internal studies on social media brain-melt. I think it also has a social component like drug epidemics often do. For most happy, thriving people, booze/weed/██████████████ / Twitter etc. are fun and harmless social lubricants.

However, if you're living in a miserable, declining town, with a miserable, declining life, you're much more susceptible to patterns of substance/internet abuse.

I lost a lot of friends and fellows to Trump Hysteria. I won't say I didn't have my own moments of panic, but I knew I needed to calm down, because panic is worse than useless.

The libs took a different approach; when they weren't hysterical, they were histrionic. Their panic wasn't just counterproductive, it was self-indulgent. Suddenly, moral and political commitment was being measured by how terrified you were.

It felt like being forced to sit through a bad play, the worst kind of play. The kind of play that demands audience participation, lest you be accused of ruining everyone's good time. But being scared is not the same thing as being smart, nor does it have anything to do with one's dedication to justice, so why was being a drama queen a prerequisite to being a leftist?

The Panic Play is enforced socially with the sort of moralistic coercion endemic to liberalism. It's a mandatory affect of panic, plus a distorted interpretation of reality that magnifies the most cinematic narrative, mirroring the right's Fox News technique of lachrymose fearmongering, which always belies the implied threat that insufficient commitment to terror and hyperbole will be noted as a moral failure. It's enough fire and brimstone to make an Evangelical blush.

Alarm itself is conflated with vigilance and compassion, while stoicism is conflated with ignorance or, worse, apathy. But panic is anathema to the sort of serious-minded, accurate analysis that would increase the likelihood of fixing the Problem. Of course, that's not the point; the point of the Panic Play is to collectively profess a debilitating vulnerability and general weakness. This weakness serves the dual purpose of excusing us from actually tackling the Problem ("What can we do? They're so big and mean, and we're so small and good!") and providing us with a familiar, reassuring bedtime story, one we know ends happily ever after. In this story, America is up against the same old enemy: fascism—we beat it before, and we are destined to beat it again. And thank God, because if this was something unprecedented, we would have no idea what the fuck to do, and that's a far more terrifying prospect than the Bad Guys we already defeated. It was a comfort— even a mantra—to insist there are no unique challenges for which we have no proven record.

As an added bonus, the Panic Play is an incredibly

entertaining way to compete in the attention economy ("I'm the most scared!" "No, *I'm* the most scared!"), and it doesn't even require a violation of social distancing! We saw it again with COVID, which made sense; everyone sort of missed having a regular Trump boogeyman, and everyone was looking for a way to hang out without actually having to hang out. It's a far less nutritious interaction, which means you have to keep doing more to get the high, something that would be alleviated by more authentic conversation. Indeed, if you were to hear some of the things said on Twitter in person, you would be deeply concerned about the speaker's grip on reality.

The truth is, fascism never came.

One of the key differences between fascism and neoliberalism is neoliberalism's tolerance for—and inevitable assimilation of—criticisms against it. Fascism, meanwhile, eliminates rather than integrates dissent. Put simply, if you don't think that Keeanga-Yamahtta Taylor, or yours truly—the Tokyo Rose of the Bernie Bros herself—is in any real danger, it's unlikely that all those mysterious "marginalized people" everyone is so fond of invoking as progressive shorthand are on the chopping block either. Were a fascist hegemony imminent, left-wing journalists, intellectuals, and, yes, even podcast nano-celebrities would be a higher priority than the sort of decent human beings who have no time for or interest in "the discourse." Thus, the Panic Play of the media class only further alienated a broader public, whose increasing distrust of institutions has been exacerbated by repeated hysteria. This is not merely annoying but dangerous; cry wolf long enough and no one listens when there's one at the door.

Indeed, the liberal media, entertainment, and political

industries are all permitted by these alleged Brown Shirts to "nevertheless, persist" in opposition to Trump and his "populist revolutionaries," who have failed to imprison Hillary Clinton or even that washed-up psycho Bette Midler. It's a curious sort of fascism that appears to take no real interest in eliminating one's enemies, preferring instead to "own" them online.

Of course, it's entirely possible that I am completely wrong and that I will be dragged off to the camps any minute now: fair enough; if you catch me in a cattle car, I owe you a Coke.

Still, this scenario begs the question: If we were really in danger of a fascist coup, isn't the Panic Play just as impotent as if we were not? If you panic when there's no emergency, you're a hysteric. If you panic when there *is* an emergency, you're irresponsible.

Indulge your terror too much, and you might leave orbit completely.

All of this is just to say that I understand that most people go nuts at some point in their life, and that yes, as Mark Fisher says, the insecurity and indignities of capitalism bear much of the responsibility, but you can't wait until the revolution to collect your fucking marbles.

12

I'M SORRY

Vietnamese is a notoriously difficult, tonal language. Even if I had taken months of immersion classes, I wouldn't have known what they were yelling at me, and I certainly wouldn't have been able to respond intelligibly.

In 2015, the Los Angeles metropolitan area had the largest Vietnamese population in the country by far, 313,000, and I doubt they all just up and left before the writing of this.[62] I'm not sure how many Vietnamese Angelenos don't speak English, but I was pretty sure they were all in the parking lot that day, trying to get the COVID vaccination they had been told would be available to them. They were almost entirely senior citizens, and I'm not sure if they believed that I could secretly speak Vietnamese and was pretending not to, or that if they yelled loud enough, I could learn it on the fly, but they were undeterred by my refusal/inability to communicate: it just made them angrier.

I was "volunteering" at one of the first drive-through vaccination sites in Los Angeles, a mass of tents and orange cones across an endless stadium parking lot. I'm not sure if the program was implemented by the state of California or LA County, or how much the private sector was involved, or really anything else. I meant to look into it, but I'm pretty allergic to anything that reminds me of COVID these days. It's not a policy, just dread, so I'll keep this brief.

My boyfriend at the time had signed me up without telling me; not only had I not volunteered to "volunteer," the gig itself was a little more tit for tat than a selfless act. You spent a day directing traffic, taking temperatures, confirming appointments and/or eligibility for early vaccine access; in return, you, the "volunteer," also got early access. I wasn't actually opposed to the transactional incentive of this not-actually-volunteer work; they didn't have enough nurses or paid medical staff, and they needed a carrot to dangle. Still, I figured, I was young enough and in good enough health that early vaccination wasn't a priority for me. The prospect of taking that shift from someone who might desperately want to visit their grandparents made me a bit squeamish, and I said as much to my boyfriend. He had signed up a lot of his friends without telling them, he replied, and had mobbed the website using an elaborate system of multiple tabs and furious clicking.

"You know they used to shoot people for shit like that in the Soviet Union," I said.

We had already broken up by the time my shift rolled around, so I was even less keen to go. I wasn't avoiding the vaccine, but I was in no rush. I could not, however, transfer the shift or gift it to anyone else, so I woke up bright and early, slapped on the sunscreen, and drove over an hour to hang out on a square mile of blacktop in the desert.

It was a shit show. State and local sources had posted conflicting information on who was eligible and what site they should go to, and both were slightly wrong. The on-line sign-up went down multiple times, and some people's appointments were lost or canceled. The bottom line was, a lot of vulnerable people were told to go to a stadium parking lot in the middle of nowhere for a vaccine, and they made the drive only to be denied.

Early in the day, I was checking in cars with four other women, and we immediately realized that a lot of people weren't going to get the jab, and that there was nothing we could do about it. Even if we had waved them through, their information would be checked a second time, and they would be rejected by the next volunteer or nurse just fifty yards away. This is what I had to tell the two different people that tried to bribe me; all three of us were ashamed of ourselves.

Those turned away were understandably upset, sometimes crestfallen, but mostly angry. On a level playing field, the Vietnamese people weren't actually more pissed than any-one else, but the language barrier exacerbated everything. If someone only spoke Spanish, a Spanish-speaking volunteer was nearby to translate, but no one spoke Vietnamese, leav-ing us all to wonder why, in this time of high unemploy-ment, didn't the state just pay amateur translators to sit safely at home by the phone for just such inevitabilities?

One Vietnamese woman, who was most certainly under five feet tall and must have been in her eighties, actually thrust her withered little finger past the face of the driver (her son?), out of the car window, and directly at me as she spat what I could only assume were curses, profanities, or both, while the driver tried to ask me a question in broken English. It was so unexpected and aggressive that I felt my-self involuntarily take a step backward. I had to admire her;

I would wager that tiny elderly immigrant women have to be tough as nails or people will walk all over them. I was as impressed as I was intimidated. At that moment, I was glad she couldn't speak English; whatever she was saying would probably devastate me.

The worst one was when I informed an older white couple they wouldn't be getting the vaccine due to an administrative error. The woman began to sob and hyperventilate from the passenger seat, while her husband closed his eyes and lowered his head with an exhausted sigh. I didn't get the impression he was exhausted with her, just that he was tired of navigating bureaucracy, tired of being scared, tired of waiting for this all to be over.

"You can't do this to people," the woman choked out her words. Without looking at his wife, the man put a reassuring hand on her back, rubbing slowly up and down, until she caught her breath. Then he raised his eyes to mine. His voice was quiet, gentle, even, when he said that he knew this wasn't my fault, that I couldn't do anything about it, and worst of all, "Thank you for coming out here and doing this. I know you must be having a hard day."

I have never felt like more of a piece of shit in my life.

The quiet compassion and gratitude of someone you're turning away is way worse than wrath.

Taking pity on me, one of the nurses moved me to thermometer duty. A lot of them didn't work, and they were nearly impossible to read in direct sunlight.

At the end of the day, I got my stupid shot and I drove home. An East Coast friend texted me that night to congratulate me on my "first jab" and ask how California's boutique, volunteer-run vaccination program was going.

★ ★ ★

When Bernie dropped out, I figured Biden would win, but even if Trump had a second term, I didn't think we were bound for any dystopia significantly worse than the present. What I really dreaded most was more of the same; the return of the old familiar dysfunctional activism endemic to a country without a strong labor movement and an organized left. The Bernie movement no longer had a North Star, and we all seemed to just sort of scatter into the wind. It wouldn't have bothered me had we not been so energized, so focused, and maybe even a little optimistic, just a few months earlier.

A lot of people just sort of disengaged, which some have called "quitting" but which I think is rational. You have to take breaks, and politics were stagnant again. I checked out as much as someone on a political podcast can: "Call me if something happens," I would say. Until then, I'd peep at the *Financial Times,* but that's about it. There was no point getting mad about Biden or the cynical careerism and overt corruption of the professional progressives; they are what they are. But with many of the most grounded Bernie people now excusing themselves from the table/discourse, the worse elements of a pre-Bernie left were proportionally more influential.

Identity politics stymied class politics again. The petulant displays of political theater, endless, meaningless marches and demonstrations with no clear goal, returned. It was back to scolding, sanctimony, paranoia, denunciations, and punitive impulses. People were cruel and vicious; so many of them were too nervous about being canceled not to participate in the cancellation of another, much less speak out against it. They had moved right back into the Vampire Castle and they were digging a new wine cellar.

But worst of all, what passes for a left in this country

had turned back inward, away from the masses, back to the LARPing little subculture we had been before Bernie. They shared a sensibility with both the anarchists of Occupy and the liberals of the Democratic Party: we're not big enough to build power, but if we make our world smaller, more insular, we don't have to grow. It can't be a coincidence that so many of them enjoyed being locked inside their houses.

★　★　★

After Hurricane Sandy hit in October of 2012, much of the activity around Occupy Wall Street collapsed, but what was left actually grew temporarily by pivoting to relief efforts. Many activists were grateful to finally have something concrete to do where time was of the essence. The absurdity and impotence of all those endless meetings, training sessions, and workshops was suddenly obvious.

Occupy Sandy wasn't really political, but it did help with the Occupy Wall Street withdrawal so many people were feeling. Like an activism methadone. This was the first time I had heard the phrase "mutual aid," and though it didn't sit right with me, I knew Zuccotti veterans were sad about Occupy Wall Street's failure, and that they felt better when they had a special name for doing regular stuff. Plus, they really were doing good work, so I shut up. As the Disaster Relief Appropriations Act of 2013 began to disburse the $49 billion allocated for Sandy, the last of the Occupy energy faded away. I didn't hear any more about mutual aid. Then people started getting sick.

★　★　★

There are a million variations on the old folktale generally known as "Stone Soup," but they all operate under the same basic story: Travelers arrive in a modest foreign town, hungry and without money for food. In some versions of the story, the travelers resort to begging, which is unsuccessful; in others, they don't try at all. But in every telling, the travelers devise a scheme to trick the townspeople into feeding them: they acquire a pot, fill it with water, throw in a stone, light a fire beneath it, and begin to watch their "stone soup" simmer. Eventually, curious townspeople approach them to ask what they could possibly be doing.

The travelers inform the locals that stone soup is the most delicious meal one could possibly imagine, although, to be honest, it would be even better with the addition of, say, carrots. A villager exclaims that they may have a few extra carrots in their cupboard at home, and the travelers happily propose to exchange some of their forthcoming soup for some of those carrots.

The travelers repeat their grift with different villagers/ingredients until the soup becomes a bounty of vegetables, meat, and spices. In the end, the crafty newcomers throw the stone away as they and the villagers enjoy a hearty and nutritious bowl of stone soup. The villagers, in short, have been conned into sharing, but with their bellies full and their prior suspicions overcome, they are either unoffended or, in most tellings of the tale, none the wiser.

At no point did the travelers persuade the villagers of the possibilities of a collective economy. Why bother? It was easier to trick them, and, in the end, all's well that ends well.

Dean Spade's COVID treatise, *Mutual Aid: Building Solidarity During This Crisis (and the Next),* imagines a similar fairy tale of "mutual aid" communities, in which resources are coordinated and distributed among the needy and shared by all, and in which outsiders are easily integrated into the larger community. In Spade's telling, such associations have the potential to become self-sufficient, to challenge power, and even to change the world. Stone soup never tasted so good.

★ ★ ★

One of the most pervasive legends on the contemporary left concerns the Black Panthers' breakfast program. Everyone and everything, from Alexandria Ocasio-Cortez to the History Channel, trots out the same story: in 1969, the Black Panthers created a school breakfast program that fed poor Black children. In so doing, the Panthers demonstrated that communities of mutual aid were not only possible but could in fact serve as a model example of a noncapitalist form of social organization. In Spade and others' tellings, if only the US government hadn't crushed the Black Panthers, a new society, based on the principle of mutual aid, could have emerged.

Unfortunately for mutual aid enthusiasts, this story is inaccurate. In actual fact, Congress passed the Child Nutrition Act in 1966, which created the national School Breakfast Program—an expansion of the National School Lunch Program, which was first initiated in 1946 and was one of the final programs of the New Deal. Indeed, Lyndon Johnson explicitly argued that his breakfast program completed the unfinished business of his democratic predecessors Franklin Delano Roosevelt and Harry S. Truman.

The first thing to notice is that the Child Nutrition Act was passed in 1966, three years before the Panthers' breakfast program. Furthermore, the fact that the National School Lunch Program began in 1946 suggests that the idea of a "free lunch" (turns out that, contra economists, such a thing is possible) had been bandied about in progressive circles for at least two decades, if not longer. In fact, the Republican

Dwight D. Eisenhower had himself expanded the lunch program. Free lunches for needy children were clearly part of US political discourse well before 1969.

So, it's impossible to argue that the Panthers inspired the school breakfast programs of the 1970s and beyond, and to insist otherwise denies historical chronology. But, even if the Panthers didn't develop the idea of free lunches, is it fair to say, as progressives often do, that they at least pressured the US government to expand its lunch programs? Alas, one cannot even proffer this milder claim: the post-1969 expansions of government food programs essentially followed the outline for expansion laid out in the original Child Nutrition Act of 1966. Unsurprisingly, the government-funded program fed far more than the Panthers' more limited program: in its first year, the former fed about 80,000 children, while the latter fed only about 10,000. Despite the racist claims of notorious paranoiac J. Edgar Hoover, who was reported to have declared the program "potentially the greatest threat to efforts by authorities to neutralize the BPP [Black Panther Party] and destroy what it stands for," it appears that most government officials either ignored the BPP program or weren't even aware of it.[63]

It's disheartening that a politician like AOC would ignore the legislative history of social democratic lunch programs and instead repeat, as she has on her Instagram, the ahistorical myth that if you "ever benefited from free & reduced school lunch, you've likely benefited from the work and legacy of the Black Panthers."[64] In affirming this, AOC is subtly advocating in favor of community "self-reliance," similar to the way a Republican politician would eschew government-mandated redistribution in favor of charity. In a follow-up post she said, "[W]e've raised and distributed over $1 MILLION in food

& direct aid to people when the Fed Gov wouldn't (and still won't) help," which begs the questions: Isn't that precisely the problem? And aren't *you* the federal government?

To be fair to AOC, she really does want to redistribute wealth . . . probably; but her fetish for apocryphal activist folklore suggests the solution to our problems does *not* lie in government redistribution. And this isn't to bash the Black Panthers, who were not politicians, and who were working to help their community in the limited, though quite impressive, ways available to them. But their legacy is more complicated than something that fits in an Instagram post.

Echoing AOC's criticism of the government she's a part of, Spade invokes a number of other misconceptions regarding the shortcomings of the New Deal, including its supposedly *inherent* racism. In brief, some scholars have argued that the exclusion of agricultural and domestic workers from Social Security benefits proves that the New Deal was racist (or even that universal programs themselves are racist). As Adolph Reed wrote, however, while it is "true that black Americans received less than whites *on the average* from many New Deal programs," they nonetheless benefited substantially; Reed himself points to the hundreds of thousands of Black Americans who in the 1930s worked for the Works Progress Administration and the Civilian Conservation Corps.[65] Moreover, Reed continues, "the percentage of African Americans who worked in the [WPA and CCC] was greater than their representation in the overall population, even though that proportion remained lower than the percentage of black people among those in greatest need of work." In addition to this incidental affirmative action, "the Public Works Administration established quotas to ensure that black workers, and particularly skilled black workers, were hired in construction projects the agency funded."

Curiously, Spade also praises the response of the Hong Kong protest movement to COVID as an example of mutual aid's superiority to state programs, even the elements that have called for government surveillance, closing borders to travel, and the relocation of the most vulnerable people from centrally located quarantine centers (which the protesters had bombed before they were occupied) to remote camps. It appears that Spade is swayed to support these actions because the "people" have demanded them, and he views them as an example of mutual aid. Again, Spade has it wrong: the protesters were in fact calling for *more* state administration to aid them in their struggle.

And if the lack of historical evidence to support mutual aid's capacity to build power is a flaw in Spade's book, then the lack of "lack" itself as an obstacle is even more damning. He doesn't mention that Hong Kong is home to "one of the worst inequality rates among developed nations."[66] Unless he's under the impression the bourgeoisie will simply "share," that leaves a bunch of poor people sharing the wealth they don't have.

★　★　★

Nothin' from nothin' leaves nothin'
And I'm not stuffin', believe you me

—BILLY PRESTON, "NOTHING FROM NOTHING"

Mad Max: Fury Road is the best criticism of the commune since Michel Clouscard (bear with me). It certainly has more relevant politics than, say, *Snowpiercer* (seriously, indulge me).

In the latter dystopia, a train is segregated according to class, inspiring a revolt among the extremely hot "grunts" in the caboose, who are relegated to hard labor, filth, and want. During the revolution, the rebels realize the entire train is powered by children, so they decide to destroy it and set out on their own into the wilderness. (They didn't have an engineer able to retrofit an expropriated child-slave-powered train?)

In *Mad Max,* however, a band of extremely hot women escape the ruling dictator's harem, fleeing their cruel empire for greener pastures. Nevertheless, when they arrive at the promised land, there are no carrots, spices, or meat—only stones. Realizing that all the wealth left in the world has been concentrated in the hands of the dictator, they return to the city and stage their revolt, expropriating the resources—including the now very precious and rare potable water—to its formerly subjugated citizens.

The reality is that the wealth of the people has already been hoarded by the elites, and what's left outside of their empire isn't enough to sustain us. If there's anything good, they probably already have it, and we need to take it. Groceries are one thing, but I cannot make insulin in my bathtub, nor can I build habitable housing on the fly. The math doesn't lie; we can't evade class conflict by slicing meager scraps thinner and thinner. That's just sharing a boiling pot of stones.

★   ★   ★

Well I wanna save the whales too
But it's a fuckin Wednesday afternoon

—BILLY NOMATES, "HIPPY ELITE"

It is worth considering *Mutual Aid* as a two-part treatise, the first being an argument in favor of mutual aid, the second a guidebook to consensus-based activism. The consensus model is not the only—or the most common—means of co-ordinating mutual aid, but Spade takes it for granted, despite the fact that groups like the Black Panthers were extremely hierarchical. Spade's innovation is to marry mutual aid to the consensus model, the criticisms of which are worth their own book entirely, but I know what the big one is for me. In brief, consensus self-selects for a "type": professional managerial class with an instinct for human resources, lots of time on their hands, loves meetings, etc. Beyond that, I will avoid any technical critiques of consensus-based decision-making and instead examine exactly why Spade favors it.

Throughout the book, he makes repeated references to "the process" and "practices," and those are his commitments. Like Barack Obama, another Harvard Law graduate, Spade fetishizes procedure rather than politics, and certainly prefers it to class conflict.

While he argues that mutual aid will build power, how this happens, exactly, remains obscure. Rather than laying out a particular plan, he insists that "communities," ill-defined but geographically situated nodes, will be the mechanism of social transformation. But as anyone familiar with the history of actually existing communities in the United States will tell you, small places offer small opportunities, and provincialism more often than not leans to the right. (There's a reason the rich use "community" when they're defending their wealth, and that "gated" is the word that comes most often before the term.) And what about those people who already have a community, or who are merely uninterested in fabricating one out of regional shared desperation? How are you going to woo/organize the people who just don't want to hang out with Dean Spade, or his readers?

★ ★ ★

> *I don't really want to be local*
>
> . . .
>
> *I don't really want to be social*
>
> —BRONCHO, "I DON'T REALLY WANT TO BE SOCIAL"

As for organizing those actually existing communities, the ones who don't read Verso books but go to church or the bar together, they prefer what Spade terms "siloes," meaning highly focused or even single-issue campaigns. Spade argues against them, favoring a whole-cloth approach, but the sort of people who want a codependent network of people with its own homegrown values, code and culture, and a prefigurative vision of utopia they believe they are trying to operate autonomously of larger authorities usually just join a cult. As lonely as the world is, there's not a lot of people who want to get involved with something so prescriptive; just look at church attendance. We don't like to be told how and who to be, at least not too much.

It may sound counterintuitive, but from a recruitment standpoint, the narrower the cause, the broader the appeal. Or, if your treehouse has five rules, you're gonna have a lot of friends. If your treehouse has five hundred rules, you're a weird kid alone in a tree. Project-based—rather than community-based—organizing does not show a preference for ideological conformity or coherence. If someone wants Medicare for All but has no interest in attending a community antiracist book club, they're still part of our team. We don't assume they're racist or reactionary. They do the work, so why should they have to live the life? To prove they're not a bad person?

In essence, Spade's community model reproduces the professional managerial class's degrading skepticism of man's inherent good faith. I.e., the masses are not prepared to fight for their own interests, they have to read *White Fragility* first. Conversely, the labor movement is predicated and focused on class conflict, has fought for more control over the national economy and resources, and recognizes the state's erosion—retrenchment, spending cuts, privatization or outright elimination of public employment workforce, etc.—as one of the major factors in their decline. Communities look inward, labor looks outward.

★ ★ ★

Long-haired preachers come out every night
Try to tell you what's wrong and what's right
But when asked how 'bout something to eat
They will answer with voices so sweet

You will eat, bye and bye
In that glorious land above the sky
Work and Pray, live on hay
You'll get pie in the sky when you die

—JOE HILL, "THE PREACHER AND THE SLAVE"

One of the curious aspects of the stone soup legend is that the townspeople never sniff out the travelers' ruse; or if they do, they clearly don't care. This both underestimates people's intelligence and their potential sense of indignation or anger should the trick be discovered. That they would either be oblivious or grateful for the bait and switch is highly implausible.

In some sense, Spade has characterized the Panthers' breakfast program accurately: It *was* a political project with an ideological agenda. It wasn't "read your Bible," but it was "read your Stokely Carmichael," and the Panthers were up front about their separatist project. For his part, Spade is never clear about how ideologically explicit he believes mutual aid should be. Either he wants to conceal the political agenda or it's the "starvation army" model sung so bitterly in Joe Hill's "The Preacher and the Slave," wherein evangelists might offer a meal in exchange for rapt attention to a sermon. It is irritating to be preached at, and make no mistake, obligatory antiracist training is a sermon for people who worship HR.

A political commitment born out of dependency, rather than free will, is not only coercive but unsustainable. Not all churches or charities evangelize or require conversion to participate, but Spade's endorsement of mutual aid is contingent on this kind of coercion, which leads to resentment, which leads to decline.

★   ★   ★

Accordingly, with admirable, though misdirected intentions, they very seriously and very sentimentally set themselves to the task of remedying the evils that they see. But their remedies do not cure the disease: they merely prolong it. Indeed, their remedies are part of the disease.

—OSCAR WILDE, "THE SOUL OF MAN
UNDER SOCIALISM"

Despite Spade's insistence to the contrary, mutual aid *is* a type of charity, and one with a peculiar, evangelizing, and covert agenda. Meanwhile, Spade describes the contemporary breakfast program as "charity" rather than redistribution at a federal level.

Charity is good, volunteering is good, but it's no replacement for state-directed programming. We don't want to survive, which is ultimately what mutual aid is—a politics of austerity. Instead, we want to thrive, and for that, we need the federal state to redistribute wealth from outside our communities into them.

Mutual aid will always be connected to a church, be it the Catholic tradition of St. Vincent De Paul, the langars of Sikh gurdwaras, the zakat of Islam, the tzedakah of Judaism, or Spade's communitarian anarchism.

Not everything that is Good is socialist; not everything socialist is Good. This is not a bad thing. Whether you donate your time, money, or resources, helping other people is important, and survival is a humane priority, if not a grand political project.

These are not political things to do; they are good things to do, and they are very urgent. Their absence of political content is not a flaw but part of their appeal. Socialists and leftists do not hold a monopoly on compassion, kindness, or generosity—and thank God, because there really aren't that many of us.

★   ★   ★

So I just spent all day trying to explain to elderly ESL people why they couldn't get their COVID vaccine in LA without an LA County address or workplace address even though the fucking spiffy new website let them sign up for one, and no I can't help them because I'm just a volunteer, and yes I agree that it's a cruel and unforgivable mistake on the city's part, and yes I agree an absurdly wealthy city like Los Angeles shouldn't be relying on volunteers who are mostly doing it for the vaccine they might get at the end of their shift during mass unemployment, and yes it's perfectly obvious this is a moment that calls for a mass public employment program including work-from-home language line support jobs, which I agree would be extremely helpful, and yes they should absolutely make life a living hell for the people who thought this up because they might as well start preparing for the actual hell that awaits them if there is anything approaching a just god in this world, and that I am so sorry—

I realize this essay is short on jokes, so here's one: Before I could start my shift at the pandemic parking lot, I was treated to a California Cold War tradition: I had to sign and verbally agree to a loyalty oath. To clarify: before trying to take people's temperatures with thermometers that didn't work, and telling them that actually we were just kidding and they don't get a COVID vaccine, I had to pledge, with pen and tongue both, that I would uphold the US Constitution. I'm not sure I can convey how surreal it was, staring out across a literal neoliberal desert and realizing that we were required to sign and say something the state of California cooked up in 1950 to prevent communists from becoming state employees. I can't imagine communists are still a concern for California politicians. It must be a sort of McCarthyite vestigial tail.

I try not to lie, especially on forms, but hell, I drove an

hour. I signed it, and I said it. They were just words. Words like,

Tôi xin lỗi.

I'm sorry.

Tôi chân thành xin lỗi.

I sincerely apologize.

Đó là lỗi của tôi.

It's my fault.

Tôi hy vọng bạn tha thứ cho tôi.

I hope you forgive me.

13

RIDING THE CREST

IOWA

> There will be a minor correction to the last batch of results and we will be pushing an update momentarily.
>
> —@IOWADEMOCRATS, 9:32 P.M., FEBRUARY 5, 2020

Iowa was freezing, but we went to Dairy Queen anyway.

After the 2016 election, there had been no real confidence that the podcast would continue under Trump. Right-wing administrations, particularly unpredictable ones, tend to narrow the field of political imagination. We did well under Obama because the obvious shortcomings of a neoliberal president had been laid bare. An anecdote I had told the boys and later recounted on the show referred to the DSA mailing lists, which we compiled by purchasing the mailing lists of progressive magazines. Before Bush, *The Nation* had been a left-wing publication, social democratically inclined at the very least. After Iraq, their readership was no longer anticapitalist, or even anti-Republican; they settled for anti-Bush, and by the time Obama rolled around, they were so relieved (and perhaps not a little self-congratulatory) that any criticism they might have had for the Obungler and his left-wing party of capital never seemed to make it to print.

The long nightmare of Dubya was over (though none of the results of his policies were), and *The Nation* lists became useless for DSA appeals to membership or donations. I assumed Chapo's lefty audience would repeat the process, receding so far into anti-Trumpism that they wouldn't have much patience for the podcast that blamed Hillary and the Dems for Trump's rise. It never happened, and I still don't totally know why. Maybe it was just that the generation screwed by the 2008 financial crisis didn't have the luxury of pretending that another yellow dog democrat would make it all better, but our audience grew. DSA grew. And a sort of ground game sleeper cell for Bernie 2020 grew, and they began organizing.

My fellow Chapo cohosts—Will, Matt, Felix, and Virgil—and I had all privately agreed to throw all the weight of the show behind the campaign prior to Bernie announcing his second run (my little birdies gave me the tip-off, but it was hardly a closely guarded secret). We had been touring with live shows across the US and found that it suited us, so we booked both a UK tour to stump for Corbyn and a primaries tour—Iowa, New Hampshire, Nevada, and a streak of California shows in San Diego, LA, Sacramento, and San Francisco.

The UK tour (plus Berlin, for a fundraising event hosted by all the boho US expats who saw what a basic social safety net had to offer) started extremely strong and energetic, but by the time we got to our last show in Liverpool, we saw dread in the faces of the audience. If I'm ever stupid enough to commit to writing another book—and if any publisher is stupid enough to let me—I'll have some things to say about the Corbyn campaign. But until then, I'll just say that the UK's loss strengthened our resolve—not just the podcast's, but the resolve of every Bernie Bro in America.

As we were trudging through the snow in Iowa to knock on doors for Bernie, I was getting texts from a UK friend who had once taken me on a tour of his hometown, pointed down an alley, and said, "That's where I got my first blow job." I managed a straight-faced "So you've been back recently, then?" which I believe earned me a true friend, a discreet source, a reliable fixer, and a pretty cinematic and romantic kiss in a picturesque train station. He had nearly destroyed his health canvassing for Corbyn—heel spurs, back issues, some sort of medieval Anglo-plague that he could never seem to shake, and general ravages of the binge-drinking necessary to nearly all British political functions of any import (the English require constant social lubrication, otherwise they rust).

He had sent a video: a crew of erstwhile Corbynistas (in a pub, of course) making gestures of vigilance, a little message of support and solidarity from comrades across the pond. I heard him cheer from behind his phone, "Bring on the Brexit!" It hadn't been two months since Labour's defeat, but at least they got to tell the EU to fuck off. It reminded me that it wouldn't be the end of the world if Bernie lost, but I really wanted to win. Mostly it reminded me that campaigning on tour would take ten years off my life if I drank like the English.

Being clever and resourceful Yankees, we learned from the Brits' mistake and supplemented our drunkenness with a balanced diet of "uppers, downers, screamers, laughers," and whatever anyone was giving us for free (which was everything short of black tar heroin, fentanyl, and adrenochrome). The level of intemperance was absurd, but I honestly don't think we could have kept pace without the benefit of chemistry. And although I joked that Chapo gets everyone laid but me, we didn't indulge in lecherous excess, so the drugs and booze powering us on the campaign trail felt pretty wholesome at the time. Besides, they were presents. And we couldn't be rude.

Drugs also helped with a good night's sleep, which is a prerequisite for the patience required to canvass in Iowa. Iowans have a chip on their shoulder that I recognize from Indiana, but the major difference is that once every four years, Iowa "matters." There were lovely people in Des Moines of course—Bernie supporters and others—who were a breeze to deal with, even when they were voting for another candidate. But there were also insecure Midwesterners—languishing in the one taste of power they ever get, and even then only every four years—who preen and lead you on, actively cultivating a dithering affect to prolong their moment in the spotlight with a "Gee, I just don't know who I'm voting for, it's a really big decision." If you don't have Xanax, you will murder these people.

But we did, so we didn't. We froze our asses off, knocked on doors, distributed literature, raised funds, did a show that doubled as a rally, and hosted an after-party to raise even more money, to which our nicest cohost invited a "friendly journalist" who proceeded to write a takedown of the entire event on the front page of *The New York Times*.[67] I got two lines in the article. No picture.

Most of Chapo's press does not mention me regardless of my participation on the show, as I'm a pretty inconvenient inconsistency in the characterization of the podcast as "a bunch of white beardy bro-dudes." So whenever anyone asks why I don't cohost the pod much anymore, I point out that being the Girl in Chapo Trap House is a lot like not being in Chapo Trap House at all (so why be a sucker when you can just get paid?).

I can't remember if this was the stop where a cohost and I ended up screaming things like, "You have *always* resented me!" and "What do I have to *do* to make *you* feel secure?"—I won't say who said what, just that we both sounded very *Days of Our Lives*—but we were wasted and running on zero sleep, and it resolved in two minutes. To be honest, being the Gendered Chapo rarely felt like a rift between us. When it did, you could usually trace it back to some sort of external scrutiny or perception of our internal dynamics; it was always someone else speculating over what was "toxic" between us. To the boys' credit, they're pretty conscientious, and they pay attention. To my own credit, I tend to complain, demand, object, etc., very loudly, very early, so I usually avoid the "I'm a fun girl!" prison of quietly filing away my resentments so no one thinks I'm a bummer until I erupt into an atomic explosion. I find that you sleep better at night and maintain your relationships better if you just regularly release a few medium-sized explosions. Say, fireworks rather than atom bombs. You want to singe their eyebrows and leave their ears ringing, not turn your friendships to dust. (And alcohol doesn't help.)

Crucially, we always maintained a united front in public, so other than little blind item teasers like the above (included only to show that we are in fact human), you're getting no dirt on the boys from me. For a while there was even an intra-media cottage industry of commentary on "the

Chapo phenomenon," usually a bunch of cynical speculation amounting to "what are they *really* getting out of this Bernie thing?" No one outside of it could ever understand. No matter how mad we might get, or how sick of each other we might be, we were an "us," and we had a mission.

And I think that is what *actually* bothered the liberal media so much about us. It wasn't really the politics, or the vulgarity, or the lack of respect for their venerable publications and credentials. I think they were jealous of us. I think they looked at us and wished that *they* had a mission, that *they* really believed in something, that *they* were unafraid. And I think they were jealous that we were having fun with our friends.

Gathered in a packed gymnasium in Iowa to hear the results, I saw reporters, journalists, poll workers, and spectators everywhere. I don't know how I got into the press stand, but I decided to go back to the floor almost immediately. I saw some journos I'd met once or twice and realized I had no idea what I'd say to them, so I slipped discreetly behind a Japanese reporter who—I swear to God in heaven—said, "Trump-u."

The candidates spoke, we waited for a count. My co-host's little birdy said Bernie's won, but not to say it out loud yet. Buttigieg and Sanders are tied. Mayor Pete makes his acceptance speech before all the ballots are counted. We know he didn't win.

Felix and I take an Uber back to the hotel. The driver pulled up in an F-350, and we had a conversation about the New World Order. We asked for more information, and he was eager to give us an outline. He enjoyed his authority in the conversation. We made a friend.

Back at the hotel, we are dizzy and frenetic. We're not sure what happened or why Buttigieg is allowed to do that. More results come in. Bernie wins the popular vote. We are rapturous. We dance, we sing, then consume chemicals that allow us to sink into the floor.

NEW HAMPSHIRE

I was even colder, with even more snow. We were getting a little ragged.

Felix fell on some black ice and had acid reflux so bad I think he slept upright in an office chair. At some point we realized that Matt had packed all his clothes and toiletries for the tour in a paper shopping bag. I did too much blow and my minor cold turned into a massive sinus infection; I sounded like Harvey Fierstein at the live show. At the hotel after-party, Will was immodestly propositioned by the ostensibly heterosexual, extremely drunk, and woozily persistent boyfriend of one of my female friends, which is the sort of thing that always happens to Will; he must emit a pheromone that attracts unwanted interest. Certain they were going to turn this tour into some sort of a documentary short, Chris and his now wife Molly never slept that I saw, always packing, toting, unpacking, setting up, and breaking down a local news studio's worth of AV equipment everywhere we went. Felix and I didn't want to be filmed (we felt fat). Virgil was missing. Virgil was back. Sinn Fein won the Irish General Election. Virgil was missing again.

I had seen the Strokes before, but it was still a good show. We were floating.

LAS VEGAS/SAN DIEGO/LOS ANGELES/SACRAMENTO/SAN FRANCISCO

None of your fucking business.

Ok, I'll give you one. We were sitting on a curb outside of a hotel, San Diego, I think. It was dusk, and it smelled like orange blossoms, and we were smoking a joint and singing

"Sad Songs and Waltzes." The hotel was clean; we had good Mexican food delivered.

"We were riding the crest of a high and beautiful wave."

We flew home, and I was as happy and exhausted as I've ever been.

Then more people got sick.

Then Bernie conceded to Biden.

Then we stayed inside.

★   ★   ★

Again, we always knew Bernie was a long shot, and all the particularist postmortems of the Sanders movement sort of miss the point: either we couldn't reach the critical mass of voters we needed to exercise "the will of the people," or the Democratic Party was so much more invested in defeating Sanders than Trump that it didn't matter how many voters we had in the first place. We knew so-called "progressive" organizations and coalitions were in the pocket of the Democratic Party.

Still, I was heartbroken, and directionless.

The cabin fever got very, very bad. I told my podcast co-hosts I had to get out of the city, and outside in nature, so if anyone wants to come with me, I'm getting an Airbnb somewhere upstate in some woods. Matt; Will and his girlfriend, Katherine; Felix; myself; and erstwhile Bernie staffer Ben Mora loaded into a rented van. We brought a fully stocked recreational pharmacy with us, and nearly killed ourselves from either food poisoning or overdose after someone accidentally basted undercooked chicken with codeine. We did acid and walked around in the woods and had conversations I'll never write about. We talked shit and laughed at the losers; my old boss at the Working Families Party, who dutifully defended their endorsement of Liz Warren and had a Harry Potter–themed wedding. (She also seems to have gone to BravoCon to promote a WFP "initiative" called "Real Housewives of Politics," described as "a multipronged approach to organize the *Real Housewives* fan base through social media, live events and watch parties."[68]) The douchebag from the *Daily Beast* who got Ben fired from the Bernie campaign by leaking screenshots from his private Twitter account ("Liz Warren is an adult diaper fetishist") was revealed to live in a $1.2-million apartment in DUMBO that his parents bought for him; he had a leather refrigerator.[69]

It felt familiar, and I was relieved, because I had been worried that we wouldn't know each other anymore, and at least as worried that we would. We had this mission, this giant thing that had tied us, our highs and our lows, together for years now, and completely changed our lives for the better. But the mission failed, and now it was just us. So what would be worse? Drifting apart, becoming strangers with familiar voices? Or, recognizing each other so well we can see our own defeat in one anothers' eyes? Neither one happened, of course. We were just left with "us," and I think that was what we needed. There were moments when we laughed so hard, we almost forgot that the wave broke and rolled back.

We better stay here. Maybe we'll get another one. . . .

afterword

I tore my hair out trying to end this book on a high note. I almost didn't finish it; it's hard to end a story about the end of something, especially when you wish it had ended differently.

I wanted to close out with a pep talk for the ages, to boost morale, rally the troops, etc., but I had nothing particularly reassuring to say, just the old "We'll get 'em next time." So I procrastinated and bought as much time as I could, scanning still waters and empty horizons for any potential new opportunities for socialism in America that I could show you. It's like I was praying for divine intervention from some literary deity who might bestow instructive yet inspiring afterwords upon her children. "Our Sacred Lady of Closure and Optimism, Restorer of Fortitude." I had convinced myself that I couldn't write about the defeat of the Bernie movement without wrapping it up in a tidy, little bow. I wanted a post-credits teaser to excite and reassure readers that victory is just around the corner: "Don't be sad, the sequel is already in development!"

But that wouldn't be true.

For now, I can't give you a happy ending. But I can give you this. . . .

In the introduction, I mentioned that I undertook this project in order to record and reflect on some of my experiences in politics thus far, because I believe that it is critically important for socialists to remember the movements of the past and learn from them. This is true, but I also firmly believe that to be a good socialist for the long run, you have to learn how to *forget*. Yes, it is essential for us to recognize patterns, weaknesses, and frailties (which we see over and over again), as well as our strengths and victories (which we will see far less often). But I can't stress enough how essential it is to cultivate an ever-so-slightly-faulty memory.

Self-induced bouts of amnesia are a prerequisite for all great ambitions—from art to romance to socialism. If we were constantly stricken with the memories and experiences of our own pasts, we would be paralyzed by defeat, failure, and betrayal, and by all the resulting disappointments that accompany such essential learning. Socialists would recede from politics, artists would eschew great work, and romantics would flee from love. No one would ever take a risk if they remembered every failure and subsequent heartbreak too acutely.

Jeremy Corbyn's campaign and the Labour Party's subsequent loss gave us a preview of failure, and a dire warning not to overestimate ourselves or start believing we could win on enthusiasm. It was a blow, but we couldn't let it slow us down. We had to take the lesson, but leave the nerves behind, because we had to keep moving.

The trouble is, after Bernie, I see no obvious path as of this writing, and blistering blindly through the thicket probably won't get you anywhere you want to go. If you're in the same painted ship upon the same painted ocean as me, I recommend taking some time away from "the discourse." At the very least, try going cold turkey off social media for a week. Step away from pundits, political essayists and podcasts, and cable news if you're that kind of pervert (but check in on labor news once in a while) to clear your head and reflect; I promise someone will let you know if everything starts back up again. Some recovery and restoration is likely in order. We (whoever "we" might be) need to build up our strength for when the next opportunity arises. The work now is more exploratory, slower and on a smaller scale, but we're in preparation, not fixation.

Apply the tourniquet between the wound and the heart; do not bleed out.

And if you've managed to read this whole book, read some actual literature next. Have you heard of novels? A lot of them are pretty good.

So as not to be overwhelmed by the library of leftist writers whose shoulders I cling to like a rhesus monkey, the book I kept turning to throughout this writing was not a memoir but a novel: *Moby-Dick*. It was the dauntless spirit of Herman Melville that buoyed my heart. If Thompson, Gornick, Wright, Freeman, Fisher, and others were cursed by the clarity of their memories, Melville was blessed with the amnesia of a romantic, one that he took great pains to cultivate.

It's with total self-awareness that I continually gravitate to a book about a motley crew embarking on the doomed mission of a madman as my political touchstone. And on a more immediate level, I have to laugh that the book was a commercial failure upon its publication, and well after its author's death. (If this thing bombs, I'll tell myself it's a sleeper; it will catch on after I cash out.) Posthumously, though, Melville won, and rereading *Moby-Dick* over and over again, I still find moments when I can convince myself that *this time*, they're gonna get that fucking whale.

Before you rush to judgment, it's not the words of the mad triumphalist Captain Ahab—his mind warped by vengeance, alienated from land, life, and sanity—that ignite me, but those of the clear-eyed Starbuck. A sober and sensible man, he believes that the ship is set for failure, but he is bound by honor and duty to proceed as if they are not. On a particularly beautiful and promising day, he gazes out onto an uncharacteristically placid sea, and the noble first mate of the *Pequod* decides to forget everything he knows about the danger that must lie ahead, saying:

> Loveliness unfathomable, as ever lover saw in his young bride's eye!—Tell me not of thy teeth-tiered sharks, and thy kidnapping cannibal ways. Let faith oust fact; let fancy oust memory; I look deep down and do believe.

Less quoted is the preceding line from the Second Mate Stubb, a wisecracking shit-talker fond of wine, women, and song, and probably a better proxy for myself. He decides to forget every woe he's ever had.

> I am Stubb, and Stubb has his history; but here Stubb takes oaths that he has always been jolly!

If you're a fellow traveler, chin up.
Find faith when you can, and always be jolly, or at least

try. I say this as someone who knows that it is very possible, if not likely, that Bernie Sanders was the only real shot we had at socialism in my lifetime. That does not mean that I am retired, but it does take some of the pressure off, as my practical political responsibilities now consist of telling people what I saw and what I know and keeping a watchful eye out for another chance without bounding at every futile spectacle and wasting everyone's time and energy in the process.

I say, learn everything you can, remember everything you learn, study experience—yours and others'—and do it together. Keep watch for anything that could actually give a leg up to the glorious cause of the workers' movement—but be picky. Remember what happened last time. And the time before that. And the time before that. Keep the memories of strategy and history in constant sight, then take a quick glance at the memories of pain, but only from the rearview mirror.

Then, floor it. There's things to do, and it's getting late. And if you ever feel your faith depleted, you can have some of mine. I've got more than anyone needs. In spite of it all, "I look deep down, and I do believe."

acknowledgments

I am deeply grateful to the many people who made this book possible, and regret that space does not permit for a full accounting of all guilty parties. The edited list is still difficult to organize, since my friends, family, colleagues, confidantes, and teachers occupy a very tangled Venn diagram. But I'm a socialist, so I figure labor should always come first.

My agent, William Callahan, who offered invaluable feedback on my proposal and maintained an incomprehensible faith in the project from the beginning; no small feat when your author is resistant to pep talks.

My long-suffering editor, Kevin Reilly (who had no idea what he was getting into with such a headcase and very much deserves a raise), who offered me invaluable feedback on the manuscript and steered me toward the pages, even as I dug in my heels the entire time.

The rest of my team at St. Martin's Press, Gabrielle Gantz, Martin Quinn, Lauren Riebs, Catherine Turiano, Laura Clark, and Rob Grom (for what might be the only cover art that could possibly make me happy), you cannot imagine what a relief it is to have a group of professionals at the helm after winging it for so many years.

To the boys, who were winging it alongside me all that time: Felix, Matt, Will, and Chris, we make something wonderful together, and I'll never know how I got so lucky to find you all.

To Lee Landey, Sarah Goldstein, and Daniel Bessner, for lending their poor ears to my neurotic editing process.

To Richard Metzger, Tara McGinley, and the gang over at Dangerous Minds for giving me the shot I needed to find my voice; Chris Lehmann, the person most responsible for my growth as a writer; Elayne Tobin, who helped me see writing in a whole new way; and Lucy Sante, for drinks at the Blue and Gold, borscht at the Ukrainian National Home, and casually letting it slip that actually, you don't need any credentials or anyone's permission to write a book.

To Bhaskar Sunkara, Remeike Forbes, Connor and Megan Kilpatrick, Ben Fong, Vivek Chibber, Alex Hochuli, George Hoare, and Philip Cunliffe, for always goading me to "engage with the discourse," but only when it made sense to wade in. To my UK fixers, Marcus Barnett, Pat Smith, and Sam Kriss.

To Barbara Ehrenreich, Cornel West, Joe Schwartz, Peg Strobel, Lee Levin, and the late, great Mike Hirsch, for keeping the fire burning. To David Duhalde, Maria Svart, Chris Maisano, Melissa Naschek, Diane Isser, Dino Guastella, and Jedidiah Slaboda, for taking up the torch.

To Adolph Reed Jr., Cedric Johnson, Mark Dudzic, and Lawrence Landerman, for their thoughts and counsel.

To my dearest Kal Hailu, Jen C. Pan, Michael Cavadias, Alexis Avedisian, Anna Khachiyan, Paul Cupo, Patrick

Sandberg, and Nick Mullen, for being resolute, and reminding me what is good and important.

To Josh Olsen and Nancy Himmel, Amber Rollo, Courtney Rawlings, Catherine Liu, and Leo and Peter Krapp, for shielding me from the blinding California sun.

To Mom and Patrick, Grandma and Grandpa, Mamaw and Papaw, and every family member who had no idea what I was doing but supported me anyway.

And finally, to Justin Hantz, the only person who was able to get me through the last mile. I couldn't write about the past until you told me my future.

To all these people and so many others who have encouraged, inspired, or indulged me: this is all your fault. Thank you.

notes

1. Hunter S. Thompson, "Fear and Loathing on the Campaign Trail '76," *Rolling Stone,* June 3, 1976, https://www.rollingstone.com /feature/fear-and-loathing-on-the-campaign-trail-76–46121/.
2. Hilton Kramer, "The Literary View," *The New York Times,* April 2, 1978, https://www.nytimes.com/1978/04/02/archives/the -literary-view-beautiful-reds-literary-view.html.
3. Joshua Leifer, "Too Close for Comfort," *Jewish Currents,* December 17, 2019, https://jewishcurrents.org/too-close-for-comfort
4. Leifer, "Too Close for Comfort."
5. Richard Wright, "I Tried to Be a Communist," *The Atlantic,* August 1944, https://www.theatlantic.com/magazine/archive/1944 /08/richard-wright-communist/618821/.
6. Jo Freeman, "The Tyranny of Structurelessness," JoFreeman.com, 1971–3, https://www.jofreeman.com/joreen/tyranny.htm.
7. Jo Freeman, "Trashing: The Dark Side of Sisterhood," JoFreeman.com, April 1976, https://www.jofreeman.com/joreen/trashing.htm.
8. Mark Fisher, "Exiting the Vampire Castle," November 24, 2013, openDemocracy, https://www.opendemocracy.net/en /opendemocracyuk/exiting-vampire-castle/.
9. Dawn Mitchell, "50 Years Ago the Justice Dept. Sued IPS to Force Desegregation," IndyStar, May 31, 2008, https://www.indystar .com/story/news/history/retroindy/2018/05/31/desegregation -indianapolis-chronology/655073002/.

10. I'll be capitalizing "Black" throughout this text to conform with current *Chicago Manual of Style* guidelines, but the following statement from Cedric Johnson's book *Revolutionaries to Race Leaders* nicely encapsulates my thoughts on this practice: "Throughout this book, I use the terms 'black' and 'African American' interchangeably. I do not capitalize 'black' or 'white' when they are used as racial descriptors. Such racial markers are not transhistorical, nor are they rooted in some biological essence. Instead, my usage reflects the view that racial identity is the product of historically unique power configurations and material conditions. This view contradicts the literary practice common to much Black Power radicalism, where racial descriptors are capitalized to denote a distinctive, coherent political community and assert an affirmative racial identity. When quoting historical texts, I maintain current usage of the author and preserve the tendency to capitalize racial descriptors that was popular during the Black Power era. Given that this period was one of considerable redefinition with respect to identity among African Americans, the reader will encounter 'Negro,' 'black,' and 'Black' as well as 'Afro-American,' 'Afrikan,' and 'African American.' I hope my presentation of these different naming practices creates a sense of historical debate and contingency over racial identity." https://muse.jhu.edu/pub/23/monograph/chapter/1272797.

11. Shannon Quinn, "The American Divorce Colonies of the 1800's," History Collection, August 2, 2018, https://historycollection.com/the-american-divorce-colonies-of-the-1800s.

12. "Indiana Minimill Shuts Down," *NWI Times*, February 7, 2001, https://www.nwitimes.com/uncategorized/indiana-minimill-shuts-down/article_c9b9f7a9-97d0-592f-8562-cd366d428725.html.

13. Area Development News Desk, "Steel Dynamics Plans $76 Million Expansion To Its Pittsboro, Indiana Mill," April 24, 2012, https://www.areadevelopment.com/newsItems/4-24-2012/steel-dynamics-pittsboro-indiana-expansion-2678901.shtml.

14. Amber A'Lee Frost and Anton Jäger, "Corbyn Lost. But Bernie Can Win," Jacobin, December 18, 2019, https://www.jacobinmag.com/2019/12/jeremy-corbyn-bernie-sanders-lessons-uk-election.

15. Vivek Chibber, "Why We Still Talk About the Working Class," Jacobin, March 15, 2017, https://www.jacobinmag.com/2017/03 /abcs-socialism-working-class-workers-capitalism-power-vivek -chibber.

16. Hunter S. Thompson, "Fear and Loathing in Las Vegas," *Rolling Stone,* November 11, 1971, https://www.rollingstone.com/feature /fear-and-loathing-in-las-vegas-204655/.

17. Gabriel Winant, "Manufacturing Isn't Coming Back. Let's Improve These Jobs Instead," *The New York Times,* March 17, 2021, https://www.nytimes.com/2021/03/17/opinion/health-care -jobs.html.

18. "All Employees, Manufacturing (MANEMP)," FRED Economic Data, Federal Reserve Bank of St. Louis, updated November 4, 2022, https://fred.stlouisfed.org/graph/?g=pFfA.

19. Gabriel Winant, *The Next Shift: The Fall of Industry and the Rise of Health Care in Rust Belt America,* Harvard University Press, 2021.

20. "United States GDP From Manufacturing," Trading Economics, https://tradingeconomics.com/united-states/gdp-from -manufacturing.

21. "Ask a Mortician," YouTube, https://www.youtube.com/c /AskAMortician.

22. Brent Scher, "ThinkProgress Senior Editor Is Scared of His Plumber," *The Washington Free Beacon,* January 9, 2017, https: //freebeacon.com/politics/thinkprogress-senior-editor-is-scared -of-his-plumber/.

23. Amber A'Lee Frost, "How to Write About Nazis," Current Affairs, August 26, 2017, https://www.currentaffairs.org/2017/08 /how-to-write-about-nazis.

24. Ken Kelley, "Penthouse Interview: Ed Sadlowski," *Penthouse,* January 1977.

25. Judith Stein, *Running Steel, Running America: Race, Economic Policy, and the Decline of Liberalism,* The University of North Carolina Press, 1998.

26. BioLife Plasma, BioLife Plasma Services, https://www .biolifeplasma.com/, accessed February 7, 2023.

27. Spivak, Gayarti. "Gayarti Spivak, YDS Winter Conference 2010, Part 1," YouTube, April 1, 2010, https://www.youtube.com/watch? v=S420CSdpj9Q.

28. Smith, Dinita. "Creating a Stir Wherever She Goes," *The New York Times*, February 9, 2002, https://www.nytimes.com/2002/02/09/arts/creating-a-stir-wherever-she-goes.html.

29. Terry Eagleton, *Figures of Dissent: Critical Essays on Fish, Spivak, Zizek and Others.*, London and New York: Verso, 2003, 158.

30. L. A. Kauffman, "The Theology of Consensus," Jacobin, May 27, 2015, https://www.jacobinmag.com/2015/05/consensus-occupy-wall-street-general-assembly/.

31. Alien Disclosure Group, "Wall Street Mocks Protestors by Drinking Champagne 2011," YouTube, September 23, 2011, https://youtu.be/2PiXDTK_CBY.

32. Trevor Loudon, "Democrat Socialists, Marxists Neck Deep in 'Occupy' Movement," Breitbart, November 4, 2022, https://www.breitbart.com/politics/2011/11/04/democrat-socialists-marxists-neck-deep-in-occupy-movement/.

33. Virginia Hotchkiss, "Ritual Protest and the Theater of Dissent," Nonsite, March 3, 2017, https://nonsite.org/ritual-protest-and-the-theater-of-dissent/.

34. Hotchkiss, "Ritual Protest and the Theater of Dissent."

35. Malcolm Harris, "I'm the Jerk Who Pranked Occupy Wall Street," Gawker, December 14, 2011, https://www.gawker.com/5868073/im-the-jerk-who-pranked-occupy-wall-street.

36. Alex Williams, "The Literary Cubs," *The New York Times,* November 30, 2011, https://www.nytimes.com/2011/12/01/fashion/new-yorks-literary-cubs.html.

37. Malcolm Harris, "I'm the Jerk Who Pranked Occupy Wall Street," Gawker, December 14, 2011, https://www.gawker.com/5868073/im-the-jerk-who-pranked-occupy-wall-street.

38. Harris, "I'm the Jerk Who Pranked Occupy Wall Street."

39. Tana Ganeva and Laura Gottesdiener, "Nine Terrifying Facts About America's Biggest Police Force," Salon, September 28, 2012, https://www.salon.com/2012/09/28/nine_terrifying_facts_about_americas_biggest_police_force/.

40. Russ Buettner, "A Brooklyn Protestor Pleads Guilty After His Twitter Posts Sink His Case," *The New York Times,* December 12, 2012, https://www.nytimes.com/2012/12/13/nyregion/malcolm-harris-pleads-guilty-over-2011-march.html.

41. Buettner, "A Brooklyn Protestor Pleads Guilty After His Twitter Posts Sink His Case."

42. Harris, Malcolm, *Kids These Days: The Making of Millennials* (New York: Little, Brown and Company, 2017), marketing copy.

43. Christopher Robbins, "Hipster Cop's Secrets Spilled By NYPD Insider," Gothamist, October 17, 2011, https://gothamist.com /news/hipster-cops-secrets-spilled-by-nypd-insider.

44. Lauren Bans, "The Hipster Cop: An Occupy Wall Street Conversation," *GQ,* October 21, 2011, https://www.gq.com/story /hipster-cop-rick-lee-interview-occupy-wall-street.

45. Colleen Curry, Mark Crudele, and Aaron Katersky, "Undercover NYPD Cop in SUV Assault Charged with Riot, Criminal Mischief," ABC News, October 8, 2013, https://abcnews.go.com /US/undercover-nypd-cop-face-charges-suv-assault/story?id =20508098 Daniel Bates, "Judge Bans Pictures of NYPD Detective Charged Over Brutal Biker Gang Attack Because He Worked Undercover in Occupy Wall Street Movement for Two Years," *Daily Mail,* October 9, 2013, https://www.dailymail.co .uk/news/article-2451451/New-York-SUV-attack-Undercover -NYPD-cop-arrested-taking-went-undercover-Occupy-Wall -St.html.

46. Richard Wright, "I Tried to be a Communist," *The Atlantic,* August 1944, https://www.theatlantic.com/magazine/archive/1944 /08/richard-wright-communist/618821/.

47. Wright, "I Tried to be a Communist."

48. The Office of Strategic Services, "Simple Sabotage Field Manual," January 17, 1944, https://www.hsdl.org/?abstract&did=750070.

49. Amber A'Lee Frost, "The Poisoned Chalice of Hashtag Activism," *Catalyst* 4, no. 2 (Summer 2020), https://catalyst-journal.com /vol4/no2/the-poisoned-chalice-of-hashtag-activism.

50. Amber A'Lee Frost, "It's Still Bernie," Jacobin, January 22, 2019, https://jacobin.com/2019/01/bernie-sanders-elizabeth-warren -democratic-primary-baffler-amber-frost.

51. Nolan, Hamilton, "Bernie Don't Run," *Splinter,* December 10, 2018, https://splinternews.com/bernie-dont-run-1830983072.

52. Cake, "Rock 'n' Roll Lifestyle," by John McCrea, recorded 1993, track 10 on *Motorcade of Generosity,* Stamen Music.

53. Arsenio, "Guardian Writer: If Burned Falklands Hero Knew Anything, He'd Still Have His Face," Falklands Harvest II, September 7, 2015, https://falklandsharvest.wordpress.com/2015/09/07/guardian-writer-if-burned-falklands-hero-knew-anything-hed-still-have-his-face/.

54. Sylvia Plath, *The Unabridged Journals of Sylvia Plath,* diary entry no. 93, 1951, Anchor Books, 2000.

55. Brigitte Amiri, "5 Things Women Should Know About the Hobby Lobby Decision," ACLU, July 2, 2014, https://www.aclu.org/news/religious-liberty/5-things-women-should-know-about-hobby-lobby-decision.

56. Amy Chozick, "Planned Parenthood, in Its First Primary Endorsement, Backs Hillary Clinton," *The New York Times,* January 7, 2016, https://www.nytimes.com/politics/first-draft/2016/01/07/planned-parenthood-in-its-first-primary-endorsement-backs-hillary-clinton/.

57. Anne Rumberger, "Bernie Sanders Is a Champion for Abortion Rights," Jacobin, July 15, 2019, https://jacobin.com/2019/07/bernie-sanders-abortion-rights-record.

58. Pema Levy, "Late-Term Abortion Debate Reveals a Rift Between Clinton and Sanders," Mother Jones, March 11, 2016, https://www.motherjones.com/politics/2016/03/hillary-clinton-late-term-abortions/.

59. "Tim Kaine on Reducing Abortions in Virginia," Tim Kaine Governor [via Wayback Machine], https://web.archive.org/web/20050919164426/http:/www.kaine2005.org/issues/abortion.php.

60. Julia M. Klein, "A Political Brat Comes of Age," *Brandeis Magazine,* Spring 2021, https://www.brandeis.edu/magazine/2021/spring/featured-stories/adams.html.

61. Philip K. Dick, *The VALIS Trilogy,* p. 61, Houghton Mifflin Harcourt, 2011.

62. "Top 10 U.S. metropolitan areas by Vietnamese population, 2015," Pew Research Center, September 8, 2017, https://www.pewresearch.org/social-trends/chart/top-10-u-s-metropolitan-areas-by-vietnamese-population/.

63. Ruth Gebreyesus, "'One of the biggest, baddest things we did': Black Panthers' free breakfasts, 50 years on," *The Guardian,* Oc-

tober 18, 2019, https://www.theguardian.com/us-news/2019/oct /17/black-panther-party-oakland-free-breakfast-50th-anniversary.

64. Vincent Barone, "AOC Rocks Black Panthers Shirt, Touts Group's Free Food Program," *New York Post,* October 7, 2020, https: //nypost.com/2020/10/07/aoc-rocks-black-panthers-shirt-touts -groups-free-food-program/.

65. Adolph Reed, Jr., "The New Deal Wasn't Intrinsically Racist," The New Republic, November 26, 2019, https://newrepublic .com/article/155704/new-deal-wasnt-intrinsically-racist.

66. Shirley Zhao and Bruce Einhorn, "How Hong Kong's Taxes Spawned Billionaires and Bred Inequality," Bloomberg UK, October 15, 2019, https://www.bloomberg.com/news/articles /2019–10–15/how-hong-kong-s-taxes-spawned-billionaires-and -bred-inequality.

67. Nellie Bowles, "The Pied Pipers of the Dirtbag Left Want to Lead Everyone to Bernie Sanders," *The New York Times,* updated March 1, 2020, https://www.nytimes.com/2020/02/29/us /politics/bernie-sanders-chapo-trap-house.html.

68. Cambria Roth, "'Real Housewives Of Politics' Makes Its Big Debut During BravoCon," HuffPost, October 20, 2022, https: //www.huffpost.com/entry/real-housewives-politics-bravo_n _63507235e4b04cf8f37f80f0.

69. TrueAnon, Twitter, February 25, 2020, https://twitter.com/ TrueAnonPod/status/1232126357817053185.